WHO ARE YOU?

. . . .

145 Easy-to-Score Quizzes that
Reveal Your Personality

Black Dog & Leventhal Publishers
Hachette Book Group
1290 Avenue of the Americas
New York, NY 10104
www.hachettebookgroup.com
www.blackdogandleventhal.com

Originally published as three individual titles: *How Smart Are You? Test Your IQ, Who
Are You? Test Your Emotional Intelligence and Who Are You? Test Your Personality*

First omnibus edition: April 2018

Black Dog & Leventhal Publishers is an imprint of Hachette Books, a division of
Hachette Book Group. The Black Dog & Leventhal Publishers name and logo are
trademarks of Hachette Book, Inc.

The publisher is not responsible for websites (or their content) that are not owned by
the publisher.

The Hachette Speakers Bureau provides a wide range of authors for speaking events.
To find out more, go to www.Hachettespeakersbureau.com or call (866) 376-6591.

Print book interior design by Elizabeth Driesbach

Library of Congress Control Number: 2017949736

ISBN: 978-0-316-41475-3

Printed in China

IM

10 9 8 7 6 5 4 3

· ·

WHO ARE YOU?

145 Easy-to-Score Quizzes that Reveal Your Personality

**SALVATORE V. DIDATO PH.D AND
THOMAS J. CRAUGHWELL**

· · · · · · · · · · · · · · · · · · · · · · · · · · · ·

Tess
Press

CONTENTS

TEST YOUR IQ

CONTENTS

PERSONALITY TESTS

CONTENTS

TEST YOUR EMOTIONAL INTELLIGENCE

TEST YOUR IQ

INTRODUCTION

IQ is shorthand for "Intelligence Quotient." Since the first years of the twentieth century, tests have been given to children to determine if they were gifted, of average intelligence, or suffered from some type of disability and would do better in special education classes. The point of the IQ test was to assess a child's intellectual ability and predict his or her chances for success in the future. A child who scored in the gifted level would be put on track for college, while a child with average scores might be marked for one of the trades or office work.

Today, an IQ test is rarely given to children, but such tests are still given to adults as a way to measure their intellectual potential. Scoring has changed, too: Instead of measuring test results against a fixed standard, the scores of those who take an IQ test are compared to scores of other adults who have taken the test.

The standard scoring system for an IQ test is:

165 Genius
148–132 Gifted/Superior Intelligence
115 Higher Than Usual Intelligence
99 Average Intelligence
83 Low Average Intelligence
70 or below Very Low Intelligence

The fifty IQ quizzes in this book are intended for high school students and adults, and they are intended to be fun. Each chapter opens with more information about the IQ test and other tests of intelligence. Your scores will not reflect your actual intelligence, or predict how successful you will be in school or in your career. Furthermore, our IQ quizzes are brief; a real IQ test given by professionals is much more complicated and takes at least an hour to complete.

So enjoy these quizzes! On the one hand, don't get caught up in your score. But on the other hand, don't be surprised if the scores indicate that you're smarter than you thought you were.

CHAPTER 1

ODD SHAPE OUT

The Origins of the IQ Test

It all began with a simple case of family rivalry. Francis Galton (1822-1911) was one of those Victorian gentlemen who seemed able to do anything: he was a explorer, geographer, inventor, anthropologist, meteorologist, statistician, and even dabbled in what was then the new science of genetics. Yet Galton was a nobody compared to his famous cousin, Charles Darwin. Eager to grab his own share of the spotlight, Galton developed a theory that human intelligence was genetic, in other words, that it was inherited—intelligent parents were likely to have intelligent children. Furthermore, Galton believed that intelligence could be measured, thereby predicting how successful a child was likely to be in school.

Unfortunately, Galton's system of measurement focused on physical attributes such as reaction time and skin sensitivity rather than cognitive skills, and of course skin sensitivity does not predict whether a child is college material. Galton's method was rejected.

In France, the French government asked psychologist Alfred Binet (1857-1911) to develop a test that would measure a child's intelligence. France had just passed a law requiring all children to attend school, and there was widespread interest in learning which children were especially promising and which would require special assistance. Working with a colleague, Theodore Simon, Binet designed a test that had nothing to do with a typical school curriculum. Instead, Binet and Simon posed questions that revealed information about a child's attention span, recall capability, and problem solving skills. The Binet-Simon method was the first IQ test.

The test was studied in the United States by Lewis Terman, a psychologist at the University of Stanford. He tweaked the Binet-Simon test, creating in 1916 the Stanford-Binet Intelligence Scale. The Stanford test's most significant contribution was the intelligence quotient score. Terman's formula was to divide the child's mental age, or skills, with its chronological age, then multiply the result by 100. So, a child with a mental age or skills of a 12 year old and the chronological age of 10 would have an IQ score of 120.

In the early part of the 20th century the Stanford-Binet IQ test was used by the U.S. government to assess the intelligence of army recruits and even to screen immigrants when they arrived on Ellis Island.

✏️ Shape Analogies

1 Examine the shapes and identify the one that is least like the others.

2 Examine the shapes and identify the one that is least like the others.

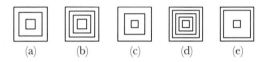

3 Examine the shapes and identify the one that is least like the others.

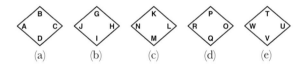

4 Examine the shapes and identify the one that is least like the others.

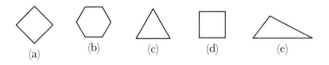

5 Examine the shapes and identify the one that is least like the others.

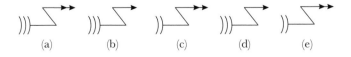

6 Cards 1 through 6 follow a pattern. Which card is next in the sequence?

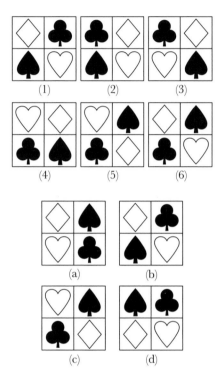

7 Examine the shapes and identify the one that is least like the others.

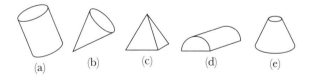

8 Which shape is next in the sequence?

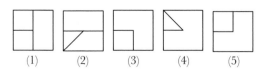

Choose from

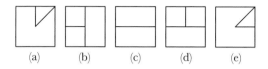

(a)   (b)   (c)   (d)   (e)

9 Which shape is next in the sequence?

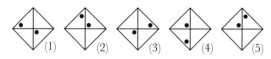

(1)   (2)   (3)   (4)   (5)

Choose from

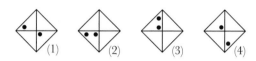

(1)   (2)   (3)   (4)

10 Examine the shapes and identify the one that is least like the others.

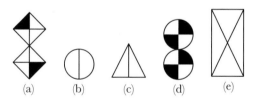

(a)   (b)   (c)   (d)   (e)

ANSWERS ·

① B. In all the other shapes, the inside figure is a smaller version of the outside figure.

② B. It is the only figure with an even number of squares. All the others have an odd number.

③ D. It is the only diamond that does not have letters running in alphabetical order from the top and moving clockwise.

④ E. It is the only shape in the series that is not symmetrical.

⑤ A. It is the only figure in the series that does not have a twin.

⑥ B. In figure 2 the top two squares from figure 1 are transposed. In figure 3 the bottom two squares are transposed. In figure 4 the two vertical squares on the left are transposed. In figure 5 the two vertical squares on the right are transposed. In figure 6 the top left square and the bottom right square have been transposed. Therefore, in the next figure in the sequence, the top square on the right will be transposed with the bottom square on the left.

⑦ C. Figure C is made only with straight lines. All the other figures are made with straight lines and curves.

⑧ E. There are two moving lines in these figures: One moves 90 degrees each time, the other moves 45 degrees. The dotted line never moves, but sometimes is covered by the moving lines.

⑨ B. The dot at the outside of the figure moves clockwise, first one triangle, then two triangles, then three triangles, etc. The dot inside the figure moves counterclockwise, first one triangle, then two triangles, then three triangles, etc.

⑩ C. All the other figures will look exactly the same when turned upside down.

SCORING ·

Award 16.5 points for each correct answer.

165 Genius
148–132 Gifted/Superior Intelligence
115 Higher Than Usual Intelligence

99 Average Intelligence
83 Low Average Intelligence
70 or below Very Low Intelligence

More Shape Analogies

1 Select the figure that best completes the analogy.

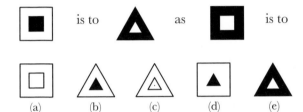

2 Select the figure that best completes the analogy.

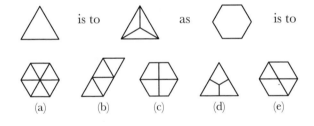

3 Select the figure that best completes the analogy.

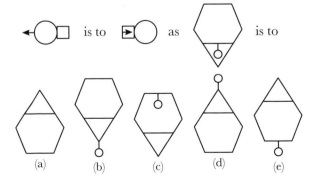

4 Select the figure that best completes the analogy.

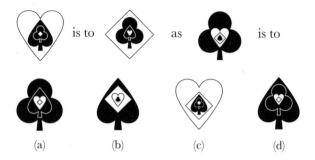

5 Select the figure that best completes the analogy.

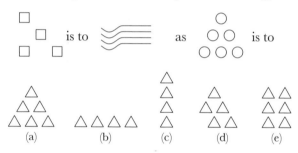

6 Select the figure that best completes the analogy.

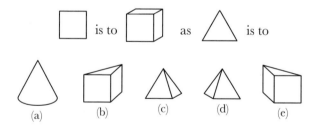

7 From the 5 figures below, choose the shape that best completes the analogy

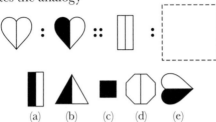

8 From the 5 figures below, choose the shape that best completes the analogy

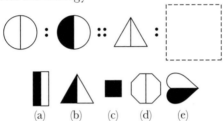

9 From the 5 figures below, choose the shape that best completes the analogy

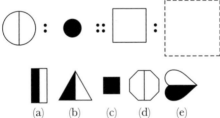

10 From the 5 figures below, choose the shape that best completes the analogy

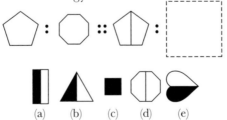

ANSWERS ·

① B The shading of the inner and outer figures is reversed.

② A The hexagon is divided into six equal parts, just as the triangle is divided into three equal parts.

③ E The short lines in the figures are reversed.

④ B The sequence is this: The tiny center figure becomes the large outer figure; the next smallest inner figure becomes the next largest outer figure; the next smallest inner figure becomes the next largest outer figure; the largest outer figure becomes the tiny center figure.

⑤ E Four squares are to four lines as six balls are to six triangles.

⑥ C Like the cube, the pyramid shows its right side.

⑦ A The rectangle is shaded on the left side.

⑧ B The triangle is shaded on the left side.

⑨ C The small shaded square corresponds to the small shaded circle.

⑩ D The split hexagon corresponds to the split pentagon.

SCORING ·

Award 16.5 points for each correct answer.

165 Genius
148–132 Gifted/Superior Intelligence
115 Higher Than Usual Intelligence
99 Average Intelligence
83 Low Average Intelligence
70 or below Very Low Intelligence

✏️ Pattern Recognition

Identify that letter or number that does not belong in each of the following series.

1
a. X
b. L
c. T
d. 7
e. 4

2
a. M
b. S
c. W
d. N
e. X

3
a. 4
b. Z
c. A
d. E
e. F

4
a. 2
b. O
c. C
d. Q
e. 8

5
a. F
b. Z
c. A
d. B
e. N

6
a. B
b. D
c. C
d. P
e. R

7
a. I
b. T
c. A
d. W
e. U

8
a. D
b. U
c. O
d. I
e. E

9 a. C   **10** a. 6

b. P   b. 2

c. I   c. 8

d. L   d. 5

e. F   e. 4

ANSWERS ·

① e. 4. All the other characters are made with two lines.

② b. S. All the other characters contain angles.

③ d. E. All the other characters are made with three lines.

④ a. 2. All the other characters are based on round shapes.

⑤ c. A. All the other letters are consonants, A is a vowel.

⑥ c. C. All the other letters are made with a straight line and a curve.

⑦ e. U. The letters are in ascending order of the number of lines necessary to write them. U is made from a curve.

⑧ a. D. Four of the letters are vowels; D is a consonant.

⑨ b. P. When you count off the letters of the alphabet by three's, the other four letters are the third in the pattern.

⑩ d. 5. The other numbers can be divided by two.

SCORING ·

Award 16.5 points for each correct answer.

165 Genius
148–132 Gifted/Superior Intelligence

115 Higher Than Usual Intelligence
99 Average Intelligence
83 Low Average Intelligence
70 or below Very Low Intelligence

More Pattern Recognition

❶ From the 6 figures below, identify the one that is significantly different from the other shapes.

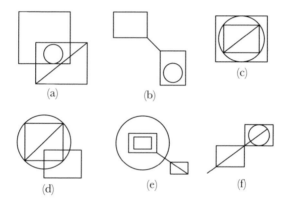

(a)　　　　　(b)　　　　　(c)

(d)　　　　　(e)　　　　　(f)

❷ The shapes on the left hand form an incomplete analogy. From the 3 figures on the right, choose the shape that best completes the analogy.

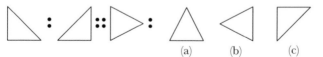

(a)　　　(b)　　　(c)

❸ The shapes on the left hand form an incomplete analogy. From the 3 figures on the right, choose the shape that best completes the analogy.

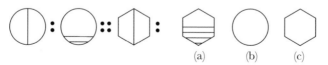

(a)　　　(b)　　　(c)

4 The shapes on the left hand form an incomplete analogy. From the 3 figures on the right, choose the shape that best completes the analogy.

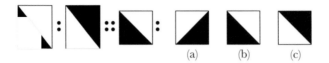

(a)   (b)   (c)

5 The shapes on the left hand form an incomplete analogy. From the 3 figures on the right, choose the shape that best completes the analogy.

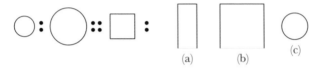

(a)   (b)   (c)

6 The shapes on the left hand form an incomplete analogy. From the 3 figures on the right, choose the shape that best completes the analogy.

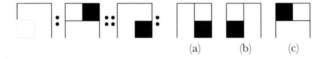

(a)   (b)   (c)

7 The shapes on the left hand form an incomplete analogy. From the 3 figures on the right, choose the shape that best completes the analogy.

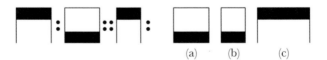

(a)   (b)   (c)

8　The shapes on the left hand form an incomplete analogy. From the 3 figures on the right, choose the shape that best completes the analogy.

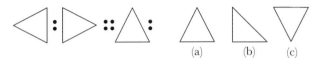

(a)　(b)　(c)

9　The shapes on the left hand form an incomplete analogy. From the 3 figures on the right, choose the shape that best completes the analogy.

(a)　(b)　(c)

10　The shapes on the left hand form an incomplete analogy. From the 3 figures on the right, choose the shape that best completes the analogy.

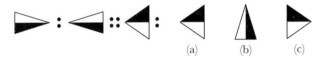

(a)　(b)　(c)

ANSWERS ·

① B. It is the only figure that does not have two triangles.

② B. It is the mirror, or reverse, image of the equilateral triangle.

③ A. It has the horizontal bar pattern of the second circle.

④ C. It is the reverse image of the small square.

⑤ B. The larger square corresponds to the larger circle.

⑥ C. The shaded box flips on a diagonal and adds a line or tail.

⑦ B. It is equal in size to the first tall rectangle.

⑧ C. It is the opposite of the second triangle.

⑨ C. The two circles are the same size, so the two triangles must be the same size, too.

⑩ C. All the figures are mirror images of each other.

SCORING ·

Award 16.5 points for each correct answer.

165 Genius
148–132 Gifted/Superior Intelligence
115 Higher Than Usual Intelligence
99 Average Intelligence
83 Low Average Intelligence
70 or below Very Low Intelligence

CHAPTER 2

MATH QUIZZES

The Wechsler
Intelligence Scales

In the 1930s an American psychologist, David Wechsler, studied human intelligence and defined it as an individual's capability "to act purposefully, to think rationally, and to deal effectively with his environment." He came to believe that the Stanford-Binet test was too limited; in an attempt to better measure intelligence over time, Wechsler created three IQ tests: the Wechsler Intelligence Scale for Children (WISC), the Wechsler Preschool and Primary Scale of Intelligence (WPPSI), and the Wechsler Adult Intelligence Scale (WAIS).

Wechsler rejected Stanford's method of scoring based on mental and chronological age. He developed a method in which test results were compared to the results of other test takers in the same age group. Wechsler found that 100 was an average score, and that two-thirds of children and adults who took his test scored between 85 and 115, which he said indicated normal intelligence.

David Wechsler's method became the standard scoring system for IQ tests in the second half of the 20th century, and is still used in IQ tests today.

Word Problems

1 On a recent test, Mary received the 11th highest and 11th lowest score in her class. How many students are in Mary's class?

A. 23   **C.** 11   **E.** 12

B. 22   **D.** 29

2 A sweater at a department store has been marked down 50 percent. For that same sweater to sell again at its original price, by what percentage must it be marked up?

A. 25%   **C.** 75%   **E.** 150%

B. 50%   **D.** 100%

3 In one day, a grocery store sold 360 kg of oranges. The store sold twice as many oranges in the afternoon as in the morning. How many kg of oranges were sold in the morning, and how many in the afternoon?

A. 80 kg in the morning, 280 kg in the afternoon

B. 90 kg in the morning, 270 kg in the afternoon

C. 120 kg in the morning, 240 kg in the afternoon

D. 100 kg in the morning, 260 kg in the afternoon

E. 140 kg in the morning, 220 kg in the afternoon

4 Morgan is 15 years old. He is 3 times older than his sister. At what age will he be twice as old as his sister?

A. 18   **C.** 24   **E.** 33

B. 21   **D.** 20

5 A car traveled 281 miles in 4 hours and 41 minutes. What was the car's average speed in miles per hour?

A. 75 miles per hour   **D.** 50 miles per hour

B. 60 miles per hour   **E.** 45 miles per hour

C. 55 miles per hour

6 Danny bought 20 baseball cards. Some cost 25 cents each, others cost 15 cents each. He spent $4.20 total. How many cards of each type did he buy?

A. 8 cards at 25 cents and 12 cards at 15 cents

B. 10 cards at 25 cents and 10 cards at 15 cents

C. 14 cards at 25 cents and 6 cards at 15 cents

D. 6 cards at 25 cents and 14 cards at 15 cents

E. 12 cards at 25 cents and 8 cards at 15 cents

7 A high school has 40 students in its senior class. Forty percent of the seniors are taking physics, 30 percent are taking chemistry, 10 percent are taking neither. How many seniors are taking neither physics nor chemistry?

A. 16 students   **C.** 18 students   **E.** 20 students

B. 17 students   **D.** 19 students

8 Two pumps working together can fill a water tank in 18 minutes. One pump works twice as fast as the other. If each pump worked alone, how long would it take to fill the water tank?

A. fast pump 20 minutes, slow pump 61 minutes

B. fast pump 23 minutes, slow pump 46 minutes

C. fast pump 27 minutes, slow pump 54 minutes

D. fast pump 30 minutes, slow pump 60 minutes

E. fast pump 33 minutes, slow pump 59 minutes

⑨ Ellie read two-thirds of a novel. The part she read was 90 pages longer than the unread portion of the novel. How many pages are in the book?

A. 300 pages   **C.** 295 pages   **E.** 250 pages

B. 270 pages   **D.** 287 pages

⑩ Taylor thought of a number, divided it by 5, then subtracted 154 and got 6. What is the number Taylor thought of?

A. 524   **C.** 400   **E.** 800

B. 774   **D.** 664

A N S W E R S ·

① A. 23
② C. 120 kg in the morning, 240 kg in the afternoon
③ D. 100 percent
④ D. 20
⑤ B. 60 miles per hour
⑥ E. 12 cards at 25 cents and 8 cards at 15 cents
⑦ A. 16 students
⑧ C. fast pump 27 minutes, slow pump 54 minutes
⑨ B. 270 pages
⑩ E. 800

SCORING ·

Award 16.5 points for each correct answer.

165 Genius
148–132 Gifted/Superior Intelligence
115 Higher Than Usual Intelligence
99 Average Intelligence
83 Low Average Intelligence
70 or below Very Low Intelligence

Number Series

For each problem, identify the next number in the series.

1 5 6 10 12 20 33 40 44

    A. 80   **C.** 24   **E.** 60

    B. 66   **D.** 128

2 5 13 21 29 37 44

    A. 53   **C.** 61   **E.** 54

    B. 52   **D.** 51

3 2 5 10 17 26 37 50 65 82

    A. 144   **C.** 88   **E.** 90

    B. 101   **D.** 89

4 503 484 465 446 427 408

    A. 398   **C.** 398   **E.** 389

    B. 308   **D.** 399

5 737 774 811 848 885

    A. 903   **C.** 922   **E.** 921

    B. 907   **D.** 897

6 4 3 5 4 7 6 10 9 14 13 19 18

    A. 21   **C.** 23   **E.** 25

    B. 22   **D.** 24

7 17 51 153 459 1,377

    A. 2,922   **C.** 3,759   **E.** 4,427

    B. 3,123   **D.** 4,131

8 431 422 413 404 395

    A. 386   **C.** 388   **E.** 385

    B. 387   **D.** 389

9 291 293 586 588 1,176 1,178 2,356 2,358

    A. 4,671   **C.** 4,716   **E.** 6,147

    B. 4,167   **D.** 4,617

⑩ 17 14 22 19 27 24 32 29 37 34 42 39 47

  A. 29   **C.** 41   **E.** 43

  B. 39   **D.** 46

ANSWERS ·

① A. 80. The series solution is: Add 1, double the first number; add 2, double the third number; add 3, double the fifth number; add four, double the seventh number.

② B. 52. The series is created by adding 8.

③ B. 101. The series is created by adding odd numbers in numerical order beginning with 3. In other words, plus 3, plus 5, plus 7, plus 9, and so forth.

④ E. 389. The series is achieved by subtracting 19 from the previous number.

⑤ C. 922. The series is achieved by adding 37 to the previous number.

⑥ E. 25. The series is minus 1, plus 2; minus 1, plus 3; minus 1, plus 4; and so on.

⑦ D. 4,131. The number triples each time.

⑧ A. 386. Each number decreases by 9.

⑨ C. 4,716. The series pattern is plus 2, double the number.

⑩ B. 39. The pattern is minus 3, plus 8.

SCORING ·

Award 16.5 points for each correct answer.

165 Genius
148–132 Gifted/Superior Intelligence
115 Higher Than Usual Intelligence
99 Average Intelligence
83 Low Average Intelligence
70 or below Very Low Intelligence

✏️ Missing Numbers

Identify the missing number in each series.

1 316 — 302 295 288 281

A. 304	**C.** 301	**E.** 310
B. 303	**D.** 309	

2 6/24 12/48 18/72 24/96 30/120 36/ —

A. 125	**C.** 143	**E.** 114
B. 144	**D.** 126	

3 39 78 117 195 312 507 —

A. 819	**C.** 624	**E.** 818
B. 737	**D.** 799	

4 2 3 5 7 11 13 17 19 — 29 31

A. 20	**C.** 22	**E.** 27
B. 21	**D.** 23	

5 148 444 1,332 3,996 11,988 —

   A. 23,000   **C.** 29,970   **E.** 35,964

   B. 23,976   **D.** 33,102

6 14,568 — 3,642 1,821 910.5 455.25

   A. 12,366   **C.** 7,284   **E.** 9,324

   B. 10,888   **D.** 8,675

7 — 246 239 232 225 218

   A. 253   **C.** 255   **E.** 257

   B. 254   **D.** 256

8 655 663 — 679 687 695

   A. 670   **C.** 675   **E.** 678

   B. 671   **D.** 680

9 926 936 931 941 936 946 — 951

   A. 937   **C.** 939   **E.** 941

   B. 938   **D.** 940

10 31/93 47/141 52/156 66/198 74/222 89/ —

   A. 231   **C.** 267   **E.** 266

   B. 243   **D.** 255

ANSWERS ·

① D. 309. The series is achieved by subtracting 7 from the previous number.

② B. 144. The denominator is 4 times the numerator.

③ A. 819. The first number is doubled. Then each succeeding number is the sum of the previous 2 numbers.

④ D. 23. The numbers are all prime numbers, each of which can only be divided by 1 or by itself.

⑤ E. 35,964. The numbers triple.

⑥ C. 7284. Each number is half the number preceding it.

⑦ A. 253. Each number decreases by 7.

⑧ B. 671. Each number increases by 8.

⑨ E. 941. The pattern is plus 10, then minus 5.

⑩ C. 267. The denominator is 3 times the numerator.

SCORING ·

Award 16.5 points for each correct answer.

165 Genius
148–132 Gifted/Superior Intelligence
115 Higher Than Usual Intelligence
99 Average Intelligence
83 Low Average Intelligence
70 or below Very Low Intelligence

✏️ More Word Problems

1 It costs a DVD manufacturer X dollars per disc to make the first 1,000 discs of a DVD title. After the first 1,000, the cost drops to only one-third of X dollars. If X = $1.50, how much will it cost the manufacturer to produce 4,000 DVD discs?

A. $2,500   **C.** $3,500   **E.** $4,000

B. $3,000   **D.** $3,750

2 A train traveling at 60 mph enters a tunnel. The tunnel is 5 miles long. The train is 1 mile long. How many minutes will it take for the entire train to travel through the tunnel?

A. 10 minutes   **C.** 8 minutes   **E.** 6 minutes

B. 9 minutes   **D.** 7 minutes

3 In a local election, the Republican candidate received one-and-a-half times as many votes as his Democratic challenger. The Democrat received one-third more votes than the Independent candidate. If the Independent received 900 votes, how many votes did the Republican receive?

A. 600 votes   **C.** 1,500 votes   **E.** 1,800 votes

B. 1,200 votes   **D.** 1,700 votes

4 The full retail price of a CD is $8.95; 800 copies were sold. Sixty percent of the CDs were sold at 50 percent off the full retail price. Twenty percent were sold at 30 percent off the full retail price. The remainder were sold at the full retail price of $8.95. Rounding off to the nearest dollar amount, how much revenue was generated by sales of this CD?

A. $4,431   **C.** $4,213   **E.** $4,114

B. $4,579   **D.** $3,999

5 Hunter's workday begins at 8:45 a.m. and ends at 5:15 p.m. He is allowed 60 minutes for lunch and 30 minutes for coffee breaks. How many hours does Hunter work in five days?

A. 40 hours   **C.** 35 hours   **E.** 37 hours

B. 39 hours   **D.** 36 hours

6 A waiter in a restaurant presented a couple with a bill for their meal. The couple were charged $12.50 for appetizers, $28.55 for entrées, and $8.95 for desserts. The waiter added a 15 percent service charge to the bill. How much did the couple pay?

A. $56.25   **C.** $55.00   **E.** $51.50

B. $57.50   **D.** $52.75

7 The full retail price for a set of pencils is $1.80. As part of a back-to-school sale, the price has been discounted by 15 percent. What is the sale price for the package of pencils?

A. $1.53   **C.** $1.35   **E.** $1.60

B. $1.30   **D.** $1.49

8 In 1964, volleyball was included in the Olympic games. Seventy-three years before volleyball became an official Olympic sport, basketball was invented. In what year was basketball invented?

A. 1873   **C.** 1907   **E.** 1900

B. 1903   **D.** 1891

9 Scott and Lisa both collect baseball cards. Scott has 248 cards. Lisa has 75 cards more than Scott. How many cards are in Lisa's collection?

A. 299 cards   **C.** 323 cards   **E.** 335 cards

B. 301 cards   **D.** 275 cards

10 A fast food restaurant pays its employees $7.95 per hour Monday through Friday. Employees who work on Saturday or Sunday are paid $9.25 per hour. Starting on Monday, Ben worked seven hours per day for six consecutive days at the restaurant. How much did he earn in those six days?

A. $343   **C.** $303   **E.** $351

B. $299.25   **D.** $314.75

ANSWERS ·

① B. $3,000
② E. 6 minutes
③ E. 1,800 votes
④ B. $4,579
⑤ C. 35 hours
⑥ B. $57.50
⑦ A. $1.53
⑧ D. 1,891
⑨ C. 323 cards
⑩ A. $343

SCORING ·

Award 16.5 points for each correct answer.

165 Genius

148–132 Gifted/Superior Intelligence
115 Higher Than Usual Intelligence
99 Average Intelligence
83 Low Average Intelligence
70 or below Very Low Intelligence

✏️ Even More Word Problems

1 The number of chickens and pigs a farmer owns totals 8. If there are 26 legs in the barnyard, how many chickens are there, and how many pigs?

A. 1 chicken and 7 pigs   **D.** 5 chickens and 3 pigs

B. 2 chickens and 6 pigs   **E.** 3 chickens and 5 pigs

C. 4 chickens and 4 pigs

2 Michael, Carol, and Claire threw a party. They each invited 1 guest. Each of these guests invited 2 friends. Each of those friends invited 3 other friends. Assuming that everyone who was invited came to the party, how many people attended (including Michael, Carol, and Claire)?

A. 30 people   **C.** 35 people   **E.** 39 people

B. 33 people   **D.** 37 people

3 The population of the town of Woodbury grows every year. The first year 3 new families moved into town. The next year 8 families, the next year 13 families, and the year after that 18 families. Assuming that this pattern continues, in what year will 43 new families have moved into Woodbury?

A. the 8th year   **C.** the 11th year   **E.** the 13th year

B. the 9th year   **D.** the 12th year

4 A patron spends $11 on a movie ticket and popcorn. The ticket cost $5 more than the popcorn. How much was the movie ticket?

A. $5   **C.** $7   **E.** $9

B. $6   **D.** $8

5 The Makos softball team has 24 players. The Bears softball team has 27 players. The Mustangs football team has 18 fewer players than the 2 softball teams combined. How many players are on the Mustangs football team?

A. 33 players   **C.** 42 players   **E.** 19 players

B. 51 players   **D.** 29 players

6 Alex has $1,000 in his checking account. Saturday he deposited $250 in his account, and on Monday he withdrew $540. What is the balance in Alex's checking account?

A. $444   **C.** $710   **E.** $715

B. $625   **D.** $801

7 A Philadelphia parking garage charges $6 for the first hour and an additional $5 for each subsequent hour or part of an hour. If a tourist drops off her car at 6 p.m. and picks it up at 10:30 p.m., how much will she pay for parking?

A. $22   **C.** $24   **E.** $26

B. $23   **D.** $25

8 As a fund-raiser, a middle school class sold stationery. A box of notepaper cost $12; a box of note cards cost $8.

Total sales for the fund-raiser were $1,236. If the students sold 55 boxes of notepaper, how many boxes of notecards did they sell?

A. 68 boxes of note cards   **D.** 71 boxes of note cards

B. 72 boxes of note cards   **E.** 82 boxes of note cards

C. 69 boxes of note cards

⑨ Four teenage boys bought a used car for $1,250. They spent $575 on parts to repair it. The boys sold the repaired and rebuilt car for $4,605. The boys agreed to split up the profits from the sale equally. How much did each boy receive?

A. $1,825   **C.** $695   **E.** $780

B. $2,780   **D.** $525

⑩ Ten teams will participate in a softball tournament. Each team in the league must play every other team once and only once. How many games will be played in the tournament?

A. 45 games   **C.** 28 games   **E.** 10 games

B. 36 games   **D.** 21 games

A N S W E R S ·

① E. 3 chickens and 5 pigs
② A. 30 people
③ B. the 9th year
④ D. $8
⑤ A. 33 players
⑥ C. $710
⑦ E. $26

⑧ B. 72 boxes of note cards
⑨ C. $695
⑩ A. 45 games

SCORING ·

Award 16.5 points for each correct answer.

165 Genius
148–132 Gifted/Superior Intelligence
115 Higher Than Usual Intelligence
99 Average Intelligence
83 Low Average Intelligence
70 or below Very Low Intelligence

CHAPTER 3

SYNONYMS, ANTONYMS, OR NEITHER

The IQ Test Controversy

As the IQ test became a standard part of American society—it was used not only for school children but also by employers to gauge the suitability of prospective employees—some patterns began to emerge that some researchers as well as the-man-and-woman-in-the-street found unsettling. Blacks and Hispanics who took an IQ test tended to score lower than whites. The well-off tended to score better than the poor. And Asian Americans tended to score higher than any other racial group.

In the 1970s, critics blamed the designers of the IQ test for formulating questions that reflected white, middle class America. For example, a child was asked to complete the phrase "cup and…." "Saucer" was assumed to be the correct answer. But if the child grew up in a house where the family had no saucers, or did not use saucers, wouldn't the child's answer "table" be valid and equally correct?

As a result, psychologists, geneticists, social scientists, and other experts in the field of human intelligence began to debate whether environmental factors—where the test taker lived and how he or she was raised—had an impact on IQ scores. And if those factors did have an impact, to what extent? Although IQ tests continue to be given to children, the debate about the type of questions that appear on the test, and the accuracy of the scores rages on.

✏ Synonyms, Antonyms, or Neither I

1 *Halcyon* and *limpid* are

A. synonyms

B. antonyms

C. neither

2 *Narcissistic* and *vain* are

A. synonyms

B. antonyms

C. neither

3 *Ravenous* and *blackbird* are

A. synonyms

B. antonyms

C. neither

4 *Inglorious* and *disgraceful* are

A. synonyms

B. antonyms

C. neither

5 *Pallid* and *ruddy* are

A. synonyms

B. antonyms

C. neither

6 *Virile* and *virulent* are

A. synonyms

B. antonyms

C. neither

7 *Affianced* and *engaged* are

A. synonyms

B. antonyms

C. neither

8 *Effrontery* and *frontage* are

A. synonyms

B. antonyms

C. neither

9 *Notable* and *significant* are

A. synonyms

B. antonyms

C. neither

10 *Porous* and *impoverished* are

A. synonyms

B. antonyms

C. neither

ANSWERS ·

① C. neither
② A. synonyms
③ C. neither
④ A. synonyms
⑤ B. antonyms

⑥ C. neither
⑦ A. synonyms
⑧ C. neither
⑨ A. synonyms
⑩ C. neither

SCORING ·

Award 16.5 points for each correct answer.

165 Genius
148–132 Gifted/Superior Intelligence
115 Higher Than Usual Intelligence
99 Average Intelligence
83 Low Average Intelligence
70 or below Very Low Intelligence

➡ Synonyms, Antonyms, or Neither II

❶ *Hidebound* and *leather* are

A. synonyms

B. antonyms

C. neither

❷ *Morass* and *quagmire* are

A. synonyms

B. antonyms

C. neither

❸ *Noisome* and *attractive* are

A. synonyms

B. antonyms

C. neither

❹ *Vignette* and *vinegar* are

A. synonyms

B. antonyms

C. neither

5 *Bauble* and *treasure* are

 A. synonyms

 B. antonyms

 C. neither

6 *Gigolo* and *flute* are

 A. synonyms

 B. antonyms

 C. neither

7 *Didactic* and *moralizing* are

 A. synonyms

 B. antonyms

 C. neither

8 *Harbinger* and *messenger* are

 A. synonyms

 B. antonyms

 C. neither

9 *Nepotism* and *despotism* are

 A. synonyms

 B. antonyms

 C. neither

10 *Nadir* and *climax* are

 A. synonyms

 B. antonyms

 C. neither

ANSWERS ·

① C. neither
② A. synonyms
③ B. antonyms
④ C. neither
⑤ B. antonyms

⑥ C. neither
⑦ A. synonyms
⑧ A. synonyms
⑨ C. neither
⑩ B. antonyms

SCORING ·

Award 16.5 points for each correct answer.

165 Genius
148–132 Gifted/Superior Intelligence
115 Higher Than Usual Intelligence
99 Average Intelligence

83 Low Average Intelligence
70 or below Very Low Intelligence

✏️ Synonyms, Antonyms, or Neither III

1 *Bane* and *nuisance* are

   A. synonyms

   B. antonyms

   C. neither

2 *Lachrymose* and *jolly* are

   A. synonyms

   B. antonyms

   C. neither

3 *Polarize* and *divide* are

   A. synonyms

   B. antonyms

   C. neither

4 *Vassal* and *flower pot* are

   A. synonyms

   B. antonyms

   C. neither

5 *Clique* and *faction* are

   A. synonyms

   B. antonyms

   C. neither

6 *Virtuoso* and *saint* are

   A. synonyms

   B. antonyms

   C. neither

7 *Forte* and *weakness* are

   A. synonyms

   B. antonyms

   C. neither

8 *Mountebank* and *fraud* are

   A. synonyms

   B. antonyms

   C. neither

9 *Risible* and *solemn* are

   A. synonyms

   B. antonyms

   C. neither

10 *Élan* and *styleless* are

   A. synonyms

   B. antonyms

   C. neither

ANSWERS

① A. synonyms
② B. antonyms
③ A. synonyms
④ C. neither
⑤ A. synonyms

⑥ C. neither
⑦ B. antonyms
⑧ A. synonyms
⑨ B. antonyms
⑩ B. antonyms

SCORING

Award 16.5 points for each correct answer.

165 Genius
148–132 Gifted/Superior Intelligence
115 Higher Than Usual Intelligence
99 Average Intelligence
83 Low Average Intelligence
70 or below Very Low Intelligence

✏️ Synonyms, Antonyms, or Neither IV

① *Immure* and *liberate* are

   A. synonyms

   B. antonyms

   C. neither

② *Diaphanous* and *sheer* are

   A. synonyms

   B. antonyms

   C. neither

③ *Maladroit* and *skillful* are

   A. synonyms

   B. antonyms

   C. neither

④ *Salubrious* and *cheesy* are

   A. synonyms

   B. antonyms

   C. neither

5 *Traumatic* and *joyous* are

    A. synonyms

    B. antonyms

    C. neither

6 *Impulsive* and *compound* are

    A. synonyms

    B. antonyms

    C. neither

7 *Portentous* and *significant* are

    A. synonyms

    B. antonyms

    C. neither

8 *Fastidious* and *sloppy* are

    A. synonyms

    B. antonyms

    C. neither

9 *Nemesis* and *archenemy* are

    A. synonyms

    B. antonyms

    C. neither

10 *Gargantuan* and *mouthwash* are

    A. synonyms

    B. antonyms

    C. neither

ANSWERS

① B. antonyms

② A. synonyms

③ B. antonyms

④ C. neither

⑤ B. antonyms

⑥ C. neither

⑦ A. synonyms

⑧ B. antonyms

⑨ A. synonyms

⑩ C. neither

SCORING

Award 16.5 points for each correct answer.

165 Genius

148–132 Gifted/Superior Intelligence

115 Higher Than Usual Intelligence
99 Average Intelligence
83 Low Average Intelligence
70 or below Very Low Intelligence

✐ Synonyms, Antonyms, or Neither V

1 *Heyday* and *harvest* are

  A. synonyms

  B. antonyms

  C. neither

2 *Prolix* and *long-winded* are

  A. synonyms

  B. antonyms

  C. neither

3 *Kudos* and *congratulations* are

  A. synonyms

  B. antonyms

  C. neither

4 *Fortnight* and *barricade* are

  A. synonyms

  B. antonyms

  C. neither

5 *Acumen* and *foolishness* are

  A. synonyms

  B. antonyms

  C. neither

6 *Lackey* and *master* are

  A. synonyms

  B. antonyms

  C. neither

7 *Liaison* and *love affair* are

  A. synonyms

  B. antonyms

  C. neither

8 *Apocryphal* and *fictional* are

  A. synonyms

  B. antonyms

  C. neither

9 *Fawning* and *haughty* are

    A. synonyms

    B. antonyms

    C. neither

10 *Patrician* and *aristocrat* are

    A. synonyms

    B. antonyms

    C. neither

ANSWERS ·

① C. neither
② A. synonyms
③ A. synonyms
④ C. neither
⑤ B. antonyms

⑥ B. antonyms
⑦ A. synonyms
⑧ A. synonyms
⑨ B. antonyms
⑩ A. synonyms

SCORING ·

Award 16.5 points for each correct answer.

> *165 Genius*
> *148–132 Gifted/Superior Intelligence*
> *115 Higher Than Usual Intelligence*
> *99 Average Intelligence*
> *83 Low Average Intelligence*
> *70 or below Very Low Intelligence*

TEST YOUR VOCABULARY

IQ Scores of People in Hisstory

What was Galileo's IQ score? Or Abraham Lincoln's? Or the ancient philosopher and mathematician Hypatia's? It sounds like a trick question, because the IQ test did not exist when these famous people were alive. Nonetheless, in the 1920s Catherine Cox Miles, an American psychologist, began to study the developmental histories of 100 geniuses. She identified 67 character traits that became her basis for calculating IQ.

In the 1990s, Tony Buzan, an English expert in intelligence and accelerated learning, confirmed Cox Miles' work, but added the IQs of several more genius to the list and in some cases gave new scores to the geniuses on Cox Miles' list. What follows is a sampling from Cox Miles' and Buzan's studies.

William Shakespeare 210 (Buzan)
Sir Isaac Newton 190 (Buzan 195)
Leonardo da Vinci 180 (Buzan 220)
Marie Curie 180 (Buzan)
George Friedrich Handel 170
Hypatia 170 (Buzan 210)
Galileo Galilei 165
Charlotte Bronte 165
Wolfgang Amadeus Mozart, 165
Albert Einstein 160 (205 Buzan)
Benjamin Franklin 160 (Buzan 185)
Thomas Jefferson, 160
Charles Darwin 153
George Eliot (Mary Ann Evans) 150 (Buzan 180)
Abraham Lincoln 150
George Washington 140
Ulysses S. Grant 130

✏ Test Your Vocabulary I

1 Something said to be *toxic* is

A. annoying

B. poisonous

C. noisy

D. oily

E. round

2 A *repast* is a(n)

A. meal

B. instant replay

C. historical event

D. nap

E. repeating rifle

3 An *obstreperous* child is

A. overweight

B. suffering from strep throat

C. defiant

D. small for his or her age

E. athletic

4 An *itinerant* person

A. wanders from place to place

B. has a short attention span

C. is poorly educated

D. asks for spare change

E. can't hold a job

5 To take *umbrage* is to

A. steal

B. feel offended

C. try a sample

D. find a shady spot

E. rest

6 A *hierarch* is a(n)

A. skydiver

B. bishop

C. ancient alphabet

D. bridge builder

E. snob

7 Someone who is *bibulous*

A. drinks too much alcohol

B. drools

C. likes lettuce

D. acts foolishly

E. is a bad dancer

8 A *fecund* field is

A. rotting

B. barren

C. full of weeds

D. overgrown

E. fertile

⑨ To act with *aplomb* is to be

    A. shy

    B. loud

    C. nervous

    D. self-confident

    E. self-conscious

⑩ A *misanthrope*

    A. hates people

    B. causes a sore throat

    C. is a female antelope

    D. is a mathematical equation

    E. studies the stars

ANSWERS

① B. poisonous
② A. meal
③ C. defiant
④ A. wanders from place to place
⑤ B. feel offended
⑥ B. bishop
⑦ A. drinks too much alcohol
⑧ E. fertile
⑨ D. self-confident
⑩ A. hates people

SCORING

Award 16.5 points for each correct answer.

165 Genius
148–132 Gifted/Superior Intelligence
115 Higher Than Usual Intelligence
99 Average Intelligence
83 Low Average Intelligence
70 or below Very Low Intelligence

✏️ Test Your Vocabulary II

1 An *augury* is a(n)

  A. stable

  B. woodworking tool

  C. prediction

  D. renowned speaker

  E. herb

2 To be *feckless* is to be

  A. incompetent or lack initiative

  B. without hair

  C. unlucky

  D. unfertile

  C. dejected

3 Something described as *tawdry* is

  A. immoral

  B. broken

  C. dry

  D. cheap or gaudy

  E. poor

4 A *boor* is a

  A. wild pig

  B. domestic male hog

  C. person with no manners

  D. small hole in fabric

  E. South African colonist

5 To *stipulate* is

  A. to sprinkle

  B. to cover with dots

  C. to drink too much

  D. to be tardy

  E. to specify

6 A fabric described as *diaphanous* is

  A. birdlike

  B. thin and transparent

  C. feathery

  D. dense

  E. cumbersome

7 To have a *penchant* is

  A. to have tendency or an inclination

  B. to pretend

  C. to write well

  D. to think carefully

  E. to dream

8 To *incise* is

    A. to dedicate a book to someone

    B. to tailor

    C. to sort clippings for a scrapbook

    D. to carve or cut into a surface, such as a stone

    E. to adorn with jewels

9 A *feint* is a

    A. swoon

    B. forgery

    C. lie

    D. masquerade

    E. pretend attack

10 To be *inured* is

    A. to be buried alive

    B. to be accustomed or hardened to suffering or pain

    C. to be covered by an insurance policy

    D. to suffer a serious injury

    E. to be falsely accused

ANSWERS

① C. prediction
② A. incompetent or lack initiative
③ D. cheap or gaudy
④ C. a person with no manners
⑤ E. to specify
⑥ B. thin and transparent
⑦ A. to have tendency or an inclination
⑧ D. to carve or cut into something, such as a stone
⑨ E. pretend attack
⑩ B. to be accustomed or hardened to suffering or pain

SCORING

Award 16.5 points for each correct answer.

165 Genius

148–132 Gifted/Superior Intelligence
115 Higher Than Usual Intelligence
99 Average Intelligence
83 Low Average Intelligence
70 or below Very Low Intelligence

✏️ Test Your Vocabulary III

1 A person described as
mettlesome is

A. interfering

B. courageous

C. stubborn

D. stingy

E. handsome

2 To be *foppish* is

A. to be a thoughtless
child

B. to be a cautious woman

C. to be a romantic girl

D. to be a wise elderly
man or woman

E. to be a man overly
concerned about
fashionable clothing
and accessories

3 A *gaffe* is a

A. type of gazelle

B. sharp metal hook

C. colloquial expression
for a father

D. social blunder or mistake

E. type of garlic

4 To be an object of
opprobrium is

A. to be admired

B. to be imitated

C. to be treated with scorn
or contempt

D. to be treated as an equal

E. to be slow or dull-
witted

5 To be *recumbent* is to

    A. lie down

    B. curtsy

    C. sit upright

    D. make a low bow

    E. straddle a chair

6 To be *culpable* is

    A. to be engaged to marry

    B. to be guilty of some wrongdoing

    C. to be romantically involved with someone else's spouse

    D. to have artistic talent

    E. to be sympathetic

7 Something described as *runic* is

    A. falling down

    B. fast or quick

    C. ancient

    D. misshaped

    E. mysterious or magical

8 An ailment described as *chronic* is

    A. incurable

    B. persistent or long-lasting

    C. fatal

    D. imaginary

    E. contagious

9 To be *discerning* is

    A. to be perceptive

    B. to be disrespectful

    C. to be confused

    D. to be careless

    E. to be prejudiced

10 A person described as *churlish* is

    A. short

    B. portly

    C. rude

    D. immature

    E. physically unattractive

ANSWERS ·

① A. interfering
② E. to be a man overly concerned about fashionable clothing and accessories

③ D. social blunder or mistake
④ C. to be an object of scorn or contempt
⑤ A. lie down
⑥ B. to be guilty of some wrongdoing
⑦ E. mysterious or magical
⑧ B. persistent or long-lasting
⑨ A. to be perceptive
⑩ C. rude

SCORING ·

Award 16.5 points for each correct answer.

165 Genius
148–132 Gifted/Superior Intelligence
115 Higher Than Usual Intelligence
99 Average Intelligence
83 Low Average Intelligence
70 or below Very Low Intelligence

✎ Test Your Vocabulary IV

1 A *demagogue* is a(n)

   A. advocate of democracy

   B. pompous schoolteacher

   C. sensitive audio system

   D. political leader who appeals to citizens' fears

   E. a community activist

2 An *interregnum* is a(n)

   A. period between two reigns or governments

   B. imperial crown

   C. official attached to a monarch's court

   D. courtroom

   E. ambassador

3 A person said to possess *dexterity* is

   A. right-handed

   B. politically and socially conservative

   C. skillful with his or her hands

   D. unshakable in his or her opinions

   E. a popular public speaker

4 A *raconteur* is a(n)

   A. nocturnal animal

   B. cat burglar

   C. French chef

   D. gangster

   E. gifted storyteller

5 To be *solicitous* of another person is

   A. to represent him or her in court

   B. to request a favor

   C. to beg for a hand-out

   D. to be thoughtful and express concern

   E. to be critical

6 To *coerce* others is

   A. to insult or belittle them

   B. to force them to do something they do not want to do

   C. to demand payment of a debt

   D. to cooperate with them

   E. to praise them

7 Something described as *iniquitous* is

   A. evil

   B. left-handed

   C. wise

   D. nosy

   E. out of balance

8 A *milliner*

   A. grinds grain

   B. mends clothes

   C. grows millet

   D. runs marathons

   E. makes hats

9 Someone described
as *dapper* is

    A. friendly and outgoing

    B. young and handsome

    C. kind and generous

    D. neat and well-dressed

    E. polite and articulate

10 Something said to be
occluded is

    A. unable to see

    B. out of date and useless

    C. blocked from moving
forward

    D. difficult to understand

    E. thick with fog

ANSWERS

① D. political leader who appeals to citizens' fears
② A. period between two reigns of governments
③ C. skillful with his or her hands
④ E. gifted storyteller
⑤ D. to be thoughtful and express concern
⑥ B. to force them to do something they do not want to do
⑦ A. evil
⑧ E. makes hats
⑨ D. neat and well-dressed
⑩ C. blocked from moving forward

SCORING

Award 16.5 points for each correct answer.

165 Genius
148–132 Gifted/Superior Intelligence
115 Higher Than Usual Intelligence
99 Average Intelligence
83 Low Average Intelligence
70 or below Very Low Intelligence

✏️ Test Your Vocabulary V

1 To be *avaricious* is

A. to strive for success

B. to desire money

C. to love birds

D. to be generous

E. to be excessively proud

2 A period or place described as *halcyon* is

A. frighteningly unfamiliar

B. mythical

C. exotic

D. aristocratic

E. happy and peaceful

3 To be *testy* is

A. to be good at taking tests

B. to enjoy giving tests

C. to be irritable

D. to be reliable

E. to be exact

4 Someone described as *maudlin* is

A. ruddy-faced

B. insincere

C. fond of children

D. sentimental to the point of weeping

E. arrogant

5 A *cumbersome* object is

A. orange in color

B. fragrant and appealing

C. bulky and hard to move or carry

D. ideally situated

E. off-putting

6 A *forward* person is

A. proud and conceited

B. presumptuous and bold

C. ahead of his or her time

D. thoughtful and considerate

E. imaginative

7 A *fortnight* is a period of

   A. fourteen days

   B. forty days

   C. four hours

   D. fourteen minutes

   E. forty years

8 To be *supine* is

   A. to sip soup

   B. to siphon liquid

   C. to be late for supper

   D. to bend over

   E. to be flat on one's back

9 A *quisling* is a

   A. teenage boy

   B. knight on a quest

   C. traitor

   D. secret agent

   E. test-taker

10 Someone described as *emaciated* is

   A. unusually attractive

   B. excessively, even dangerously thin

   C. taller than average

   D. freed from slavery

   E. elderly and feeble

ANSWERS ·

① B. to desire money
② E. happy and peaceful
③ C. to be irritable
④ D. sentimental to the point of weeping
⑤ C. bulky and hard to move or carry
⑥ B. presumptuous and bold
⑦ A. two weeks or fourteen days
⑧ E. to be flat on one's back
⑨ C. a traitor
⑩ B. excessively, even dangerously thin

SCORING ·

Award 16.5 points for each correct answer.

165 Genius
148–132 Gifted/Superior Intelligence
115 Higher Than Usual Intelligence
99 Average Intelligence
83 Low Average Intelligence
70 or below Very Low Intelligence

CHAPTER 5

RECOGNIZING PATTERNS

IQ Scores of Famous Contemporary People

Just about everyone who was born in the second half of the 20th century took an IQ test, so it is much easier to learn their scores than the scores of people from the distant past.

Gary Kasparov, chess champion, 190
Bobby Fischer, chess champion, 187
Benjamin Netanyahu, prime minister of Israel, 180
Bill Gates, founder of Microsoft, 160
Stephen Hawking, physicist and author, 160
Reggie Jackson, professional baseball player, 160
Richard Nixon, former president of the United States, 143
Hillary Clinton, US secretary of state and former First Lady, 140

Bill Clinton, former US president, 137
George W. Bush, former US president, 125
Gerald Ford, former president of the United States, 121

Recognizing Patterns I

In each of the following groups of words, select the word that is not like the others.

1. **A.** novel
   B. poem
   C. painting
   D. flower
   E. sculpture

2. **A.** radish
   B. tomato
   C. pear
   D. apple
   E. orange

3. **A.** shredder
   B. knife
   C. razor
   D. chainsaw
   E. grater

4. **A.** heron
   B. swan
   C. penguin
   D. duck
   E. goose

5. **A.** euro
   B. dollar
   C. diamond
   D. pound
   E. franc

6. **A.** bus
   B. cab
   C. train
   D. subway
   E. monorail

7. **A.** lion
   B. tiger
   C. cougar
   D. puma
   E. bear

8. **A.** azure
   B. cobalt
   C. emerald
   D. navy
   E. sapphire

9 **A.** malbec

   B. chardonnay

   C. burgundy

   D. shiraz

   E. pilsen

10 **A.** chamois

   B. gabardine

   C. calico

   D. twill

   E. denim

ANSWERS

① D. flower
② A. radish
③ E. grater
④ A. heron
⑤ C. diamond
⑥ B. cab
⑦ E. bear
⑧ C. emerald
⑨ E. pilsen
⑩ A. chamois

SCORING

Award 16.5 points for each correct answer.

165 Genius
148–132 Gifted/Superior Intelligence
115 Higher Than Usual Intelligence
99 Average Intelligence
83 Low Average Intelligence
70 or below Very Low Intelligence

✏️ Recognizing Patterns II

In each of the following groups of words, select the word that is not like the others.

1 **A.** dictionary
B. atlas
C. almanac
D. encyclopedia
E. memoir

2 **A.** cup
B. gill
C. bushel
D. firkin
E. hogshead

3 **A.** courage
B. security
C. perseverance
D. fortitude
E. patience

4 **A.** plot
B. table of contents
C. index
D. chapter
E. cover

5 **A.** yam
B. cucumber
C. potato
D. sunchoke
E. shallot

6 **A.** whale
B. dolphin
C. porpoise
D. tuna
E. seal

7 **A.** breach
B. break
C. brooch
D. fissure
E. gap

8 **A.** conductor
B. author
C. ballerina
D. engraver
E. contractor

9 **A.** numeracy
  B. empty set
  C. cosine
  D. radius
  E. matrix

10 **A.** dig
  B. pot shard
  C. stratosphere
  D. midden
  E. in situ

ANSWERS

① E. memoir
② C. bushel
③ B. security
④ A. plot
⑤ B. cucumber
⑥ D. tuna
⑦ C. brooch
⑧ E. contractor
⑨ A. numeracy
⑩ C. stratosphere

SCORING

Award 16.5 points for each correct answer.

165 Genius
148–132 Gifted/Superior Intelligence
115 Higher Than Usual Intelligence
99 Average Intelligence
83 Low Average Intelligence
70 or below Very Low Intelligence

✏️ Recognizing Patterns III

In each of the following groups of words, select the word that is not like the others.

1. **A.** grape seed oil
   B. aloe
   C. lanolin
   D. glycerin
   E. astringent

2. **A.** stamen
   B. petal
   C. stem
   D. tannin
   E. stigma

3. **A.** cowardice
   B. anxiety
   C. jealousy
   D. rapaciousness
   E. vanity

4. **A.** eulogy
   B. doggerel
   C. haiku
   D. sonnet
   E. epic

5. **A.** equilateral
   B. isosceles
   C. obtuse
   D. acute
   E. hypotenuse

6. **A.** polenta
   B. faro
   C. barley
   D. quinoa
   E. wheat berries

7. **A.** balloon
   B. fixed rate
   C. adjustable rate
   D. reverse
   E. truth-in-lending

8. **A.** carnation
   B. cyan
   C. fuchsia
   D. magenta
   E. rose

9. **A.** awl

   B. fabric shears

   C. bias

   D. mannequin

   E. seam ripper

10. **A.** repel

    B. retort

    C. oppose

    D. withstand

    E. weather

ANSWERS

① E. astringent
② D. tannin
③ B. anxiety
④ A. eulogy
⑤ E. hypotenuse

⑥ A. polenta
⑦ E. truth-in-lending
⑧ B. cyan
⑨ C. bias
⑩ B. retort

SCORING

Award 16.5 points for each correct answer.

165 Genius
148–132 Gifted/Superior Intelligence
115 Higher Than Usual Intelligence
99 Average Intelligence
83 Low Average Intelligence
70 or below Very Low Intelligence

✎ Recognizing Patterns IV

In each of the following groups of words, select the word that is not like the others.

1. **A.** antic
   B. frivolous
   C. exploit
   D. eccentric
   E. amusing

2. **A.** epistolary
   B. bildungsroman
   C. dime
   D. Gothic
   E. burlesque

3. **A.** festivals
   B. mores
   C. customs
   D. traditions
   E. practices

4. **A.** globe
   B. sphere
   C. orb
   D. rotunda
   E. ball

5. **A.** falchion
   B. scimitar
   C. gladius
   D. foil
   E. stiletto

6. **A.** apt
   B. absorbed
   C. apposite
   D. appropriate
   E. fitting

7. **A.** lilac
   B. aubergine
   C. lavender
   D. vermilion
   E. violet

8. **A.** intransigent
   B. inflexible
   C. insufferable
   D. unyielding
   E. uncompromising

9 **A.** cubist
   B. still life
   C. landscape
   D. genre
   E. portrait

10 **A.** guru
   B. mystic
   C. shaman
   D. yeti
   E. sage

ANSWERS

① C. exploit
② E. burlesque
③ A. festivals
④ D. rotunda
⑤ E. stiletto

⑥ B. absorbed
⑦ D. vermilion
⑧ C. insufferable
⑨ A. cubist
⑩ D. yeti

SCORING

Award 16.5 points for each correct answer.

165 Genius
148–132 Gifted/Superior Intelligence
115 Higher Than Usual Intelligence
99 Average Intelligence
83 Low Average Intelligence
70 or below Very Low Intelligence

Recognizing Patterns V

In each of the following groups of words, select the word that is not like the others.

1. **A.** evening
   B. cocktail
   C. prom
   D. bridesmaid
   E. vintage

2. **A.** chambermaid
   B. gardener
   C. butler
   D. valet
   E. footman

3. **A.** excoriate
   B. berate
   C. upbraid
   D. criticize
   E. exculpate

4. **A.** square
   B. plaza
   C. cube
   D. piazza
   E. quadrangle

5. **A.** fork
   B. junction
   C. intersection
   D. crossroads
   E. bypass

6. **A.** genius
   B. muse
   C. inspiration
   D. motivation
   E. stimulation

7. **A.** teal
   B. lemon
   C. mustard
   D. saffron
   E. gold

8. **A.** adolescent
   B. tot
   C. youth
   D. youngster
   E. teenager

⑨ **A.** souvenir

　B. keepsake

　C. memento mori

　D. trinket

　E. knickknack

⑩ **A.** reference

　B. checkout

　C. stacks

　D. narthex

　E. periodical room

ANSWERS ·

① E. vintage
② B. gardener
③ E. exculpate
④ C. cube
⑤ E. bypass

⑥ A. genius
⑦ A. teal
⑧ B. tot
⑨ C. memento mori
⑩ D. narthex

SCORING ·

Award 16.5 points for each correct answer.

165 Genius
148–132 Gifted/Superior Intelligence
115 Higher Than Usual Intelligence
99 Average Intelligence
83 Low Average Intelligence
70 or below Very Low Intelligence

CHAPTER 6

FILL IN THE MISSING LETTERS

Hollywood IQ Scores

There is a common perception that when it comes to intellectual achievement, Hollywood actors run the gamut from dumb to dumber. That's an unfair characterization. The breathtakingly beautiful Hedy Lamarr, for example, was also incredibly intelligent—she was the co-inventor of a spread spectrum technique used in wireless communication. Of course, not everyone in Hollywood rises to that level of brilliance, but there are plenty of highly intelligent actors and actresses.

James Wood, 180
Judy Holliday, 172
Dolph Lundgren,160
Quentin Tarantino, 160

Sharon Stone, 154
Jayne Mansfield, 149
Steve Martin, 142
Geena Davis, 140
Madonna, 140
Shakira, 140
Arnold Schwarzenegger, 135
Jodie Foster, actress, 132
Nicole Kidman, 132

✏️ Fill in the
Missing Letters I

Fill in the missing letters to create words associated with comedy.

❶ ___ U ___ LE ___ QU ___

❷ F ___ RC ___

❸ ___ U ___ O ___

❹ ___ ES ___ IN ___

❺ C ___ OW ___ IN ___

❻ ___ OS ___

❼ S ___ A ___ S ___ IC ___

❽ ___ A ___ S

❾ P ___ EA ___ A ___ T ___ Y

❿ ___ A ___ P ___ O ___

ANSWERS ·

❿ LAMPOON
❻ PLEASANTRY
❽ GAGS
❼ SLAPSTICK
❾ JOSH

❺ CLOWNING
❹ JESTING
❸ HUMOR
❷ FARCE
❶ BURLESQUE

SCORING ·

Award 16.5 points for each correct answer.

165 Genius
148–132 Gifted/Superior Intelligence
115 Higher Than Usual Intelligence
99 Average Intelligence
83 Low Average Intelligence
70 or below Very Low Intelligence

Fill in the Missing Letters II

Fill in the missing letters to create words associated with romance.

1 A ___ F ___ I ___

2 ___ A ___ S ___ O ___

3 A ___ FE ___ T ___ O ___

4 ___ E ___ O ___ I ___ N

5 Y ___ AR ___ IN ___

6 ___ E ___ D ___ R

7 A ___ O ___ O ___ S

8 ___ O ___ I ___ G

9 S ___ A ___ RY-E ___ E ___

10 A ___ D ___ N ___

ANSWERS ·

⑩ ARDENT

⑥ STARRY-EYED

⑧ LOVING

⑦ AMOROUS

⑨ TENDER

⑤ YEARNING

④ DEVOTION

③ AFFECTION

② PASSION

① AFFAIR

SCORING ·

Award 16.5 points for each correct answer.

165 Genius
148–132 Gifted/Superior Intelligence
115 Higher Than Usual Intelligence
99 Average Intelligence
83 Low Average Intelligence
70 or below Very Low Intelligence

✐ Fill in the
Missing Letters III

Fill in the missing letters to create words associated with innocence.

① I ___ E ___ P ___ R ___ E ___ C ___

② ___ I ___ T ___ E

③ P ___ R ___ T ___

④ ___ N ___ O ___ R ___ P ___

⑤ B ___ A ___ E ___ E ___ S

6 ___ O ___ D ___ E ___ S

7 C ___ I ___ D ___ I ___ E

8 ___ N ___ E ___ U ___ U ___

9 N ___ Ï ___ E

10 ___ R ___ S ___ I ___ G

ANSWERS ·

⑩ TRUSTING

⑨ NAÏVE

⑧ INGENUOUS

⑦ CHILDLIKE

⑥ GOODNESS

⑤ BLAMELESS

④ INCORRUPT

③ PURITY

② VIRTUE

① INEXPERIENCE

SCORING ·

Award 16.5 points for each correct answer.

165 Genius
148–132 Gifted/Superior Intelligence
115 Higher Than Usual Intelligence
99 Average Intelligence
83 Low Average Intelligence
70 or below Very Low Intelligence

✏️ Fill in the Missing Letters IV

Fill in the missing letters to create words associated with work.

1. ___ O ___ L

2. R ___ P ___ T ___ T ___ O ___ S

3. ___ E ___ A ___ D ___ N ___

4. L ___ B ___ R

5. ___ O ___ A ___ I ___ N

6. O ___ C ___ P ___ T ___ O ___

7. ___ U ___ E ___ V ___ S ___ R

8. S ___ L ___ R ___

9. ___ E ___ E ___ I ___ S

10. U ___ I ___ N

ANSWERS ·

1. TOIL
2. REPETITIOUS
3. REWARDING
4. LABOR
5. VOCATION
6. OCCUPATION
7. SUPERVISOR
8. SALARY
9. BENEFITS
10. UNION

SCORING ·

Award 16.5 points for each correct answer.

165 Genius
148–132 Gifted/Superior Intelligence
115 Higher Than Usual Intelligence
99 Average Intelligence
83 Low Average Intelligence
70 or below Very Low Intelligence

✏️ Fill in the Missing Letters V

Fill in the missing letters to create words associated with entertainment.

1 A ___ U ___ E ___ E ___ T

2 ___ H ___ A ___ E ___

3 D ___ N ___ E

4 ___ O ___ I ___

5 P ___ A ___

6 ___ E ___ F ___ R ___ A ___ C ___

7 S ___ O ___

8 ___ A ___ D ___ V ___ L ___ E

9 A ___ P ___ A ___ S ___

10 ___ A ___ G ___ T ___ R

ANSWERS

① AMUSEMENT
② THEATER
③ DANCE
④ MOVIE
⑤ PLAY

⑥ PERFORMANCE
⑦ SHOW
⑧ VAUDEVILLE
⑨ APPLAUSE
⑩ LAUGHTER

SCORING

Award 16.5 points for each correct answer.

165 Genius
148–132 Gifted/Superior Intelligence
115 Higher Than Usual Intelligence
99 Average Intelligence
83 Low Average Intelligence
70 or below Very Low Intelligence

CHAPTER 7

THE RIGHT WORD

Mensa International

Have you heard of Mensa? It is an organization of people with impressively high IQ scores. To qualify for membership, your IQ score must be in the top 2 percent of the population. In other words, 98 percent of people who have taken an IQ test are not eligible to join Mensa.

The society was founded in 1946 by Lancelot Ware, a graduate student who was studying law at Oxford University, and Roland Berrill, an Australian barrister who hung around the university, although his application for admission to Oxford had been rejected. Initially they called their society the High IQ Club. The name did not have much panache, so Ware and Berrill considered changing it to Mens, the Latin term for mind. Unfortunately, Mens was also the name of a racy men's magazine. So they chose Mensa,

Latin for "table," because the organization was to be a round table where no one was judged on the basis of their background or belief system. (Ironically, Ware and Berrill learned later that in Mexican slang, mensa means idiot).

Mensa has about 110,000 members in 100 countries across the globe. And they're not all brain surgeons and Nobel Prize-winning physicists. Sure, there are professors and scientists who are members of Mensa, but there are also firefighters, musicians, farmers, police officers, truck drivers, and members of the military.

This diverse group of people doesn't just sit around trying to impress one another with how smart they are. Nor do they promote any particular political, religious, or social agenda. According to the Mensa website, the organization is committed to three goals:

1. "To identify and foster human intelligence for the benefit of humanity.
2. To encourage research in the nature, characteristics and uses of intelligence.
3. To promote stimulating intellectual and social opportunities for its members."

Mensa publishes a journal for its members that features articles on a wide range of topics. The organization also publishes a newsletter that spotlights special events and activities that may be of interest to Mensa members. There is also the *Mensa Research Journal*, published for non-members, which addresses the nature of human intelligence.

✏️ The Right Word I

Identify the word that fits the definitions.

1. A strand or fiber of material.

   F _____

2. To be important or well-known.

   P _____

3. Something that stands for or represents something else.

   S _____

4. To be happy or optimistic.

   C _____

5. In geometry, a four-sided figure with four angles.

   T _____

6. A nonstick coating often used for cookware.

   T _____

7. Money collected by a government from its citizens.

   T _____

8. An informal term for a dirty or disreputable tavern, bar, or restaurant.

   D _____

9. Squares of pasta filled, typically, with meat or cheese.

   R _____

10. A cold-blooded animal that lives on land and in the water, but breeds exclusively in water.

    A _____

ANSWERS ·

⑩ Amphibian

⑨ Ravioli

⑧ Dive

⑦ Tax

⑥ Teflon

⑤ Tetragon

④ Cheerful

③ Symbol

② Prominent

① Filament

SCORING ·

Award 16.5 points for each correct answer.

165 Genius
148–132 Gifted/Superior Intelligence
115 Higher Than Usual Intelligence
99 Average Intelligence
83 Low Average Intelligence
70 or below Very Low Intelligence

✏️ The Right Word II

Identify the word that fits the definitions.

① An artifact, the remains of a building, or the remains of someone or something considered holy.

   R _____

② The organ enclosed inside the cranium that controls the nervous system.

   B _____

③ An expert who leads groups of visitors around a tourist destination.

   D _____

④ A corm, tuber, or rhizome from which a flowering plant grows every year.

   B _____

5 A liquid, often thickened, served to enhance the flavor of meat, fish, vegetables, or other dishes.

S _____

6 To be well-spoken, but in an insincere way.

G _____

7 A person who has a condition that it makes it challenging to perform common tasks of daily life.

D _____

8 A mechanism typically found in rivers to raise or lower ships.

L _____

9 A hard, underwater organism, famous for its distinctive colors; often made into jewelry.

C _____

10 A small open-sided structure often found in gardens or other scenic locations.

G _____

ANSWERS · · · · · · · · · · · · · · · · · ·

10 Gazebo

9 Coral

8 Lock

7 Disabled

9 Glib

5 Sauce

4 Bulb

3 Docent

2 Brain

1 Relic

SCORING ·

Award 16.5 points for each correct answer.

165 Genius
148–132 Gifted/Superior Intelligence
115 Higher Than Usual Intelligence
99 Average Intelligence
83 Low Average Intelligence
70 or below Very Low Intelligence

✏️ The Right Word III

Identify the word that fits the definitions.

1 A diplomat sent to a foreign nation to represent his or her nation's interests.

A _____

2 A crease in the skin or in fabric.

W _____

3 Kernels of a type of grain that puff up when heated.

P _____

4 A deer less than a year old.

F _____

5 Office machinery that destroys documents.

S _____

6 An edible, thin-skinned tuber, usually orange in color.

C _____

7 An athlete who works to increase the size of his or her muscles.

B _____

8 To be silly, unwise, or show a lack of judgment.

F _____

9 A violent emotion, usually in response to being insulted or offended.

A _____

10 A foreigner who settles in a new country.

I _____

ANSWERS ·

10 Immigrant
9 Anger
8 Foolish
7 Bodybuilder
6 Carrot

5 Shredder
4 Fawn
3 Popcorn
2 Wrinkle
1 Ambassador

SCORING ·

Award 16.5 points for each correct answer.

165 Genius
148–132 Gifted/Superior Intelligence
115 Higher Than Usual Intelligence
99 Average Intelligence
83 Low Average Intelligence
70 or below Very Low Intelligence

✏️ The Right Word IV

Identify the word that fits the definitions.

1 Describing a wound that oozes pus.

S _____

2 Criminal involved in organized crime.

M _____

3 An alcoholic beverage made by fermenting grapes.

W _____

4 To shake or tremble, often from cold or fear.

S _____

5 The Sun and its planets, satellites, asteroids, meteors, and comets.

S _____

6 The inability to make a decision. Also a breakfast pastry.

W _____

7 The level of moisture in the atmosphere.

H _____

8 A virtue that demonstrates sound judgment in making decisions in practical matters.

P _____

9 Something lethal or fatal.

D _____

10 To be kind and courteous.

G _____

ANSWERS

1 Septic
2 Mobster
3 Wine
4 Shudder
5 Solar System
6 Waffle
7 Humidity
8 Prudence
9 Deadly
10 Gracious

SCORING

Award 16.5 points for each correct answer.

165 Genius
148–132 Gifted/Superior Intelligence
115 Higher Than Usual Intelligence
99 Average Intelligence
83 Low Average Intelligence
70 or below Very Low Intelligence

✏ The Right Word V

Identify the word that fits the definitions.

1. Someone who arranges romantic relationships intended to lead to marriage.

   M _____

2. Water in its solid form.

   I _____

3. An area covered with dense tropical vegetation.

   J _____

4. A work of fiction with a long, complicated plot, usually involving many characters.

   N _____

5. To receive a guest or visitor happily.

   W _____

6. Characteristic of someone who endures a delay or long wait or even a form of suffering without complaint.

   P _____

7. Characteristic of being frugal.

   E _____

8. To be intelligent and creative in solving problems.

   C _____

9. An enclosed area where spectators watch athletes.

   S _____

10. A measure of someone's intelligence, based on a test score.

    I _____

ANSWERS

10. IQ
9. Stadium
8. Clever
7. Novel
6. Patience

5. Welcome
4. Economical
3. Jungle
2. Ice
1. Matchmaker

SCORING

Award 16.5 points for each correct answer.

165 Genius
148–132 Gifted/Superior Intelligence
115 Higher Than Usual Intelligence
99 Average Intelligence
83 Low Average Intelligence
70 or below Very Low Intelligence

CHAPTER 8

WORD PAIRS

Famous Members of Mensa

Jean Auel is the author of the best-selling novels *Clan of the Cave Bear*, *Valley of Horses*, and *Plains of Passage*.

Richard Bolles' book, *What Color is Your Parachute?*, was *The New York Times* Bestseller List for 228 weeks.

Adrian Cronauer is a radio personality made famous in the movie *Good Morning Vietnam*.

Geena Davis is an Academy Award-winning actress who starred in *A League of Their Own* and *Thelma and Louise*.

Maurice Kanbar invented and owns Skyy Vodka.

Richard Lederer is a renowned "pun-master," has appeared often on National Public Radio. He is the author of numerous books on word play.

Harry Milligan is a boxer who won the 1983 National Amateur Heavyweight championship.

Ellen Morphonios is a former model and beauty queen who serves as a judge in Florida, where her strict rulings have earned her the nickname, "Maximum Morphonios."

Barry Nolan is co-anchor of the TV program *Hard Copy*.

Donald Petersen was chairman of the Ford Motor Company where he was involved in the development of the Mustang and the Maverick—two of Ford's most successful automobiles.

Julie Peterson is a chiropractor and former Playboy Playmate.

Marilyn Vos Savant is featured in the Guinness Hall of Fame for having the world's highest recorded IQ score—228. She writes the "Ask Marilyn" column in *Parade* magazine.

Linda Warwick created and produced the wildly popular Babymugs! and Toddler TOGS videos.

Deborah Yates dances with the Radio City Rockettes.

Word Pairs I

Pair one word from Column A with one word from Column B to create a common two-word expression. For example, Big + Top forms Big Top.

COLUMN A	COLUMN B
1 Well	Times
2 Left	Hearted
3 Thin	Mail
4 Warm	Movie
5 Cold	Face
6 Happy	Five
7 Express	Skinned
8 High	Day
9 Dirty	Fish
10 Hard	Heeled

ANSWERS

10 Hard Times
9 Dirty Movie
8 High Five
7 Express Mail
6 Happy Day

5 Cold Fish
4 Warm Hearted
3 Thin Skinned
2 Left Face
1 Well Heeled

SCORING

Award 16.5 points for each correct answer.

165 Genius
148–132 Gifted/Superior Intelligence

115 Higher Than Usual Intelligence
99 Average Intelligence
83 Low Average Intelligence
70 or below Very Low Intelligence

Word Pairs II

Pair one word from Column A with one word from Column B to create a common two-word expression. For example, Big + Top forms Big Top.

COLUMN A	COLUMN B
1 Never	Kennel
2 Every	Cream
3 Pickup	Show
4 Wake-up	Mind
5 Puppet	Fountain
6 Dog	Call
7 Doll	Chocolate
8 Soda	Truck
9 Ice	Day
10 Hot	Hospital

ANSWERS

1) Never Mind
2) Every Day
3) Pickup Truck
4) Wake-up Call
5) Puppet Show

6) Dog Kennel
7) Doll Hospital
8) Soda Fountain
9) Ice Cream
10) Hot Chocolate

SCORING ·

Award 16.5 points for each correct answer.

165 Genius
148–132 Gifted/Superior Intelligence
115 Higher Than Usual Intelligence
99 Average Intelligence
83 Low Average Intelligence
70 or below Very Low Intelligence

 Word Pairs III

Pair one word from Column A with one word from Column B to create a common two-word expression. For example, Big + Top forms Big Top.

COLUMN A	COLUMN B
1 Movie	Scan
2 Thumb	Crumbs
3 Fig	Court
4 Independent	Teller
5 Pocket	Pot
6 Brain	Star
7 Flower	Watch
8 Bread	Tack
9 Basketball	Leaf
10 Bank	Contractor

ANSWERS ·

⑩ Bank Teller
⑨ Basketball Court
⑧ Bread Crumbs
⑦ Flower Pot
⑥ Brain Scan

⑤ Pocket Watch
④ Independent Contractor
③ Fig Leaf
② Thumb Tack
① Movie Star

SCORING ·

Award 16.5 points for each correct answer.

165 Genius
148–132 Gifted/Superior Intelligence
115 Higher Than Usual Intelligence
99 Average Intelligence
83 Low Average Intelligence
70 or below Very Low Intelligence

Word Pairs IV

Pair one word from Column A with one word from Column B to create a common two-word expression. For example, Big + Top forms Big Top.

COLUMN A	COLUMN B
❶ Gregorian	Plane
❷ Gold	Color
❸ Character	Exam
❹ Living	Standard
❺ Lay	Chicken
❻ Sitting	Television
❼ Prop	Chant
❽ Fried	Claim
❾ Public	Pretty
❿ Bar	Assassination

ANSWERS

① Gregorian Chant
② Gold Standard
③ Character Assassination
④ Living Color
⑤ Lay Claim
⑥ Sitting Pretty
⑦ Prop Plane
⑧ Fried Chicken
⑨ Public Television
⑩ Bar Exam

SCORING

Award 16.5 points for each correct answer.

165 Genius
148–132 Gifted/Superior Intelligence

115 Higher Than Usual Intelligence
99 Average Intelligence
83 Low Average Intelligence
70 or below Very Low Intelligence

✏️ Word Pairs V

Pair one word from Column A with one word from Column B to create a common two-word expression. For example, Big + Top forms Big Top.

COLUMN A	COLUMN B
① Bar	Body
② Public	Temperature
③ Best	Off
④ Merry	Start
⑤ Love	Pepper
⑥ Hands	Man
⑦ Head	Widow
⑧ Bell	Affair
⑨ Student	None
⑩ Daytime	Enemy

ANSWERS · · · · · · · · · · · · · · · · · ·

① Bar None
② Public Enemy
③ Best Man
④ Merry Widow
⑤ Love Affair

⑥ Student Body
⑦ Head Start
⑧ Bell Pepper
⑨ Hands Off
⑩ Daytime Temperature

SCORING ·

Award 16.5 points for each correct answer.

165 Genius
148–132 Gifted/Superior Intelligence
115 Higher Than Usual Intelligence
99 Average Intelligence
83 Low Average Intelligence
70 or below Very Low Intelligence

CHAPTER 9

ENGLISH IDIOMS

The Origins of the SAT Test

Carl Brigham, an American psychologist, invented the Scholastic Aptitude Test (SAT) in the late 1890s to eliminate a common problem in college admissions department—bias against applicants based on their race, ethnicity, religion, or economic background. The first test was given in 1901 to 973 students. The test asked very specific questions on such subjects as English, French, German, Latin Greek, history, chemistry, and physics. For example, this question came from the Latin section of the 1901 test:

Write the rules for the following constructions and illustrate each by a Latin sentence:

A. Two uses of the dative.
B. The cases used to indicate the relations of place.
C. The cases used with verbs of remembering.
D. The hortatory (or jussive) subjunctive.
E. The supine in um.

By 1926 the SAT had evolved into an examination that tested logical thinking and reading comprehension rather than specific knowledge. It was still very demanding—test-takers were given only 90 minutes to answer 315 questions. The SAT has continued to change over the years; in 2005, for example, the Math section was made harder in response to the rising number of test takers who were getting 800—a perfect score.

Like the IQ test, the SAT has its share of critics. In California, a study found that students whose family had an annual income of $20,000 or less on average scored 1310 (out of a possible 1600), while students whose family had an income of $200,000 or more scored on average 1715. Critics found evidence of cultural bias in the questions. For example, students were asked to complete the analogy, "Runner is to marathon as oarsman is to. . . ." The correct answer is "regatta," a reference to the sport of crew. A study found that 53 percent of white students answered that question correctly, but only 22 percent of black students. In response to these critics, many colleges no longer require the SAT as part of the admissions process.

✏️ English Idioms 1

English idiomatic expressions often pair two words to express a single idea; for example, *dead and gone* to convey that someone is deceased. Fill in the missing word or words in the following pairs.

1 _____ and drakes

2 a gentleman and _____ _____

3 all bark and _____ _____

4 _____ _____ and no steak

5 _____ and beyond

6 an arm and _____ _____

7 _____ and battery

8 bag and _____

9 _____ _____ and sevens

10 _____ and bull

ANSWERS ·

1 ducks and drakes
2 a gentleman and a scholar
3 all bark and no bite
4 all sizzle and no steak
5 above and beyond
6 an arm and a leg
7 assault and battery
8 bag and baggage
9 at sixes and sevens
10 cock and bull

SCORING ·

Award 16.5 points for each correct answer.

165 Genius
148–132 Gifted/Superior Intelligence
115 Higher Than Usual Intelligence
99 Average Intelligence
83 Low Average Intelligence
70 or below Very Low Intelligence

English Idioms II

English idiomatic expressions often pair two words to express a single idea; for example, *dead and gone* to convey that someone is deceased. Fill in the missing word or words in the following pairs.

1 _____ and call

2 high and _____

3 between a rock and _____ _____ _____

4 _____ and fancy free

5 between Scylla and _____

6 _____ and mean

7 _____ _____ and end all

8 _____ and whistles

9 dribs and _____

10 neck and _____

ANSWERS ·

⑤ between Scylla and Charybdis

④ footloose and fancy free

⑩ neck and neck

a hard place

⑥ dribs and drabs

③ between a rock and

⑧ bells and whistles

② high and mighty

⑦ be all and end all

① beck and call

⑨ lean and mean

SCORING ·

Award 16.5 points for each correct answer.

165 Genius
148–132 Gifted/Superior Intelligence
115 Higher Than Usual Intelligence
99 Average Intelligence
83 Low Average Intelligence
70 or below Very Low Intelligence

✏️ English Idioms III

English idiomatic expressions often pair two words to express a single idea; for example, *dead and gone* to convey that someone is deceased. Fill in the missing word or words in the following pairs.

① _____ and bothered

② blood and _____

③ _____ and needles

④ _____ and balances

5 chapter and _____

6 _____ and dried

7 crash and _____

8 dog and _____ _____

9 _____ and gloom

10 birds and _____

ANSWERS ·

10 birds and bees   **5** chapter and verse

6 gloom and doom   **4** checks and balances

8 dog and pony show   **3** pins and needles

7 crash and burn   **2** blood and guts

9 cut and dried   **1** hot and bothered

SCORING ·

Award 16.5 points for each correct answer.

165 Genius
148–132 Gifted/Superior Intelligence
115 Higher Than Usual Intelligence
99 Average Intelligence
83 Low Average Intelligence
70 or below Very Low Intelligence

✏️ English Idioms IV

English idiomatic expressions often pair two words to express a single idea; for example, *dead and gone* to convey that someone is deceased. Fill in the missing word or words in the following pairs.

1 _____ _____ _____ and the deep blue sea

2 fits and _____

3 _____ and center

4 _____ and go

5 hard and _____

6 _____ and blue

7 here and _____

8 _____ and outs

9 kit and _____

10 _____ and between

ANSWERS ·

5 hard and fast

10 betwixt and between

4 grab and go

9 kit and caboodle

3 front and center

8 ins and outs

2 fits and starts

7 here and now

1 between the devil and the deep blue sea

9 black and blue

SCORING ·

Award 16.5 points for each correct answer.

165 Genius
148–132 Gifted/Superior Intelligence
115 Higher Than Usual Intelligence
99 Average Intelligence
83 Low Average Intelligence
70 or below Very Low Intelligence

✏️ English Idioms V

English idiomatic expressions often pair two words to express a single idea; for example, *dead and gone* to convey that someone is deceased. Fill in the missing word or words in the following pairs.

1. meat and _____

2. _____ and oranges

3. _____ and cranny

4. _____ and dime

5. born and _____

6. once and _____ _____

7. _____ and parcel

8. _____ _____ and pound foolish

9. _____ and tumble

10. _____ and save

ANSWERS

10 scrimp and save
9 rough and tumble
8 penny wise and pound foolish
7 part and parcel
6 once and for all

5 born and bred
4 nickel and dime
3 nook and cranny
2 apples and oranges
1 meat and potatoes

SCORING

Award 16.5 points for each correct answer.

165 Genius
148–132 Gifted/Superior Intelligence
115 Higher Than Usual Intelligence
99 Average Intelligence
83 Low Average Intelligence
70 or below Very Low Intelligence

CHAPTER 10

CORRECT THE MISSPELLED WORDS

SAT Scores of the Rich and Famous

These SAT scores are easy to find online, but no one can say with any certainty if they are accurate. We reproduce them here purely for entertainment value.

Paul Allen, co-founder of Microsoft, 1600

Bill Gates, co-founder of Microsoft, 1590

Bill O'Reilly, journalist, author, social and political commentator, 1585

James Woods, actor, 1579

Ben Stein, actor, writer, political commentator, 1573

Rush Limbaugh, radio personality and social
and political commentator, 1530

Al Gore, former vice president of the United States, 1355

George W. Bush, former president of the United States, 1206

Courtney Cox, actress, 1150

Amy Tan, author, 1110

Kobe Bryant, basketball star, 1080

Bill Clinton, former president of the United States, 1032

Al Franken, comedian, U.S. senator, 1020

✏️ Correct the Misspelled Words I

Each of the following words is misspelled. Spell each word correctly.

1 phalsetto

_____

2 accomodate

_____

3 destinashun

_____

4 acolyght

_____

5 cantancerous

_____

6 harrass

_____

7 decieve

_____

8 enfranchize

_____

9 civilizaytion

_____

10 sibilante

_____

ANSWERS ·

10 sibilant

9 civilization

8 enfranchise

7 deceive

6 harass

5 cantankerous

4 acolyte

3 destination

2 accommodate

1 falsetto

SCORING

Award 16.5 points for each correct answer.

165 Genius
148–132 Gifted/Superior Intelligence
115 Higher Than Usual Intelligence
99 Average Intelligence
83 Low Average Intelligence
70 or below Very Low Intelligence

✏ Correct the Misspelled Words II

Each of the following words is misspelled. Spell each word correctly.

1 seege

_____

2 catalist

_____

3 respectible

_____

4 verminus

_____

5 akaline

_____

6 embarass

_____

7 voyour

_____

8 delikacy

_____

9 centriphigal

_____

10 grammarion

_____

ANSWERS

(10) grammarian
(6) centrifugal
(8) delicacy
(7) voyeur
(9) embarrass

(5) alkaline
(4) verminous
(3) respectable
(2) catalyst
(1) siege

SCORING

Award 16.5 points for each correct answer.

165 Genius
148–132 Gifted/Superior Intelligence
115 Higher Than Usual Intelligence
99 Average Intelligence
83 Low Average Intelligence
70 or below Very Low Intelligence

✏️ Correct the Misspelled Words III

Each of the following words is misspelled. Spell each word correctly.

1 newstand

_____

2 crapulus

_____

3 sarcofagus

_____

4 vermichelli

_____

5 propertyed

_____

6 fortifys

_____

7 crannial

_____

9 locomoshun

_____

8 scaberous

_____

10 sinequre

_____

ANSWERS ·

10 sinecure

9 locomotion

8 scabrous

7 cranial

6 fortifies

5 propertied

4 vermicelli

3 sarcophagus

2 crapulous

1 newsstand

SCORING ·

Award 16.5 points for each correct answer.

165 Genius
148–132 Gifted/Superior Intelligence
115 Higher Than Usual Intelligence
99 Average Intelligence
83 Low Average Intelligence
70 or below Very Low Intelligence

✏️ Correct the
Misspelled Words IV

Each of the following words is misspelled. Spell each word correctly.

1. mysticue

   _____

2. harmmonium

   _____

3. burlezque

   _____

4. institutionel

   _____

5. quandarry

   _____

6. quary

   _____

7. querey

   _____

8. perilus

   _____

9. phantastical

   _____

10. ballisticks

    _____

ANSWERS ·

10. ballistics

9. fantastical

8. perilous

7. query

6. quarry

5. quandary

4. institutional

3. burlesque

2. harmonium

1. mystique

SCORING· ·

Award 16.5 points for each correct answer.

165 Genius
148–132 Gifted/Superior Intelligence
115 Higher Than Usual Intelligence
99 Average Intelligence
83 Low Average Intelligence
70 or below Very Low Intelligence

Correct the Misspelled Words V

Each of the following words is misspelled. Spell each word correctly.

1 blith

_____

6 harbinnger

_____

2 reminicent

_____

7 victuial

_____

3 voraycious

_____

8 hummungous

_____

4 whiste

_____

9 relikuary

_____

5 tremulos

_____

10 sinonim

_____

ANSWERS

10. synonym
9. reliquary
8. humungous
7. victual
6. harbinger

5. tremulous
4. whistle
3. voracious
2. reminiscent
1. blithe

SCORING

Award 16.5 points for each correct answer.

165 Genius
148–132 Gifted/Superior Intelligence
115 Higher Than Usual Intelligence
99 Average Intelligence
83 Low Average Intelligence
70 or below Very Low Intelligence

CHAPTER 11

UNSCRAMBLE THE LETTERS

The LSAT

Frank Bowles, an admissions officer at the Columbia University Law School in New York City created the Law School Aptitude Test (LSAT) in 1945 as a reliable way to gauge the suitability of law school applicants. Until 1945, almost every law school in the United States had relied primarily on the grade point average of applicants. Bowles invited admission officers from other major law schools to work with him in developing a prototype. Representatives from Harvard and Yale signed on, however the admissions officers at New York University were sceptical that such a test would serve any purpose. But by 1947 other law schools were working with Bowles and his colleagues, and the first LSAT was administered in 1948. Today the test is offered four times a year to prospective law school applicants.

The test measures reading comprehension, logical reasoning, analytical reasoning, and requires a writing sample. A perfect score is 180, and such a score is extremely rare.

Since 1998, Michael Nieswiadomy, an economist at the University of North Texas, has conducted several studies which attempt predict the college majors of law school applicants who do best on the LSAT. He studied LSAT test scores by major and found . . .

UNDERGRADUATE MAJOR	AVERAGE SCORE
1. Mathematics/Physics	160
2. Economics and Philosophy/Theology	157.4
3. International Relations	156.5
4. Engineering	156.2
5. Government service and Chemistry	156.1
6. History and Interdisciplinary studies	155.5
7. Foreign languages	155.3
8. English	155.2
9. Biology/Natural sciences	154.8
10. Arts	154.2

What do the scores mean? The Ivy League law schools, as well as top-tier law schools such as Stanford, generally require scores of 160 or above. Scores in the 159-150 range may gain the applicant admission to a state university law school. Applicants who score below 150 will probably have trouble gaining admission to a law school.

Unscramble the Letters I

Unscramble the letters to create an English word or name.

1. talictan

   A. Atlantis
   B. athletic
   C. autism
   D. Atlantic

2. recrog

   A. retro
   B. grocer
   C. gawker
   D. Oscar

3. thilezabe

   A. Elizabeth
   B. errand
   C. errant
   D. barrage

4. xnvie

   A. vicious
   B. vixen
   C. never
   D. Nineveh

5. lydarceptt

   A. Pericles
   B. lethargic
   C. pterodactyl
   D. pictogram

6. calios

   A. social
   B. solar
   C. calico
   D. solicit

7. quasashuenn

   A. seaquake
   B. succotash
   C. suspenseful
   D. Susquehanna

8. delif

   A. fled
   B. flies
   C. delight
   D. field

9 revnima

    A. monetary

    B. moument

    C. Minerva

    D. marvelous

10 krabey

    A. crabby

    B. bakery

    C. kraken

    D. bicker

ANSWERS

1 D. Atlantic

2 B. grocer

3 A. Elizabeth

4 B. vixen

5 C. pterdactyl

6 A. social

7 D. Susquehanna

8 D. field

9 C. Minerva

10 B. bakery

SCORING

Award 16.5 points for each correct answer.

165 Genius
148–132 Gifted/Superior Intelligence
115 Higher Than Usual Intelligence
99 Average Intelligence
83 Low Average Intelligence
70 or below Very Low Intelligence

Unscramble the Letters II

Unscramble the letters to create an English word or name.

1 eenurve

   A. renovate

   B. revenue

   C. revive

   D. nervous

2 sriragon

   A. garrison

   B. dragon

   C. garnish

   D. garish

3 giacoch

   A. jester

   B. Chicago

   C. gigantic

   D. cherish

4 stivior

   A. visor

   B. Swedish

   C. visitor

   D. variant

5 tryucen

   A. censure

   B. century

   C. triplicate

   D. triangle

6 clanhios

   A. Nicholas

   B. choleria

   C. churlish

   D. nascent

7 iusceni

   A. cousin

   B. cuisine

   C. scenery

   D. squish

8 slaitoe

   A. salivate

   B. icicles

   C. cuisine

   D. isolate

⑨ theckin

    A. thicken

    B. chicken

    C. check-in

    D. kitchen

⑩ rateric

    A. erratic

    B. rated

    C. terrific

    D. exotic

ANSWERS

① **B.** revenue
② **A.** garrison
③ **B.** Chicago
④ **C.** visitor
⑤ **B.** century
⑥ **D.** kitchen
⑦ **B.** cuisine
⑧ **D.** isolate
⑨ **A.** Nicholas
⑩ **A.** erratic

SCORING

Award 16.5 points for each correct answer.

165 Genius
148–132 Gifted/Superior Intelligence
115 Higher Than Usual Intelligence
99 Average Intelligence
83 Low Average Intelligence
70 or below Very Low Intelligence

PERSONALITY TESTS

INTRODUCTION

Welcome to your personal quiz book! With some 3,000 personality tests in use today, we are certainly the most analyzed creatures on earth. We are also among the most self-conscious. We never tire of putting our abilities to the test—whether it be at a simple game of Monopoly or poker or whether it's trivia on every conceivable subject from animal life to zodiac signs.

The one topic that commands our overwhelming attention is our self. Anything that sheds light on the fascinating mystery of our emotions—why we feel and behave as we do, why we do what we shouldn't and don't do what we should—compels our interest. We revel in knowing what makes us tick.

And although the sages of old have intoned, "know thyself," in this hectic, non-contemplative society, with its many distractions from our inner selves, self-knowledge is perhaps the most difficult of all tasks to achieve. Still, our search hasn't diminished one mite. We're ever attuned to how we compare with others, always eager to steal a glimpse of who we are, why we feel and act as we do and, more importantly, what we might become if given the opportunity.

Quizzes have been known to be great party starters. They can stimulate discussion at the dinner table, at a picnic, beach outing, or cocktail party. They are capable of raising an eyebrow over a controversial point or two or smashing a sacred cow we've nurtured all our life.

How to Get the Most Out of This Book

In planning this book, I felt that the quiz format would be an interesting and entertaining way to impart understanding on a wide range of human psychology subjects. The tests are drawn from the research studies, surveys, and clinical experience of some of the finest minds in social science, psychology, and psychiatry.

Although everything is open to interpretation and these tests are therefore not foolproof or the final word, I am confident that they do have more scientific credibility than the average quiz in the daily tabloids. Indeed, many of the questions in this book might very well be those that a professional psychologist would ask during an evaluation.

Test the Tests for Fun

To verify any given test's conclusions, try to rate yourself on the particular trait being tested before you begin. For added interest, ask a friend to join you in your self-ratings, then compare answers. But please be aware that if you disagree with your score, it might mean that either you slanted your responses (unintentionally or not) or that you may not have an accurate view of yourself. If this happens, go back and review your answers. Considering how you might have responded differently often provides insights that will help you pinpoint your answers the next time around.

To Thine Own Self Be True

Will this book really give you a window into your true self? A lot depends on you. To get the most from a quiz, don't fudge your answers. No one's peering over your shoulder, so be straightforward. Usually it's best to respond without too much deliberation. And though it's tempting, try not to minimize weaknesses or maximize strengths. If you're honest and accurate in your answers, you should come away with a fairly realistic picture of yourself as you really are. Enjoy the tests!

—Salvatore V. Didato, Ph.D.

ACKNOWLEDGEMENTS

I would like to thank my wife, Dr. Paulette Didato, for her assistance in editing and proofreading this book; and my son, David Didato, for his valuable help in the technical computer adjustments required to prepare effective copy.

Also, I wish to thank authors Wayne Dyer and Evan Hunter (a.k.a. Ed McBain) for their sound advice about the finer points of book publishing; and Walter Anderson, CEO of Parade Publications, for his encouragement in pursuing the quiz as a format to convey psychological understanding.

I especially wish to honor the memory of the late Dr. Norman Vincent Peale, who over the years provided this writer with incomparable insights into the human condition.

—Salvatore V. Didato, Ph.D.

CHAPTER 1

THE REAL YOU

✐ How Daring Are You?

Though they may not be daredevils in the strictest sense of the word, some people enjoy the public image associated with being adventurous. When we think of such types, certain characters come to mind, like Mario Andretti, speed car racer; Sir Richard Branson, Virgin Group C.E.O. and hot air balloonist; and Robby Knievel, stunt motorcyclist. Studies show that daring persons often have more self-confidence and higher IQ levels than those who are more reluctant. But this is only part of the picture.

At the Institute of Psychiatry at the University of London, H. J. Eysenck and S. G. Eysenck performed extensive research on adventuresome people. In their sample of 1,200 subjects they found that daredevils are more extraverted and impulsive on average, but that contrary to popular belief, their risk-taking is not necessarily a sign of a neurotic personality. The psychologists concluded that about one-half to two-thirds of our capacity for derring-do is probably inherited.

TEST

How much of an Andretti or Knievel are you? The following quiz lists items similar to those presented by the Eysencks. Respond "True" or "False" to the items below to determine how daring you are.

1. When shopping, I usually stick to brands I am know.
   True False

2. It upsets me when one of my friends is upset.
   True False

3. Unhappy people who feel sorry for themselves irritate me.
   True False

4. It is silly for people to cry out of happiness.
   True False

5. Many animal lovers are too concerned about the comfort and feelings of animals.
   True False

6. I feel better after having a few cocktails.
   True False

7. I would probably feel sympathetic to a stranger in a group.
   True False

8. Public displays of affection annoy me somewhat.
   True False

9. I would prefer a job that required travel and change to one that kept me at home most of the time.
   True False

10. I save money regularly.
    True False

SCORING

To tally your score, give yourself 1 point for each response that matches yours. An average score on adventurousness falls between 4 and 6.

① *False* ② *False* ③ *True* ④ *True* ⑤ *True* ⑥ *True* ⑦ *False* ⑧ *True* ⑨ *True* ⑩ *False*

EXPLANATION ·

The Eysencks found that men tend to be more adventure-seeking than women. Daring types have a strong need for variety and change in their everyday activities. Their capacity for excitement is above average, and for them, boredom is a recurring problem.

Adventurous people shy away from public displays of affection or other emotions and tend to be uncomfortable with the open expression of feelings by others. They are somewhat thick-skinned, and generally prefer to act rather than emote.

The daring among us are generally impatient for movement and gravitate toward those who seek novelty and are willing to take risks to achieve it. Strangely though, activities that the average person might deem risky, such as mountain climbing or sky diving, are often viewed by daredevils as relatively benign.

How bold or adventurous we are can vary with our social surroundings. Studies of group dynamics confirm that a pattern called "risky shift" occurs when members bolster each other's daring and shift to more risk taking than when they are alone. When committees form to decide an issue, for example, members may take more extreme stands because they are shielded by peer support. Social psychologist I. L. Janis calls this phenomenon "groupthink." In his book, Victims of Groupthink, he gives a telling example of how groupthink functions, citing the United States strategy committee's ill-conceived decision to invade Cambodia during the Vietnam War.

There are always extremes on the human continuum. Biochemists have dubbed strongly adventurous types "adrenaline junkies," because they seem to have a physical need to maintain high adrenaline levels in order to feel satisfaction. But as much as these outer bounds of the human psyche are influenced by psychological factors, family forces also play a crucial role in determining how daring one will be. The pulls of nature and nurture make it difficult to discern which, if either or both, is responsible for risky behavior. Studies show that parents who provide stimulating environments for their kids are likely to be adventuresome types themselves. But, if the children turn out the same way, it is tough to tell which was more influential, their inherited traits or their upbringing.

✏ Are You a People Person or a Wallflower?

What makes people get up on stage when the call goes out for volunteers from the audience? Chances are they're extraverts—those who enjoy doing things with and for others.

As far back as 1921, Carl Jung, the Swiss psychoanalyst, first coined the terms introversion and extraversion. The notion that all of mankind could be divided into these two types has been around for several centuries, but Jung did the most extensive study and writing on the subject. He maintained that we are born with two "innate attitudes," one which focuses inwardly on ourselves and the other, outwardly toward others.

Jung felt that both of these tendencies exist in everyone. But one attitude gets the upper hand while the other lies submerged deep in the unconscious, exerting a counterforce that may show up in dreams and fantasies. So, according to Jung every extravert on the outside is an introvert on the inside, and vice versa.

While extraverts need heavy doses of social stimulation and are less interested in their inner experiences, such as feelings, imagination, and ideas, introverts are just the opposite.

One orientation is not healthier than the other, although different cultures may encourage one or the other. Introverts are among the world's best researchers, scientists, and writers, while extraverts excel as business managers, teachers, and salespeople.

TEST ·

If you wonder where you fall on the Introvert-Extravert scale, the following quiz might provide some clues.

1 I am more of a listener than a talker.
A. *Very true*
B. *Largely true*
C. *Slightly true*
D. *Not True*

2 Compared with others, I am difficult to get to know.
A. *Very true*
B. *Largely true*
C. *Slightly true*
D. *Not True*

3 I find it difficult or unpleasant to make small talk.
A. *Very true*
B. *Largely true*
C. *Slightly true*
D. *Not True*

4 I am a worrier.
A. *Very true*
B. *Largely true*
C. *Slightly true*
D. *Not True*

5 I would not want to be in charge of a large group.
A. *Very true*
B. *Largely true*
C. *Slightly true*
D. *Not True*

6 I would feel very self-conscious if someone pointed out a large stain on my clothes in front of people.
A. *Very true*
B. *Largely true*
C. *Slightly true*
D. *Not True*

7 I have a tendency to daydream.
A. *Very true*
B. *Largely true*
C. *Slightly true*
D. *Not True*

8 It makes me feel uneasy when strangers watch me doing something.
A. *Very true*
B. *Largely true*
C. *Slightly true*
D. *Not True*

9 It takes me a long time to get over an embarrassment.
A. *Very true*
B. *Largely true*
C. *Slightly true*
D. *Not True*

10 I would feel embarrassed if I stumbled in public.
A. *Very true*
B. *Largely true*
C. *Slightly true*
D. *Not True*

SCORING ·

To tally your score, give yourself 1 point for each "a" response, 2 points for each "b" response, 3 points for each "c," and 4 points for each "d."

A score of 29–40 points: You are highly extraverted. You enjoy being around and interacting with people. However you may want to guard against acting too spontaneously in certain settings in which your gregarious side might best be kept under control.

A score of 21–28 points: You fall somewhere between both Introvert-Extravert extremes, as do most people. You like being part of the social set but you also enjoy time alone.

A score of 10–20 points: You tend to be on the introvertive side. You can cope with people when necessary but for the most part prefer to be alone. You're not highly dependent on others to uplift your mood, but instead tend to rely on your inner mental life for inspiration.

EXPLANATION ·

Western society tends to foster extravertive behavior. We approve of children who are outgoing and socially assertive and disapprove of the absence of these traits. In some non-occidental societies, however, introversion is a more acceptable personality style.

Professor Hans Eysenck, in his work at Maudsley Hospital in London, concluded that the introvert-extravert conflict is better explained in biological, rather than cultural terms. He believes introverts have a more sensitive nervous system than extraverts, causing them to withdraw in order to prevent their brains from being overwhelmed. Introverts tend to follow their own mind set and are not overly swayed by the opinions of others. Extraverts, on the other hand, physically require lots of stimulation, and actively seek out others whose opinions and ideas are influential.

Despite someone's natural propensity toward one extreme or the other, they can alternate between the two attitudes, depending upon the situation. For example, at a party someone who is generally introvertive may be more outgoing, talkative, and responsive if he or she knows the other guests. But if he or she knows no one except the hostess—who is busy taking coats and freshening drinks—the gregarious side of his or her personality may not surface as readily.

While each of these types possesses positive characteristics, extremes of either type can present problems in certain settings. The strong extravert needs contact and feedback from others, and grows restless when working or studying quietly alone. He yearns to be near others. A strong introvert seeks solitude and feels nervous when dealing with others even in the most casual way. As always, moderation is key.

✏ How Time-Conscious Are You?

Time sense differs around the world. The culture we live in shapes our attitudes about time, and gradually we set our inner clocks to conform to its tempo. Many tropical nations have a slower daily rhythm—while nations in northern climates tend to move much faster.

In his work at the California State University at Fresno, psychology professor Robert Levine surveyed a cross-section of nations (Japan, England, Italy, Indonesia, Taiwan, and the United States). He found that by many measures, Japan has the fastest pace of life, while Indonesia assumes the most relaxed attitude about timed activities.

TEST ·

In Western society we value promptness and are very focused on time. Those people who handle time efficiently tend to be in great demand and are generally successful in life. What pace do you set for yourself? The following quiz, similar to those used in the Stanford University Time Perspective Inventory, should help to gauge your sense of time urgency.

1 It bothers me when I am late for an appointment.
 A. *Rarely or very little*
 B. *Sometimes or moderately*
 C. *Often or very much*

2 I am disoriented when I forget to wear my watch.
 A. *Rarely or very little*
 B. *Sometimes or moderately*
 C. *Often or very much*

3 It is hard for me to let time go by and do absolutely nothing.
 A. *Rarely or very little*
 B. *Sometimes or moderately*
 C. *Often or very much*

4 It irritates me to be kept waiting.
 A. *Rarely or very little*
 B. *Sometimes or moderately*
 C. *Often or very much*

5 It is upsetting for me to put off finishing a task.
 A. *Rarely or very little*
 B. *Sometimes or moderately*
 C. *Often or very much*

6 I make lists of things to do.
 A. *Rarely or very little*
 B. *Sometimes or moderately*
 C. *Often or very much*

7 I am on time for appointments and meet deadlines and obligations that involve others.
A. *Rarely or very little*
B. *Sometimes or moderately*
C. *Often or very much*

8 I enjoy doing many things within a short period of time.
A. *Rarely or very little*
B. *Sometimes or moderately*
C. *Often or very much*

9 When I have a few hours on my hands I think of how to best use the time.
A. *Rarely or very little*
B. *Sometimes or moderately*
C. *Often or very much*

10 If I expect a long wait, I bring work or something to read.
A. *Rarely or very little*
B. *Sometimes or moderately*
C. *Often or very much*

11 I like to allocate blocks of time to specific projects.
A. *Rarely or very little*
B. *Sometimes or moderately*
C. *Often or very much*

12 I carry a pad on which to jot down to-do lists.
A. *Rarely or very little*
B. *Sometimes or moderately*
C. *Often or very much*

SCORING

To tally your score, give yourself 1 point for each "a" response, 2 points for each "b" response, and 3 points for each "c." Keep in mind that neither extreme of time consciousness is particularly beneficial when it comes to respecting your scheduling constraints. If you are too easygoing, you may miss the chance to accomplish worthwhile goals. If you are too driven to "honor" time, then you've made a potentially valuable personality trait into a liability.

A score of 12–19 points: You are time-carefree. You don't pay enough attention to the limits that time imposes on your life. You probably frustrate others by your lax attitude and low sense of time urgency. Strive to make and keep deadlines for completing tasks.

A score of 20–29 points: You have a sensible attitude about time and a realistic sense of urgency about getting things done when you should.

A score of 30–36 points: You are on your way to becoming a compulsive clock-watcher. Train yourself to put things into perspective and tackle important tasks first. Relax and get used to feeling comfortable with the idea that some things can be put off until tomorrow without dire consequences.

EXPLANATION

While culture affects our perception of time, being time-conscious is an individual matter. It doesn't depend on a timepiece on the wall. Our subjective clock can be habitually slower than objective time. So, in addition to our society's view of time, we are strict or lax about it depending on factors such as what we are doing at the moment, the people we are with, and our prevailing mood. Professor Levine and his associates found that people tend to live in different time frames. A few live in the past, some live in the present, and most live in the future. As teenagers, we live in the here and now, enjoying each passing hour as it arises. But as we grow to adulthood, we become more future-oriented, putting off immediate pleasures for the sake of future goals.

Those of us in Western society have a special preoccupation with what lies ahead. Our savings banks and insurance companies thrive on fostering a sense of an extended future. But any extreme time perspective could work against us. The mismanagement of time is usually a significant factor in what causes much of our stress. We give ourselves only a limited period in which to accomplish our goals and often miscalculate how much time we'll really need.

Alan Lakein, time consultant and the author of *How to Get Control of Your Time and Your Life*, advises that we prioritize the things we do. In order to minimize stress and maximize productivity, we should give top billing to the most crucial tasks, then work our way down the list to the least-important projects.

Are Thrills Your Thing?

The statement "truth is stranger than fiction" may be a cliché, but it tells it best. A few years ago a twenty-nine-year-old student from Long Beach, California, pushed his hang glider off a cliff and promptly slammed to earth six hundred feet below. He wasn't wearing a helmet. After several days spent near death in an intensive care unit, he was discharged from the hospital and soon returned to his favorite sport—hang gliding.

Why do people take chances? Humans, it seems, have an unexplained urge for stimulation. Call it thrill seeking, if you will—it exists in degrees in every person, from high-wire artists to children on skateboards. The appetite for thrills peaks in our teens, then gradually decreases as we grow older, but some of us never quite lose the desire to experience new and exciting kicks.

Dr. Marvin Zuckerman calls this phenomenon "sensation seeking." He believes it is a universal trait that probably has a biological basis. Through extensive research, Zuckerman has devised a number of questionnaires that identify those who actively seek to bombard their senses as a means of sparking up their lives. For these people, paths to the sensational could include such simple activities as ordering an exotic dish, speeding, or reading adventure stories instead of romance novels.

TEST ·

To test your sensation-seeking tendencies, try the following quiz. It is based on one of Dr. Zuckerman's tests.

1. I enjoy stories about medical breakthroughs.
   A. *Disagree*
   B. *Agree*
   C. *Strongly agree*

2. When on a vacation trip, I prefer to camp out.
   A. *Disagree*
   B. *Agree*
   C. *Strongly agree*

3. I would enjoy work that requires a lot of travel.
   A. *Disagree*
   B. *Agree*
   C. *Strongly agree*

4. On a hot day, I like jumping into the ocean or a cold pool.
   A. *Disagree*
   B. *Agree*
   C. *Strongly agree*

5. I enjoy spicy foods.
   A. *Disagree*
   B. *Agree*
   C. *Strongly agree*

6. I would enjoy working to help people solve problems.
   A. *Disagree*
   B. *Agree*
   C. *Strongly agree*

7. I prefer scary movies.
   A. *Disagree*
   B. *Agree*
   C. *Strongly agree*

8. I enjoy being out on a cold day.
   A. *Disagree*
   B. *Agree*
   C. *Strongly agree*

9. I get bored seeing the same familiar faces.
   A. *Disagree*
   B. *Agree*
   C. *Strongly agree*

10. I like emotionally expressive people even if they're eccentric or somewhat unstable.
    A. *Disagree*
    B. *Agree*
    C. *Strongly agree*

⑪ I would enjoy being
hypnotized.
   A. *Disagree*
   B. *Agree*
   C. *Strongly agree*

⑫ I would prefer working on
a commission basis to
being on salary.
   A. *Disagree*
   B. *Agree*
   C. *Strongly agree*

SCORING ·

To tally your score, give yourself 1 point for each "a" response, 2
points for each "b" response, and 3 points for each "c."

A score of 30–36 points: You are a thrill seeker.

A score of 20–29 points: You have about average needs for
adventure and new sensations.

A score of 12–19 points: You are somewhat conservative in
your tastes and less daring than most people.

EXPLANATION ·

Most sensation seekers answer the items as true of themselves. Compared to the average, they tend to be more adaptable to fast-moving
situations and show strong preferences for entering the helping
professions such as medicine, social service, and teaching.

After some forty years of work, Dr. Zuckerman concluded that
very high scorers differ from low scorers in four basic ways:

① Thrill and adventure seeking: They look for new thrills by
engaging in risky and adventurous activities such as sky diving,
riding roller coasters, and motorcycling.

② Experience seeking: They continually seek excitement by adopting a non-conventional style, i.e., by making unusual (eccentric) friends, traveling frequently, or taking drugs.

③ Disinhibition: They tend to be socially uninhibited and are drawn to social drinking, gambling, and sexual experimentation.

④ Boredom susceptibility: They have low tolerance for experiences that are constant or repetitious, such as routine work or association with predictable, "boring" people.

In the journal *Psychology Today*, Professor Frank Farley reported experiments that demonstrate thrill seekers' need to maintain a high level of arousal in their nervous system. Sometimes called "adrenaline junkies," these people choose to be hyped up rather than calmed down. Males tend to dominate this category. Because men often equate risk-taking with courage, they generally score higher than women on assessments of thrill-seeking levels. This can be attributed in part to social attitudes: Boys are encouraged to take chances and engage in risky behavior more often than girls. When it comes to thrill seeking, this gender split tends to bear out.

✏️ Could You Become Assaultive?

When laboratory animals receive electrical shocks they tend to vent their anger by pouncing on those nearby. The effects of frustration on human behavior are not much different. Our frustration often spells trouble for others, especially those closest to us.

Handling hostile impulses is a never-ending, lifelong challenge. Unfortunately, some of us never quite adopt a satisfactory way of managing our hostility. The evidence shows that we learn to be aggressive in stages. As a child one may strike a playmate or parent during a tantrum. But if this type of behavior persists later in life, it can spill over into everyday situations in undesirable proportions. It is through a lifetime of learning that violence is adopted as a solution to social conflicts.

T E S T ·

The following quiz is based on the findings of Dr. Richard Parlour and others who have written about aggressive behavior. It may help to gauge your susceptibility to being assaultive.

1 I fall into moods of irritability for no apparent reason.
  A. *Rarely*
  B. *Sometimes*
  C. *Often*

2 I don't work hard enough to improve myself.
  A. *Rarely*
  B. *Sometimes*
  C. *Often*

3 If someone yells at me, I yell right back.
  A. *Rarely*
  B. *Sometimes*
  C. *Often*

4 I drink frequently and often get drunk.
  A. *Rarely*
  B. *Sometimes*
  C. *Often*

5 I do things on impulse.
  A. *Rarely*
  B. *Sometimes*
  C. *Often*

6 When others cross me, I don't forgive and forget easily.
  A. *Rarely*
  B. *Sometimes*
  C. *Often*

7 When I'm angry, I slam or break things.
  A. *Rarely*
  B. *Sometimes*
  C. *Often*

8 I engage in physical activity or use some other outlet to "let off steam."
  A. *Rarely*
  B. *Sometimes*
  C. *Often*

⑨ If someone annoys me,
I'm quick to tell them off.
A. *Rarely*
B. *Sometimes*
C. *Often*

⑩ After an outburst I regret
having lost my temper.
A. *Rarely*
B. *Sometimes*
C. *Often*

SCORING ·

To tally your score, give yourself 1 point for each "a" response, 2 points for each "b" response, and 3 points for each "c."

A score of 10–14 points: You tend to express your anger peacefully, but may suppress it on occasion.

A score of 15–21 points: You have an average amount of control when it comes to inhibiting your angry feelings.

A score of 22–30 points: You have a short fuse when under stress and may want to exercise more self-control. It might help to review the items that you responded "Often" to and try to work on changing those behaviors.

EXPLANATION ·

In his work, Dr. Parlour found that destructive actions are common in our society. He identified early predictors of aggressive outbreaks, some of which are in our quiz. He concluded that each of us has a breaking point and that if enough stress is placed on us, we are likely to vent our anger in an aggressive way. But Parlour is quick to note that too often those who act out attribute their behavior to some sort of "last straw," when actually we all have much more self-restraint than we realize.

Can psychologists predict an outbreak of anger in a family? Dr. J. Monahan, author of *The Clinical Prediction of Criminal Behavior*, says that it is not possible to predict violence with much accuracy. However, he notes, there are some characteristics that help predict whether a husband might strike his wife. They include whether the husband himself had a history of family violence, whether his peers were violent, and whether he has had a history of steady unemployment. Monahan advises that people with the tendency to act out steer clear of situations that might trigger impulsive behavior.

Our quiz is based on a list of traits that correlate with poor self-control. Some experts believe that giving in too easily to "alien" impulses is behavior learned through role models, such as parents, siblings, or peers, in our formative years. But it must be said that most domestic upsets do not involve violence.

It is important to note that if you have the potential to anger quickly, it is always intensified by alcohol. At Yale University, professor A. B. Hollingshead did a survey of five hundred divorce cases and found that more than 26 percent of the complaints filed were based on excessive drinking by a spouse, usually the husband.

✐ Can You Keep Yourself in Check?

A hard-bitten oil tycoon was once asked if he had stomach ulcers. His reply, " I don't get ulcers, I give them." Living intensely is a way of life for some people. More than 80 million prescriptions for tranquilizers are written annually to help us keep our emotions in check, but still some of us don't succeed. Our blow-ups often cause detrimental results for ourselves and for others.

Researchers have devised lengthy questionnaires designed to identify individuals who don't handle stress well. The following quiz is based on studies by Leonard Derogatis at Johns Hopkins University, which assess your style of handling difficult situations.

TEST ·

To determine if you are likely to drop a bomb when irritated, take the following test.

1. You grow quite impatient when you must wait in line.
   A. *Rarely*
   B. *Sometimes*
   C. *Often*

2. You work very hard, play very hard, and try to be the best at what you do.
   A. *Rarely*
   B. *Sometimes*
   C. *Often*

3. You easily become annoyed when held up by someone in traffic.
   A. *Rarely*
   B. *Sometimes*
   C. *Often*

4. You are more of a go-getter than most of your friends.
   A. *Rarely*
   B. *Sometimes*
   C. *Often*

5. You slam and break things when angry.
   A. *Rarely*
   B. *Sometimes*
   C. *Often*

6. It irritates you when people don't take their job seriously.
   A. *Rarely*
   B. *Sometimes*
   C. *Often*

7. You snap at strangers when you become annoyed, for example while driving, shopping or working.
   A. *Rarely*
   B. *Sometimes*
   C. *Often*

8. You become angered when you fail at things you attempt to do.
   A. *Rarely*
   B. *Sometimes*
   C. *Often*

9 When angry, you speed up and do things like driving, eating, and walking faster.
A. *Rarely*
B. *Sometimes*
C. *Often*

10 You don't easily forgive and forget someone who has offended you.
A. *Rarely*
B. *Sometimes*
C. *Often*

SCORING

To tally your score, give yourself 1 point for each "a" response, 2 points for each "b" response, and 3 points for each "c." The higher you score, the more you tend to be an intensive adaptor to daily life.

A score of 0–15 points: You are low-key and easy-going.

A score of 16–23 points: You are in the average range of emotional response to life's ups and downs.

A score of 24–30 points: You're living in a pressure cooker. It's time to ease up, relax, and gain a better perspective on your life.

EXPLANATION

The items included in the quiz generally depict over-reactions to fairly typical situations. They display an intensity that is usually not needed to cope with the matter at hand.

A healthy personality engages in a kind of psychic economy of its own. It responds to life with the effort and energy reasonably appropriate to deal with events—not much more and not much less. Here are just a few examples at the other extreme: a homemaker who jumps up and rushes to answer the doorbell every time it rings, a teenager who gulps his food, a manager who slams her desk or repeatedly jabs the elevator button. These are all over-extended behaviors. Psychologists look for this "too muchness" quality and typically judge it as neurotic.

It's fair to say that occasionally everyone acts intensively, but just because someone exhibits this behavior doesn't necessarily mean that he or she is maladjusted. However, some high-tension types actually unwittingly strive to maintain a constant level of stress. These so-called "adrenaline junkies" spew more of the stuff than most of us. To them, life just isn't exciting unless it is lived in a state of urgency.

Work at Harvard University shows that high-tension types drive hard to gain mastery over their lives. They are argumentative, competitive, and over-sensitive to slights by others (as touched upon in quiz items 3, 6, and 10). They make up for shortcomings by overcompensating (see items 2, 4, and 8) and they tend to scapegoat others as well (items 1, 5, 7, and 9).

✐ Do Your Parents' Hang-Ups Psych You Out?

How would you compare yourself with your parents on traits like sociability, assertiveness, and optimism? If you rate yourself as very similar to them, you might be tempted to conclude that your personality is inherited. But, aside from genes, your own experiences have also had much to do with shaping who you are.

It's a centuries-old question: Is nature or nurture more responsible for human development? This debate really kicked into high gear after Charles Darwin published *On the Origin of the Species* in 1859, in which he held that inheritance plays a significant role in determining a being's characteristics. Darwin theorized that advantageous physiological mutations naturally propogate themselves by enabling beings to survive and procreate, thereby passing along adaptations to subsequent generations.

Years later, in sharp contrast, Johns-Hopkins University behaviorist J. B. Watson argued that one's characteristics are acquired more than inherited. He remarked that given a dozen healthy infants (from various backgrounds), he'd guarantee he could turn them into doctors, lawyers, beggars, or thieves.

Our view of genetics is much more sophisticated now than it was then. Today, for example, we study identical twins who've been separated at birth to determine what personality traits they share. Comparative studies have also been conducted with orphans, adoptive families, and fraternal twins. Some of the findings are included in the following quiz.

TEST ·

How much do you think you've inherited from your parents? Take the following quiz to find out.

1 An insecure mother's thoughts and beliefs can influence the character of her unborn infant.
True False

2 People are born with an urge to be aggressive.
True False

3 We inherit our ability in art, music, and sports.
True False

4 Psychoneurosis, or more seriously, insanity, is caused by genes.
True False

5 An aversion to snakes, bats, bugs, etc., is instinctive (i.e., not learned).
True False

6 If close relatives marry, their children will be in some way underdeveloped.
True False

7 How excitable or emotional I am depends upon the disposition I inherited from my parents.
True False

8 Competitiveness is instinctive in human nature.
True False

9 Girls usually inherit more traits from their mothers than from their fathers.
True False

10 We can inherit our parent's alcoholism.
True False

SCORING ·

To tally your score, give yourself 1 point for each "False" response.

A score of 1–5: You may think that many of your quirks and idiosyncrasies were genetic gifts, but they probably owe more to where you've been, what you've done, and who you've known than to your DNA.

A score of 6 points or more: You have a good grasp of what is or isn't inherited from your folks.

EXPLANATION ·

The evidence shows that our life experience determines much of who we are. An item-by-item explanation of the quiz follows.

① *False*. An expectant mother's insecurity probably will not influence her baby. But the emotions she experiences, such as elation, depression, or fear, will temporarily affect her fetus's physiology through her nervous system and hormone levels.

② *False*. We do not have an "aggression" gene. Rather, it is societies that engender aggression and even violence in their children, or teach them to avoid or suppress it.

③ *False*. We may inherit the physiology that gives us a predisposition to excel at art (like strong eye receptors for increased color perception) or music (such as sensitive auditory neurons for greater tone discrimination) but that is about all. The actual talent must then be trained and developed.

④ *False*. Some mental illnesses have a strong hereditary component (for example, certain neurological disorders and forms of epilepsy and psychosis), but the vast majority of mental disturbances are the result of life experiences.

⑤ *False*. Our specific fears are not inherited but are more likely adopted from those around us who displayed particular fear reactions to certain stimuli.

⑥ *False*. There is no strong evidence that underdevelopment results when parents are closely related.

⑦ *False*. This is true of animals but not of humans. Much of how we respond in the face of stress will depend upon how our role models (mostly our parents) reacted when confronted with stress.

⑧ *False*. Competitiveness is culturally acquired and not passed on through the genes.

⑨ *False*. A child will not always identify with the same sex parent. If a girl tends to act more like her mother than her father, chances are that she spent more time with her mother and modeled herself after her.

⑩ *False*. Alcoholism is not genetically caused. In families where drinking is frequent, a child may learn to use it as a remedy for frustration as others around him have done.

So, if you ever wonder whether your hang-ups have been handed down to you, think again. You're probably not the innocent victim of your genes. Chances are you yourself played the major role in the formation of your weaknesses. Incidentally, this goes for your strengths as well. One way to explain genetic influence is to say that our genes set the limits of our abilities and traits and our own experience does the rest.

CHAPTER 2

IN THE MOOD FOR LOVE

✏️ Are You Free to Fall in Love?

Like it or not, trust is a condition for survival in human society. Even in such simple acts as eating a candy or boarding a bus we have to trust that the candy hasn't been tampered with, or that the bus's brakes have been checked. The bottom line is that enjoying the benefits of societal living requires that we build a "believing dependence" upon one another. And, in our sometimes impersonal world, being trusted may well represent a greater compliment than being loved.

Obviously, your willingness to trust others depends upon the setting. You might trust a stranger at a religious function more readily than you would at a bar. Placing your faith in someone depends upon judgment as well. You might rely on a friend to feed your pet

175

in your absence but would not trust the same friend to keep a secret. Yet trusting isn't completely reliant on setting or judgment.

At Tufts University in Medford, Massachusetts, psychologists C. Johnson-George and W. Swap identified a general personality trait they call "impersonal trust"—it applies to one's ability to fall in love. Their extensive investigations found that women are more willing to trust others than men (though this need not suggest that people should be categorized as trusting or untrusting by gender alone). They also concluded that if you approach a relationship with a high level of distrust, it willprobably be harder for you to trust unconditionally and fall in love. Of course, the amount you confide in and depend on other people can vary over time—a reluctance to trust at one point in your life may be in response to a variety of factors and does not mean you'll be that way forever.

TEST ·

If you are wondering whether you have the capacity to fall in love, the quiz below may provide some insight. It's based on the research at Tufts. Respond "True" or "False" to each item below to determine your "love-trust index."

1 I am reluctant to lend money to others because of the hassle often involved in getting it back.
True False

2 Most people who compliment others are only flattering them for their own gains and don't really mean what they say.
True False

3 The majority of people would intentionally misrepresent their point of view if it benefited them.
True False

4 Most people who borrow something and return it slightly damaged probably wouldn't mention it to their lender.
True False

5 Most people today are too dependent on others.
True False

6 In general, I can take people or leave them.
True False

7 If a company told its employees that profits were too low to grant pay raises, I would tend to doubt the firm's honesty.
True False

8 Most politicians have taken bribes in some form or another.
True False

9 Most successful people get ahead more as a result of whom they know than what they know.
True False

10 People today tend to have lower moral standards than people a generation ago.
True False

SCORING ·

To tally your score, give yourself 1 point for each "False" response.

A score of 8–10: You are a trusting person who accepts others as you see them. You fall in love easily. You may have a tendency to be so accepting of others that you are gullible or naïve.

A score of 5–7: You have a balance between trust and caution. You're open to new relationships but can maintain a fair amount of objectivity when it comes to trusting others and falling in love.

A score of 0–4: You are more guarded and suspicious than most people. You probably analyze others' motives too much. Your desire to protect yourself at all costs may prevent you from having meaningful relationships with honest people who deserve your trust.

EXPLANATION ·

Interpersonal trust involves risk. When beginning a friendship or romantic relationship, people often wonder if the possible gain will outweigh the chance of betrayal or rejection. After much research, Dr. Carl Rogers—founder of the humanist movement in psychology and the former director of the Center for the Study of the Human Person in La Jolla, California—concluded that a measure of trust is fundamental to being a balanced individual. Realistic trust and a willingness to accept others usually indicate self-acceptance, and are signs of a well-adjusted personality.

Is Your Romantic Bond Unbreakable?

With marriages occurring at the rate of about two million per year, and divorces or annulments totaling about a third of that number, it's no wonder that psychologists and other experts are giving considerable thought to what makes for wedded bliss or a marital miss.

Operating on the notion that "forewarned is forearmed," psychologists have attempted to divine the factors that forecast compatibility and those that betoken a future split. They have learned that among the reasons given in court for divorce, few bear any resemblance to the true reasons for a marital break-down. A number of expert studies have been conducted in the quest to learn more about what keeps couples together and what tears them apart. Thousands of single and married persons have answered elaborate, lengthy questionnaires designed to predict their chances of maintaining a successful long-term relationship. Having pored over the masses of data, behavioral scientists have finally unearthed what they believe to be the markers of possible future romantic incompatibility.

TEST ·

The following quiz measures your ability to spot the warning signs of breakup and divorce. Rate each statement "True" if you think it is a significant romantic-bond breaker, and "False" if you do not think it's significant.

1 Age difference of ten years or more between partners.
True False

2 Significant difference in religious background.
True False

3 Heavy and varied dating experience by either or both partners before marriage.
True False

4 High education level (some college) for both spouses.
True False

5 A strong attachment to parents by either spouse before marriage.
True False

6 Virginity before marriage.
True False

7 Both partners were under 21 when married.
True False

8 An unemployed spouse who feels he or she doesn't get enough money for him or herself and the children.
True False

9 The husband establishes himself as the dominant personality.
True False

10 One spouse does not desire children.
True False

S C O R I N G ·

To tally your score, give yourself 1 point for each response that matches yours.

① *False* ② *False* ③ *True* ④ *False* ⑤ *False* ⑥ *True* ⑦ *True* ⑧ *True*
⑨ *False* ⑩ *True*

E X P L A N A T I O N ·

① *False.* In three independent studies, psychologists L. Terman, E. Burgess, and L. Cottrell concluded that even if age differences between spouses are considerably larger than average, this factor is not related to unhappiness and divorce to any important degree.

② *False.* Studies by psychologist H. Locke failed to reveal that religious differences are a major source of divorce. Apparently, differences great enough to disrupt a marriage are generally great enough to prevent it from occurring in the first place.

③ *False.* In research conducted with more than five hundred couples, there was less need for marital adjustment among those couples who had had many steady relationships prior to marriage.

④ *False.* Partners with a high level of education generally have better marriages and fewer divorces than those who have lower levels of education.

⑤ *False.* Perhaps contrary to popular assumption, studies have found that the chances of divorce decrease if partners had close ties to their parents when they were single.

⑥ *True.* Exhaustive work by L. Terman at Stanford University and A. Kinsey at the Indiana Institute for Sex Research demonstrated that the chances of having a lasting marriage are somewhat better if individuals have sexual experience prior to marriage.

⑦ *True.* The bulk of divorces, more than 50 percent, occurs between partners who are under twenty-one years old. There are six times as many occurrences of divorce among couples who are under twenty-one than among those who are over thirty-one years of age.

⑧ *True.* Consistent findings indicate that poor family economics is a major cause of divorce. In fact, non-support is the number-one stated cause in divorce courts.

⑨ *False.* There is abundant evidence that a marriage is more successful and less divorce-prone if the husband is not more dominant than the wife or only somewhat so.

⑩ *True.* There is considerable evidence that disagreement between partners about wanting children leads to marital disruption. It is surprising how often this crucial point is not thrashed out before marriage.

✏️ Will You Win the Battle of the Sexes?

The late Frank Sheed once quipped that there are two basic ways to waste time—by reading subway-car advertisements, and by spitting over a bridge. With all due deference to the noted author-publisher, there is probably a third contender in the race to squander seconds: the battle of the sexes.

These feisty contests tend to generate heat rather than shed light. The truth is that neither sex is superior. In fact, marriage experts find that the strengths and weaknesses of men and women complement each other perfectly in this beautiful game of life and love.

TEST ·

It's likely that if your beliefs were probed, some outlandish notions about the opposite sex would emerge. The following quiz will help you gauge whether your opinions are on target or way off base.

1 If a woman exercised as often and with as much intensity as a man, she would develop muscle strength equal to that of a man.
True False

2 Women get the blues more often than men do.
True False

3 The rate of suicide is higher among women than among men.
True False

4 Men make better hypnosis subjects than women.
True False

5 Women are shier than men.
True False

6 Men are better able to detect the motives of others than women are.
True False

7 Women daydream more often than men.
True False

8 Fathers are more likely than mothers to physically abuse their children.
True False

9 Females engage in sexual activity at an earlier age than males do.
True False

10 In same-sex friendships, men are more helpful to their male friends than women are to their female friends.
True False

SCORING ·

To tally your score, give yourself 1 point for each response that matches yours.

① *False* ② *True* ③ *False* ④ *False* ⑤ *False* ⑥ *False* ⑦ *False* ⑧ *False* ⑨ *False* ⑩ *False*

A score of 7 points or more: Your insight into the differences between the sexes is good. You have fewer distortions than most people.

A score of 4–6: You have an average degree of understanding of men and women.

A score of 0–3: Chances are you are relying too heavily upon stereotyped notions about the differences between men and women.

EXPLANATION ·

① *False*. The male body produces more testosterone than the female body. This hormone adds bulk to muscle fiber, and programs men for larger bones. Men's bodies are 40 percent muscle, compared with 23 percent for women, and exercise won't change this very much.

② *True*. Women suffer depression more often than men, and are treated for this condition more frequently than men.

③ *False*. The suicide rate is higher among men than women by a ratio of 3 to 1.

④ *False*. Studies show that at any age level females are somewhat more hypnotizable than males.

⑤ *False*. Shyness is found equally among men and women. Philip Zimbardo, a leading authority on the subject, claims there is no difference between the sexes in shyness.

⑥ *False*. Generally, women are more aware of social cues than men are. They show more sensitivity than men in picking up such non-verbal messages as body language, facial expression, and tone of voice.

⑦ *False*. Studies by Jerome Singer at Yale University show that there are very few major differences between men and women in how often and when and where they daydream.

⑧ *False*. Sociologists summarized several surveys that showed that mothers abuse their children more than fathers do. Mothers were cited as being the abusive parent in 50 to 80 percent of the cases studied, and mothers kill their children about twice as often as fathers do.

⑨ *False*. Males have sex at a younger age than females do. Once they begin their sexual activity, they engage in sex more often than females. In general, men are more responsive to sexual stimuli and are more likely to engage in self-stimulation than women.

⑩ *False*. Research done at the University of Utah shows that since women are more self-disclosing, verbal, and affectionate, they tend to have more of a "therapeutic" effect on each other than men have on other men.

What's Your Intimacy Index?

The search for intimacy is the lonely quest of the human heart. Intimacy is an inborn biological need we first encounter early in life when we are cuddled by our mothers—we never outgrow its powerful lure.

But interpersonal closeness is not as prevalent as you might think. Too often, we learn to adjust to having little meaningful emotional interaction, and it becomes our personalized "love style" to have little or no intimacy at all. This is when the trouble begins.

Studies show that people who are lonely tend to suffer more physical and mental breakdowns than those who are close to someone. Unmarried individuals, compared with those who are married, have higher rates of maladjustment. Children who experience lengthy separations from their parents and family can develop asthma, respiratory disorders, and other diseases, and ill people who fall in love are more likely to recover faster than those who don't. Some experts go so far as to conclude that an intimate love style is just as crucial to a person's well-being as food or water.

Sadly, a world that now rewards uniqueness and independence makes it that much harder to achieve closeness. Many of us are socialized to fend off the attempts of others who try to draw close to us. How intimate would you say you are with the closest person in your life? Are your love styles compatible? Do you ever feel that you are missing a sense of closeness or depth of understanding with your partner?

TEST

The following quiz will help reveal how socially intimate you are. As you answer the questions below, keep in mind your relationship with someone close to you. Perhaps they should also take the quiz.

1 How much of your leisure time do you spend with your partner?
A. *Not much*
B. *A little*
C. *A lot*

2 How often do you feel it is important for your partner to show you physical affection?
A. *Not often*
B. *Sometimes*
C. *Often*

3 Would you feel hurt if he/she didn't share deep, intimate feelings with you?
A. *Not much*
B. *A little*
C. *Very much*

4 Do you understand his/her innermost feelings?
A. *Not much*
B. *A little*
C. *Very much*

5 How encouraging and supportive are you when your partner is unhappy?
A. *Not much*
B. *A little*
C. *Very much*

6 How much do you show him/her affection?
A. *Not much*
B. *A little*
C. *Very much*

7 Do you feel close to your partner?
A. *Not much*
B. *A little*
C. *Very much*

8 When you disagree strongly, how much does it hurt your relationship?
A. *Not much*
B. *A little*
C. *Very much*

9 How much time do you spend alone with him/her?
A. *Not much*
B. *A little*
C. *A lot*

10 How satisfying is your relationship with your partner?
A. *Not very satisfying*
B. *Somewhat satisfying*
C. *Very satisfying*

11 When you quarrel heatedly, does it actually make you physically ill?
A. *Not much*
B. *A little*
C. *Very much*

12 Do your arguments last two days or longer?
A. *Often*
B. *Sometimes*
C. *Not often*

SCORING

To tally your score, give yourself 1 point for each "a" response, 2 points for each "b" response, and 3 points for each "c" response.

A score of 27 points or less: Your intimacy level with your partner is fairly low. This may not necessarily mean that either of you is displeased. Both of your closeness needs may be low, and you may be suited to each other. However, if a low scorer is unhappy, it might mean that he/she has difficulty achieving intimacy, and counseling should be sought.

A score of 28–32 points: You have an average degree of intimacy in your relationship compared with other couples.

A score of 33 points or more: You have an intensely close relationship. One thing to be aware of is that you might be too sensitive to each other's feelings and easily hurt when ignored.

EXPLANATION

The quiz is based on social-intimacy research conducted by R.S. Miller and H.M. Lefcourt of the University of Waterloo, Ontario, who tested hundreds of single and married couples. Should you conclude that marriage will take care of all of your intimacy needs, be aware that this is not necessarily the case. Although marriage might seem like an appropriate way to increase a couple's closeness, it can be destructive if a couple has incompatible love styles. In fact, studies show that unhappily married couples who take the quiz come out with low intimacy scores.

CHAPTER 3

A HAPPY HOME

✏ Can You Spot a Troubled Child?

"**S**ince Sammy has been in Ms. Hamway's class, he is doing better. She seems to sense when something is bothering him and knows how to help him." A mother recently told me this, and it raised a question: Why do kids respond better to some teachers than to others?

Children are sensitive to how a teacher judges their behavior. A teacher's attitude—what the teacher believes to be "good" or "bad" behavior—can have a bearing on the development of the personality of a pupil. A classic study done more than fifty years ago found that there were great incongruities between how teachers and conservative parents defined "serious" behavior problems and how child experts did.

Could you be out of step with the experts' opinions? Are you aware of the most predictive signs of maladjustment in your child, or are you focusing on relatively unimportant behavior your child will probably outgrow?

TEST ·

An opinion survey asked teachers, parents, and child psychology experts to rank certain behaviors as indicators of future maladjustment. The ten behaviors listed below were included in the survey. To take this quiz, rank the behaviors in terms of their relative seriousness, with "1" being extremely serious and "10" being not serious—place your rankings in the column marked "Your response." Then move on to the "Scoring" section to see how well you can spot a troubled child.

YOUR RESPONSE	EXPERTS	DIFFERENCE	
_____	_____	_____	Unsocial, withdrawn
_____	_____	_____	Suspicious
_____	_____	_____	Unhappy, depressed
_____	_____	_____	Resentful
_____	_____	_____	Fearful
_____	_____	_____	Cruel
_____	_____	_____	Easily discouraged
_____	_____	_____	Suggestible
_____	_____	_____	Overly-critical of others
_____	_____	_____	Sensitive
		_____	YOUR SCORE

SCORING ·

The behavior patterns you just ranked were taken from a list of fifty characteristics rated by child psychologists, psychiatrists, social workers, and counselors. The order in which the items appear concurs with the position in which they were ranked, with "unsocial" being the most problematic behavior a child can exhibit. To tally your score, write the numbers "1" through "10" down the "Experts" column, beginning with "1" in the first row and ending with "10" in the last. This will give you the specialists' rankings. Then, for each item, calculate the difference between your ranking and that of the experts and place that number in the "Difference" column. Add up all the numbers in the "Difference" column—the sum of the numbers is your score. The lowest possible score is 0 and the highest is 50. A score of 25 is the average between these extremes. The closer your score is to 0, the more you agree with child experts about what constitutes serious deviant behavior.

EXPLANATION ·

Unfortunately, adults who are responsible for healthy mental traits in kids are often oblivious to the most important signals of trouble ahead. All ten behaviors in our quiz are, to some degree, serious reflections of something wrong in the child, but those that fall among the first three or four ranks are the most serious. In all fairness, it must be said that what teachers consider to be a serious problem is an action which upsets the teacher, the school, and the classroom routines, not necessarily that which behaviorists consider a predictor of neurosis.

When other studies using the traits above were repeated some thirty years later, the findings showed that the ratings of teachers and parents had shifted and become more similar to the experts' opinions. But the experts themselves also became more conservative in their judgments. Current surveys show that all three groups are now more concerned with behavior like withdrawal, unhappiness, depression, and fearfulness. The most encouraging result of these studies is that, compared with their predecessors fifty years ago, more highly trained teachers and better informed parents are beginning to focus on deviant patterns before they get out of hand.

CHAPTER 4

SOCIAL SENSES

✏️ Are You a
Con Artist in Disguise?

At some time or another, we've all been in a position to persuade others. Whether it's a child who beguiles his parents for another cookie or a wily con artist who bilks the innocent out of their hard-earned money, both behaviors require a certain degree of shrewdness.

In their work at Columbia University in New York, psychologists Charles Turner, Daniel Martinez, and Richard Christie independently probed the personal characteristics that mark a person for either social or professional success. Several factors came to the fore: IQ, education level, school achievements, social background, and the personality of one's parents. But the investigators learned that it's not these traits alone that predict success. As a matter of fact, these traits account for only 65 percent, at most, of one's success in the business world. The other 35 percent is attributable to a personality factor loosely defined as getting others to do what you want.

TEST

Whether you're at the top of the success ladder, struggling midway, or angling for a toehold on that first rung, the following quiz will help reveal whether, unwittingly or not, you rely on manipulation to get ahead.

1. There is nothing wrong with telling a white lie in order to avoid hassles.
True False

2. It is probably shrewd to flatter important people who are in a position to help you.
True False

3. As a child, I was known as a bully.
True False

4. In this strongly competitive world, most anything short of being unethical is justified in getting ahead.
True False

5. Most successful people lead clean, honest lives.
True False

6. P. T. Barnum was right when he said, "there's a sucker born every minute."
True False

7. It is not possible to abide by all the rules and still get ahead in this world.
True False

8. Most people are brave.
True False

9. The biggest difference between law violators and others is that the violators were not smart enough to avoid being caught.
True False

10. Don't tell anyone your real reason for doing something unless it is useful to do so.
True False

SCORING ·

The quiz was adapted from the work of professors Turner and Martinez. For want of a better term, the quiz measures your "manipulativeness," or Machiavellian tendencies (more about Machiavelli later). To tally your score, give yourself 1 point for each response that matches yours.

① *True* ② *True* ③ *True* ④ *True* ⑤ *False* ⑥ *True* ⑦ *True* ⑧ *False* ⑨ *True* ⑩ *True*

A score of 3 points or less: You are a low Machiavellian and tend to be more than willing to entertain another person's viewpoint. You are a harmonizer and, at times, may be even too submissive in carrying through your own ideas and goals.

A score of 4–6 points: You are average when it comes to conning others. You are likely to push your ideas moderately, but not to the point of overruling or manipulating others.

A score of 7 points or more: You are a high Mach. You do not share traditional notions about social rights and wrongs. You are an independent thinker who dislikes conforming to your peers. According to the researchers at Columbia, you are cool and at times even distant. You might sometimes treat others as objects. If this is you, it might be time for a change.

EXPLANATION ·

The term "Machiavellian" is derived from the military, government, and business tactics proposed by Niccolo Machiavelli, an influential politician-writer of the 16th century. As counsel to royalty, he advocated the use of cunning and contrivance when needed to assure one's political goals. Compared to his other ideas, these amoral aspects of his doctrines have always attracted the greatest attention, yet he also devised brilliant strategies to make Italy a free republic. Nonetheless, his name is equated with power and manipulation.

You don't have to be smart to be Machiavellian. Manipulative tendencies do not correlate with IQ, as many might believe. Both bright and dull people can be high Mach types. The difference is that the bright high Mach types are more likely to succeed, while those less crafty can't conceal their motives as readily. High Machs tend to be credible and charming, with an action-oriented message. Their easiest target is a person with low IQ and little self-esteem who is taken by surprise by the ruse. High Machs succeed mostly when their prey is distracted or indecisive. Body language experts tell us not to look for shifty eyes as a sign of insincerity. Those who are experienced at deception actually have a steadier gaze than those who are honest. Also, it is not true that "con artist" drives go hand in hand with psychopathology; many normal people use power tactics because they work for them.

Manipulativeness is probably learned from our parents. This is confirmed by Dr. F. Geis and Richard Christie in their book, *Studies in Machiavellianism*. In homes where parents are high Machs, the child who escapes this influence is likely to be the first-born, who often develops traits diametrically opposed to the tactics of his or her canny parents. And although Machs are found among both sexes, studies show that men are more manipulative than women.

✏️ Are You Socially Anxious or Socially Secure?

Comedian Robin Williams once said that even with all his years of performing, he still gets nervous when facing a new audience. Social anxiety is a burden everybody endures, from childhood through old age. Many never shake it no matter how hard they try, though some of us have learned to disguise it quite well.

When unusual or special social situations arise, how high is your social angst? Take the following quiz to find out. You may also want to ask someone who knows you well to respond to the items as he or she thinks you might answer. When you're both finished, compare results.

T E S T ·

This quiz will help you evaluate whether you simply have slightly sweaty palms or if you suffer from social anxiety. Rate how tense or uncomfortable you would feel under the following conditions.

1 Being approached by a policeman.
   A. *Not tense at all*
   B. *Slightly tense*
   C. *Quite tense*

2 In a casual get-together with acquaintances and co-workers.
   A. *Not tense at all*
   B. *Slightly tense*
   C. *Quite tense*

3 When sitting with a group of strangers in the waiting room at the doctor's office.
   A. *Not tense at all*
   B. *Slightly tense*
   C. *Quite tense*

4 Talking to your boss about a raise or a teacher about your grade.
   A. *Not tense at all*
   B. *Slightly tense*
   C. *Quite tense*

5 Speaking to an attractive person of the opposite sex whom you've just met at a cocktail party.
   A. *Not tense at all*
   B. *Slightly tense*
   C. *Quite tense*

6 Talking sweetly to your lover over the phone with strangers nearby.
   A. *Not tense at all*
   B. *Slightly tense*
   C. *Quite tense*

7 Being interviewed for an important job.
   A. *Not tense at all*
   B. *Slightly tense*
   C. *Quite tense*

8 Arguing about politics, ethics, or other non-personal issues among your friends.
   A. *Not tense at all*
   B. *Slightly tense*
   C. *Quite tense*

9 Being in a new group where you are the only one of your race, nationality, or religious background.
   A. *Not tense at all*
   B. *Slightly tense*
   C. *Quite tense*

10 Meeting a friend by chance while shopping for something personal and potentially "embarrassing," such as underwear, feminine products, or condoms.
   A. *Not tense at all*
   B. *Slightly tense*
   C. *Quite tense*

SCORING

To tally your score, give yourself 1 point for each "a" response, 2 points for each "b" response, and 3 points for each "c" response. To determine your level of social unease, refer to the scores below.

A score of 24–30 points: You are very anxious socially and probably too worried about what others will think of you. Too much concern about your impact on others might indicate personal insecurity or a sagging self-image.

A score of 18–24 points: You have an adequate amount of social sensitivity to what others look for and expect from you. You feel accepted by others and are satisfied enough with your social image to function passably well in new social circumstances.

A score of 10-17 points: You are quite self-assured and very relaxed when around others. You may even be oblivious to how they view you. Your self-image is shaped by your own internal standards and very little by what society may judge as acceptable behavior.

EXPLANATION

According to research by Mark Leary at Eastern Illinois Universty, one of the greatest difficulties in studying social anxiety is that it is manifested in two distinct ways: a person's self-report (what our quiz measures), and actual behavior, as demonstrated by withdrawal, speaking in a low voice, and being passive.

The quandary is that one may feel socially anxious but also be good at covering it up. People with these characteristics—labeled "shy extraverts" by Dr. Philip Zimbardo of Stanford University—have learned to appear sociable and relaxed while feeling awkward. Research shows that the less self-esteem we have, the more likely we are to experience anxiety in the presence of others.

This finding is also backed up by the work of Professors R. E. Glasgow and H. Arkowitz conducted at the University of Oregon, who found that people with high social anxiety tend to date little. The main reason underlying their reluctance is their poor self-perception. These types would score low on the quiz and are often called "avoidant personalities" because they are acutely sensitive to humiliation and deprecation by others and actively avoid people in order to protect themselves. Social angst is actually a fairly prevalent problem in our culture, and as a result, a number of shyness clinics have formed to help people learn to feel more comfortable in their own skin.

How Popular Are You?

When Groucho Marx quipped, "I'd never join a club that would have me as a member," it was a funny way of saying that his self-esteem was at zero level. Fortunately, most of us are not in this category and have enough good feelings about ourselves to be reasonably happy. One powerful means of gaining self-esteem is through social acceptance. It's like getting a vote of confidence from others about our value. In a way, others validate our sense of worth.

Psychologists find that those who are popular are "middle-of-the-roaders" who strongly accept the attitudes and ideas of their group; they are not extremists in their thinking. Further, they have the social skills to form mature and lasting relationships with others.

TEST

How popular are you? The following quiz will suggest how well you get along with people and/or if you have the potential to boost your social skills.

1 In the past month, I have received two or more social invitations.
True False

2 My friends seek my advice about their problems.
True False

3 When the joke is on me, I usually laugh along with the rest without feeling resentment.
True False

4 Some friends divulge their intimate secrets to me.
True False

5 When something is bothering me, I readily turn to friends for help.
True False

6 I have participated actively in at least two social groups for the past two years.
True False

7 I usually make friends through people I already know rather than on my own.
True False

8 I choose to be friendly with someone mostly on the basis of common interests.
True False

9 I am late for at least one out of three social engagements.
True False

10 I don't like to be dependent on others and don't encourage others to be dependent on me.
True False

SCORING ·

To tally your score, give yourself 1 point for each response that matches yours.

① *True* ② *True* ③ *True* ④ *True* ⑤ *True* ⑥ *True* ⑦ *False* ⑧ *False* ⑨ *False* ⑩ *False*

Read on to see where you fall on the popularity meter.

A score of 8–10 points: You are, or have the potential to be, above average in popularity and enjoy a wide circle of friends.

A score of 5–7 points: Like most of us, your popularity is solidly in the average range.

A score of 0–4 points: You are more of a private person than the popular type.

EXPLANATION ·

Research on the topic of popularity is scant, but some facts are known. Popular people tend to attract others and are role models for us to emulate. Often they are leaders. At work, a boss who is popular has strong advantages over one who isn't. His or her workers will show less absenteeism, higher morale, less tension, and more productivity. Popular people tend to be born later in the family lineup. They develop more social skills because they interact with their siblings and others for a longer time.

Disliked boys often compensate by fighting with peers and by bullying them. Girls, on the other hand, sometimes drift into promiscuity in order to be accepted. Dr. Philip Zimbardo has called this "a physical means of achieving an illusion of psychological security."

Other social scientists have shown that children can improve their popularity levels. Third and fourth graders were trained on such things as manners, listening skills, and other social-interaction techniques. Their studies yielded marked results. The children who received training mixed better with their peers, showing more concern, listening more intently when spoken to, and other traits that up one's popularity quotient. On the adult level as well, social interaction is a skill like reading and writing that can be learned through the use of videotapes, talks, and group counseling.

✏ Do You Listen or Leave 'Em Hanging?

They say that listening well is an art form. But do you recall how frustrating it was the last time you spoke with someone who was only partly present? Being an effective listener isn't just about hearing what's said; it also involves conveying your interest and understanding.

Good communication keeps human relations going. But too often there is a breakdown at the receiving end. A prime example would be parents who are at a loss when their teenager "tunes out" during a conversation. Parents don't know what to focus on in the two-way exchange and don't profit enough from the experience. But according to Dr. Thomas Gordon, author of *Parent Effectiveness Training*, parents can break through this impasse and get their children to talk with them by "active listening." The technique can be learned and applied to conversations with adults, too.

TEST ·

To discover how well you listen, take the following quiz.

1 When my friends have something on their mind, they usually use me as a sounding board.
True False

2 I don't mind listening to the problems of others.
True False

3 In a social gathering, I move from one conversation to another, often feeling that there is a better partner across the room.
True False

4 I grow impatient with someone who doesn't come to the point quickly.
True False

5 I tend to complete the jokes or stories that others tell.
True False

6 While people are speaking to me, I find myself thinking of the next thing to say to them.
True False

7 Most people are boring conversationalists.
True False

8 I usually do more talking than whomever I am with.
True False

9 People repeat things once or twice when speaking to me.
True False

10 I would rather give a talk than hear one.
True False

SCORING

To tally your score, give yourself 1 point for each response that matches yours.

① *True* ② *True* ③ *False* ④ *False* ⑤ *False* ⑥ *False* ⑦ *False* ⑧ *False*

A score of 8 points or more: You are an above-average listener. Friends most likely seek you out when they have a problem they need to discuss, and you are probably popular at social gatherings.

A score of 5–7 points: Your listening skills are average. You are like most people—sometimes you listen very well, and at other times you probably let your mind wander. Remember, there is always room for improvement.

A score of 0–4 points: Frankly, you are not the best listener. You tend to tune out more often than you tune in. Read the "Explanation" section that follows for some tips on how you can improve your skills.

EXPLANATION

Why do trained counselors relate to people better than laymen do? What do these pros do differently to help others to grow? Dr. Gordon calls it "active listening." He has taught this technique to parents who have been "written off" by their children, and has found that it can be used equally well in "adult" arenas such as professional environments and social situations.

Dr. Gordon's method, which he has taught to more than 100,000 parents, is based on the work of Dr. Carl Rogers, founder of client-centered therapy, who taught that active listening focuses sharply on creating empathy, an essential element for good ties with others. Active listening involves entering the private perceptual world of the speaker, seeing things from his or her point of view, and becoming thoroughly at home in it. It means paying attention to the underlying feelings being expressed and not so much to the statements themselves.

For example, if a downcast youngster says: "Won't my friend come over to play with me today?" it would be only partly correct to respond to the content of his remark by replying, "No, he had to go to the dentist." In responding in that way, you are missing his underlying feelings. Using active listening, you would answer something like this: "I know you're disappointed that your friend isn't coming today, but don't feel blue. Let's plan a good time with him for tomorrow." Active listening enables you to immediately get to the heart of what's bothering someone. It demonstrates that you really understand. Granted, it will take a little more time to discover exactly what underlying emotion is being expressed, but it will bring good results in the end.

To train yourself for better listening, take these three steps:

1. Commit yourself to being a better listener.
2. Read up on the subject and practice skills like active listening.
3. Determine what your defective habits may be by studying the quiz items. Hopefully this will get you started on attaining better communication know-how.

✏️ How Thoughtful Are You?

Can you recall the good feeling you had when someone carried your bulky package, held a heavy door, or allowed you to cut ahead of a long line? In a world of chaos, favors granted by perfect strangers remind us that social graces are still well and thriving. But we humans are variable creatures, and a host of conditions influence whether or not we will choose to render aid to others. Some mitigating factors include our relationship to the afflicted, our mood, or even the weather. A needy person's age also influences our generosity. In one experiment at the New School for Social Research in New York City, unsuspecting subjects were asked to help various people in distress. Researchers found that elderly persons were helped more readily than those who were middle-aged or younger. Also, the study showed that it's more likely we'd come to the aid of a woman than a man, to a woman who is pretty than one who is plain, or to one who is well-dressed, compared with one who is sloppy in appearance.

Then there are the other, more subtle facilitators or inhibitors that bring out the best or worst in us. If we have a good self-image and if we perceive ourselves as helpful, it's more likely that we will extend a helping hand. We're less likely to help if others nearby are watching than if we are alone or if there is a high noise level nearby, as on a subway or near a churning lawn mower.

T E S T ·

Below are some questions that will gauge your thoughtfulness. Respond "Yes" or "No" to each one. Be honest!

1 Do you, when instructed, write your account number on your checks when paying bills?
Yes No

2 When you meet someone, do you usually turn so that the sunlight will not be in their eyes?
Yes No

3 When a waiter clears the table, do you readily hand him items that are hard for him to reach?
Yes No

4 When stopping to speak with someone on the street, do you remove your sunglasses?
Yes No

5 After reading the newspaper at home, do you put it back together?
Yes No

6 When picking fruit from a fruit bowl, do you usually take the piece that is over-ripe or about to go bad?
Yes No

7 Do you push your chair in close to the table when leaving a restaurant?
Yes No

8 Do you give your teeth a good scrubbing before you visit the dentist?
Yes No

9 Do you hesitate to take the last appetizer on the platter?
Yes No

10 When you buy a small item, do you often carry it as is, to save the clerk the trouble of wrapping it?
Yes No

11 At the checkout counter, do you turn items so the cashier can see the price or bar code?
Yes No

12 When you dial a wrong number, do you usually hang up without saying anything?
Yes No

SCORING ·

To tally your score, give yourself 1 point for each answer that matches yours.

① *Yes* ② *Yes* ③ *Yes* ④ *Yes* ⑤ *Yes* ⑥ *Yes* ⑦ *Yes* ⑧ *Yes* ⑨ *Yes* ⑩ *Yes* ⑩ *Yes* ⑫ *No*

A score of 8 points or more: You have a great willingness to be helpful to others, and don't hesitate to lend a hand when it is needed.

A score of 5–7 points: You rank about average on the trait of thoughtfulness. You will give help if someone asks for it, but don't always think to offer.

A score of 0–4 points: You exhibit little interest in being of help to those who might benefit from it. You may be oblivious to the needs of others. Try to pay more attention to those around you.

EXPLANATION

Doing a good deed is called "social compliance" in psychology, and often the manner in which a favor is asked is crucial to how someone will respond. Researchers have found that people comply more often if the requester states his or her request openly, and if he or she follows it with a plausible reason. When it comes to granting wishes, we are guided by a simple formula: Request plus reason equals greater compliance. This is a good thing to remember. For example, if you asked to cut in line at the grocery store, you'd probably get a better response if you explained that your child is not feeling well and that you would like to get her home quickly. In addition, compliance has a ripple effect. Researchers at Manhattanville College in Purchase, New York, studied shoppers at a department store and found that when requests were accompanied by even such a trifling offering as a warm smile, shoppers tended to be kind and helpful to those nearby.

How responsive you are to the needy is learned behavior instilled by your childhood role models. The National Institute of Mental Health in Washington, D.C., found that some babies as young as one year old are capable of comforting others who are crying or in pain. You can increase your level of thoughtfulness if you encourage yourself to become more conscious of people, and practice daily the niceties that make for smoother interpersonal relationships.

✏️ Are You a "Take-Charge" Type?

It seems that whenever two people meet, the issue of who is dominant is the first one to be settled, most often very subtly. Between students, who gets better grades? Between executives, who earns more or has the larger office? Between tomboys, who is tougher? Among animals, the case is clear. Birds, in particular, size each other up and then decide who shall henpeck whom to show superiority.

Dominance-submissiveness is probably the most basic of all interactions between creatures great and small. In Western culture, submissive behavior is not rewarded. We tend to push our children ahead with notions of the "go-getter," and expressions like "Never say die," all of which reflect our belief in the value of personal dominance.

TEST ·

Where do you stand on the dominant-submissive scale? The following quiz may provide the answer.

1 I could bluff my way past a guard without feeling uneasy.
True False

2 I have heckled or sharply questioned a public speaker.
True False

3 I wouldn't feel uneasy about scolding a workman who didn't complete a job I asked him to do.
True False

4 I would feel timid about starting a conversation with a stranger.
True False

⑤ I don't mind the job of introducing people at gatherings.
True False

⑥ I can cut into a long line without feeling guilty.
True False

⑦ When I drive, it doesn't bother me to follow a long line of cars.
True False

⑧ When dining with friends, I would complain if a waiter brought me a somewhat small portion of food.
True False

⑨ When I'm at odds with someone, I don't call him or her. I usually wait until he or she calls me first.
True False

⑩ I like to instruct people on how to do things.
True False

SCORING ·

To tally your score, give yourself 1 point for each response that matches yours.

① *True* ② *True* ③ *False* ④ *False* ⑤ *True* ⑥ *True* ⑦ *False* ⑧ *True* ⑨ *True* ⑩ *True*

A score of 0–4 points: You're low on dominance, high on submissiveness. If you enjoy this laid back style of life, great. But if you feel unhappy with the way you often come out in encounters with others, consider getting help to become more assertive. Dominance can be enhanced through assertiveness training, a trend that was kicked off in the 1960s and persists today.

A score of 5–7 points: You have an average balance of dominance and submissive tendencies. You probably respond to different situations on a case-by-case basis, and not with any set type of behavior.

A score of 8–10 points: You are high on dominance. If people accept this in you and follow your lead (many leaders are high dominants), then you should be happy. However, if your high levels of dominance are causing friction in your day-to-day interactions, it may be time to back off, be more empathetic, and let others win some points every now and then, too.

EXPLANATION

One question that has tickled the brains of scientists for years is this: Is a dominant personality inherited or learned? Among animals, it is a strongly inherited trait. Among humans, genes seem to play only a minor role in our levels of boldness or timidity. They are largely patterns learned from family and peers.

Nowhere has the interplay of dominant and submissive roles been studied more than in marriage, the most interdependent of all human partnerships. Here there is almost always one spouse who tips the dominant/submissive scale in his or her favor. But it isn't as totalitarian as it sounds, for as long as mutual love and respect are there, spouses are generally happy to accept their respective roles and feel comfortable in them. At the same time, children usually adopt the attitudes of parents. They copy their parents' role-playing style and accept it as the norm when they themselves marry. Studies of families conducted at Cornell University in New York by Dr. Hazel Ingersoll showed that boys with dominant fathers tended to follow in their fathers' footsteps when they themselves had families. Likewise, if a girl grew up with a timid mother, she would likely fall back on such behavior when handling conflicts, and act accordingly.

An interesting note about dominance has to do with birth order. An only child tends to be dominant among his peers. In homes where there is more than one child, however, dominance is more random among the siblings. Tests show that the strongest, most intelligent people (and animals, too), are usually the ascendant ones in their group. Of course, people aren't always just dominant or just submissive. The role we take depends on a host of factors: the people near us, our relation to them, the mood we're in, the circumstances of the occasion, and what role is expected of us, among others.

CHAPTER 5

ON THE JOB

✐ Would You Be an Understanding Boss?

Job dissatisfaction is rampant these days, running as high as 70 percent in some industries. In a tight job market, the figure is probably even higher. Most of the time workers are disgruntled because they feel misunderstood by those in charge. Often, supervisors don't accurately read the signals of workers who are growing progressively discontent with their work. Furthermore, because many supervisors are job-oriented rather than people-oriented, they sometimes lack the skills to react appropriately when they do spot employee unrest.

Chances are that if you work for a company, you've thought of leaving it a few times in the past year. Or perhaps you've had a fantasy or two of how you could run the whole corporation better than your president does. So let's say that by some stroke of magic, you're suddenly placed in charge of your department or company. How well would you fare? Would you be perceptive enough to identify symptoms of worker unrest before they eroded into labor-management chaos?

Your judgments as manager would be influenced by how you perceive your workers and what you believe is important to them.

TEST ·

Below is a ten-statement quiz that relates to happiness on the job. How understanding a boss would you be?

1 Men enjoy their jobs more than women do.
True False

2 If a worker is dissatisfied he will produce less.
True False

3 Job satisfaction tends to increase with age.
True False

4 Men tend to rely upon their supervisors for job satisfaction more than women do.
True False

5 New employees tend to show high job satisfaction.
True False

6 Increasing workers' salaries improves their level of job contentment most of the time.
True False

7 Compared with high performers, low performers will do better if you provide them more chances to socialize on the job.
True False

8 The more intelligent a worker, the more satisfied he or she tends to be.
True False

9 Job dissatisfaction tends to increase with a worker's level of responsibility.
True False

10 Hours and work conditions are generally not important factors in job satisfaction.
True False

SCORING ·

This is a difficult quiz and you may be in for a few surprises. To tally your score, give yourself 1 point for each response that matches yours. All the statements were drawn from recent industry surveys.

① *False* ② *False* ③ *False* ④ *False* ⑤ *False* ⑥ *False* ⑦ *True* ⑧ *True* ⑨ *True* ⑩ *True*

A score of 5 is average. Anything above 5 indicates that you have a better-than-average understanding of what makes workers happy.

EXPLANATION ·

The major studies on job satisfaction in the U.S. go back to just after World War II. The Conference Board, a non-profit research organization formerly known as the National Labor Relations Board, did a significant and still much quoted study in 1947. Basically, it found that management had little idea about what workers considered the most satisfying aspects of their jobs.

For example, management put more emphasis on wages than workers did. On a list of the top ten most important aspects of the job, workers ranked salary third on the list, while managers assumed it was workers' number one aspect of job satisfaction. Workers actually ranked security the most important aspect of their jobs, while managers ranked it second on the list. Similarly, workers placed the possibility of advancement higher on their list than management did. The largest discrepancy between workers and management was in the importance placed on job benefits: workers ranked this their fourth most pressing concern, while management considered this only eighth in order of importance.

As if these disparities in work values weren't enough to cause friction between labor and management, a report by the Department of Health, Education and Welfare, called "Work in America," yielded other previously ignored factors found to cause job blahs. It stated that worker frustration is only partially due to poor management philosophy and work conditions. Worker alienation is also related to a variety of social problems such as physical and mental health, family stability, and community acceptance.

So, given all this, it's plain to see that the boss who tries to keep everyone happy must bear a lot in mind. Still think you'd like to be one?

✏ Does Your Job Satisfy Your Personality Needs?

Lifelong satisfaction in a job is rare. Some 70 percent of all workers are dissatisfied with what they do and would welcome a change. For the remaining relatively content 30 percent, there's a significant reason why we continue in our jobs. The fact is we enjoy work that fulfills our deeper needs and thinking styles. Unfortunately, most of us don't probe our psychodynamics before we choose a job. We all might be better off if we did.

While a professor of management at the University of Southern California, Dr. Alan Rowe uncovered several crucial factors that relate to happy work adjustment. He identified four basic thinking styles. When we match these styles with what our job requires, the chances are good we'll be professionally satisfied.

If you feel unhappy with your position and wonder if a change will help you live up to more of your potential, the quiz below might help. It is based on a test devised by Rowe after some six years of research, and it will suggest whether you and your job are meant for each other.

TEST ·

For each of the ten items below, choose two answers from among the lettered choices. Put the number 5 next to your first letter choice for each item, and the number 1 next to your second letter choice. (It may help to make a table with the letters a, b, c, and d across the top and the question numbers 1 through 10 along the left-hand side; then, for each question, simply place the 5 and 1 beneath the letter choices you've picked.)

1 I enjoy jobs that:
   A. *Have much variety*
   B. *Involve people*
   C. *Allow independent action*
   D. *Are technical and defined*

2 My main objective is to:
   A. *Be the best in my field*
   B. *Feel secure in my job.*
   C. *Get recognition for my work*
   D. *Have a status position*

3 When faced with a problem, I:
   A. *Apply careful analysis*
   B. *Rely on my feelings*
   C. *Look for creative paths*
   D. *Rely on proven approaches*

4 When uncertain about what to do, I:
   A. *Search for facts*
   B. *Delay making a decision*
   C. *Explore a possible compromise*
   D. *Rely on hunches and intuition*

5 Whenever possible, I avoid:
   A. *Incomplete work*
   B. *Conflict with others*
   C. *Using numbers or formulas*
   D. *Long debates*

6 In social settings I generally:
   A. *Think about what is being said*
   B. *Listen to conversations*
   C. *Observe what is going on*
   D. *Speak with others*

7 I am good at remembering:
   A. *Places where I met people*
   B. *People's personalities*
   C. *People's faces*
   D. *People's names*

8 Others consider me:
   A. *Disciplined and precise*
   B. *Supportive and compassionate*
   C. *Imaginative and perfectionist*
   D. *Aggressive and domineering*

9 I dislike:
   A. *Boring work*
   B. *Being rejected*
   C. *Following rules*
   D. *Losing control of others*

10 I am especially good at:
   A. *Solving difficult problems*
   B. *Interacting with others*
   C. *Seeing many possibilities*
   D. *Recalling dates and facts*

SCORING

Tally up the number values you've assigned to each letter. The two letters that have the highest scores correspond to your two major thinking styles, as defined in the "Explanation" section that follows.

EXPLANATION

A. Analytical. Analytical people are problem solvers. They have a desire to find the best possible answers. They examine lots of details and use large amounts of data. They are innovative, creative, and enjoy variety.

B. Behavioral. Behavioral people need human contacts. They are supportive, empathic people. They use little data in making decisions, preferring to talk things out with others. They communicate easily and prefer to use persuasion instead of pressure to win their point of view.

C. Conceptual. Conceptual people are broad-minded thinkers who like to contemplate the "big picture." They are future-oriented and achievement-oriented and tend to be independent, humanistic, and creative.

D. Directive. Directive people are authoritarian taskmasters. They need power and expect results. They act decisively and are rule- and regulation-minded. They are highly verbal and tend to rely on intuition.

These patterns predict the kind of work that might suit a person best. Businesspeople, for example, tend to score high on the analytical and conceptual scales. They like to consider many options and develop broad plans for their companies. Technical people, engineers, scientists, and others in similar lines of work are analytical and directive. They enjoy solving problems logically, working with numbers, and finding mathematical and scientific answers.

Those in the helping arts, like nurses, doctors, and social workers, combine conceptual and behavioral frames of mind. They like to work closely with people in developing an understanding of human affairs. People who combine the analytical-behavioral frameworks tend to go into the fields of education and law, while directive-behavioral people are often found in sales and politics.

The highest score obtainable in any category is 50, but few people ever make this. The closer your score is to 50, the stronger your thinking style is in that category. Match your thinking style with your current job, and consider how well your work satisfies your personality needs.

✐ What's Your Pecuniary Profile?

Money. Throughout history, wars have been fought over it, religions have denounced it as a danger to one's soul, and most crimes have been committed for it, in one way or another. Money is a powerful motivator. When it beckons, many people have difficulty resisting its call.

No matter what our economic level, we all have a "dollar personality," a cluster of attitudes about money. There are three basic "money personalities"—perhaps you'll see yourself in one of them.

Compulsive spenders: This group feels uneasy about holding on to money. They believe that if they accumulate earnings, then they must also bear the unwelcome responsibility for its management. This generates anxiety. Compulsive spenders feel emotionally secure when they're free to spend. Through buying and owning items, they gain a false sense of assurance and security.

Compulsive hoarders: Hoarders perceive money as an extension of their egos, and to them, giving up money is like losing a part of themselves. They have a compelling drive to keep and protect their cash as if it were their very lifeblood.

Compulsive risk-takers: These people are basically magical thinkers guided by a grandiose notion that they can win the universe if they wish hard enough for it. For them, winning at a game, gambling, or engaging in speculative business or stock ventures symbolizes immortality.

TEST ·

What is your dollar personality? The following quiz items measure specific attitudes you might possess but of which you are perhaps unaware.

1. To be rich means to be powerful.
True False

2. The bottom line is, money is the ultimate symbol of success.
True False

3. I like to buy top-of-the-line products.
True False

4. I often use money to persuade others to do what I want.
True False

5. When I discover that I earn more than someone I previously believed made more than I, I feel satisfied.
True False

6. I'm likely to tell people how much I paid for an expensive item, even if they don't ask.
True False

7. I have been told or have later realized that I boasted about how much money I earn.
True False

8. I feel flattered when people notice a prestigious label on something I own.
True False

9. I try to find out who makes more money than I do.
True False

10. I catch myself admiring those who have more money than I have.
True False

11. When I shop, I am frequently mindful of what others will think about the quality of my purchases.
True False

12. I really enjoy it when I'm complimented on my expensive possessions.
True False

SCORING

To tally your score, give yourself 1 point for each "True" response. Read on for an explanation of your spending style.

A score of 10–12 points: You believe that money equals power and prestige, which mean a lot to you. External recognition and regard by others are vital to your feelings of importance and success. You might look down on those whom you think are worth less than you or decline to consider them for friendship. You might want to soften your attitudes.

A score of 6–9 points: You are average in your tendency to use money for social power and status. You probably try to satisfy those needs through other channels, such as personal achievement and relationships.

A score of 0–5 points: No matter how much money you have, you don't use money to enhance your image with others. You evaluate yourself and others by their intangible qualities, not by their possessions. If you do pursue money, it is for reasons other than the need for social power and prestige.

EXPLANATION

The quiz above is based on research conducted by K. T. Yamauchi and D. I. Templer at the California School of Professional Psychology in Fresno. In an effort to develop a scale for measuring attitudes towards money, Yamauchi and Templer tested three hundred people at various economic levels. The quiz taps into the tendency to regard money as a means to social power, prestige, and status.

In an interesting aside, attitudes about money are an important predictor of marital compatibility. If you're married, or plan to be, and you and your partner have very different "money personalities," there may be trouble ahead. It has been noted that couples argue most often about money, and it is the number one cause of divorce. These rifts usually have more to do with who has the power to make important decisions than about the money itself. It might be wise for couples to compare their attitudes towards money before they get married in order to pinpoint potential areas of disagreement.

✏️ Are You Slotted for Job Success?

Are you dissatisfied with your career? Do you wish you could do better? If so, do you sometimes wonder what's holding you back?

Career pros consistently find that job success is strongly related to a particular cluster of attitudes, habits, and personality traits. If you already have an impressive work history, you possess something a prospective employer wants. But if you're still in the process of building a solid background, you would benefit from knowing as much as possible about the traits that prospective employers value and reward.

TEST ·

The following quiz will gauge your grasp of what it takes to be a success on the job.

1 I get to work on time.
   A. *Rarely*
   B. *Sometimes*
   C. *Often*

2 I try hard to give a full day's work each day.
   A. *Rarely*
   B. *Sometimes*
   C. *Often*

3 I plan an alternate means of getting to work in case there's a transportation breakdown.
   A. *Rarely*
   B. *Sometimes*
   C. *Often*

4 I feel tired and sometimes even ill at work and yearn to have a good nap.
A. *Rarely*
B. *Sometimes*
C. *Often*

5 I get along well with my co-workers and my boss.
A. *Rarely*
B. *Sometimes*
C. *Often*

6 I accept supervision and rules without resistance or opposition, unless the situation calls for debate.
A. *Rarely*
B. *Sometimes*
C. *Often*

7 I have enough education, training, and job know-how for the position I now hold.
A. *Rarely*
B. *Sometimes*
C. *Often*

8 I have loyalty and respect for my company and its products.
A. *Rarely*
B. *Sometimes*
C. *Often*

9 My grooming and appearance are always appropriate and attractive.
A. *Rarely*
B. *Sometimes*
C. *Often*

10 My behavior is ethical, unpretentious, and courteous.
A. *Rarely*
B. *Sometimes*
C. *Often*

SCORING

To tally your score, give yourself 1 point for each "a" response, 2 points for each "b" response, and 3 points for each "c" response.

A score of 24–30 points: You possess the attitudes and traits that make employers want to hire you.

A score of 17–23 points: A score in this range shows that you have an average number of job success traits. You should do as well as most of your peers.

A score of 10–16 points: You lack many of the job success traits necessary for a career upgrade, and it's probably apparent to your employer. You might benefit from reading a book or two about how to move up the corporate ladder. You might also want to go over your answers with a friend who can help you find your weak spots.

EXPLANATION

This quiz consists of the ten basic job success traits found to be most important in the minds of bosses. They were compiled by the U.S. Department of Labor from a survey of thousands of employers conducted in 2000. Read on for an expanded explanation of each item.

① Surprisingly, many work hours are wasted by those who believe it is okay to be several minutes late. Employers are especially unhappy about the example such workers set for those who get to work on time or arrive early.

② Nearly all businessmen in the survey spoke out emphatically about expecting a full day's work for a full day's pay. Some employees settle for just trying to look busy when someone is watching.

③ Successful workers plan ahead for those emergency situations when a car breaks down or the bus is late, and get to work on time despite obstacles.

④ Companies lose millions each month due to employee illness. Thus, a poor attendance record can ruin your chances for promotion. It's a sensitive issue among employers. Consequently, more firms offer "wellness" programs to promote mental and physical fitness. Incidentally, the data show that these programs improve production significantly.

⑤ A large percentage of those not promoted or fired fail because they lack the social skills needed to get along with co-workers or supervisors. Work flows better from person to person when people are compatible.

⑥ Unfortunately, many workers who hit a snag have not resolved their early conflicts with authority. At heart they are still restless adolescents who buck the system and resist following rules. Mature adults, on the other hand, show flexibility and do not feel diminished when accommodating the demands of their bosses.

⑦ The most common requirements for most jobs are education and training. Are you one of the millions who succeed by getting the schooling needed to qualify for better positions? (For example, by taking computer, business, or secretarial courses?)

⑧ If you honestly cannot feel in favor of your company and its products or services, it will be tough to make a wholehearted job commitment. Think twice before signing on with a firm where your loyalty will be difficult to give.

⑨ The kind of appearance that is valued by employers varies from job to job. Receptionists, for example, must be well dressed, groomed, and attractive, while file clerks and others who work in the "background" of a company can usually adapt more casual dress codes. But no matter what the job, appearance is a powerful factor that influences your supervisor's evaluation of you.

⑩ Companies spend millions using lie detectors, reference checks, and personal interviews in screening applicants. In this day and age of computer banks loaded with information on work histories, it does not pay to be anything but honest and ethical on your job or when presenting your work history to a prospective boss.

✏️ Do You Suffer from Sunday Neurosis?

It's a Sunday morning, and you have a free day ahead of you. But you're already worrying about how you'll fill it up—will you do errands, tinker around the house, make plans with friends? For many of us who work full-time, figuring out how to spend our free time becomes a job in itself. We eagerly await the arrival of the weekend, but when it finally comes, we feel threatened by the idea of being leisurely.

Many of us long for free time, but then fail to truly enjoy it. Why? Because we're living in the imperative mood! We've been swallowed up by the quick tempo of our society. We must be doing something, anything, just to fill up empty time and relieve some indefinable sense of guilt. It's what psychoanalyst Karen Horney has called "the tyranny of the should": I should be doing this or I should be doing that—but above all, I shouldn't waste time.

This behavior has been called the "Sunday Neurosis." It attacks on weekends and vacations, when we're faced with time on our hands. It makes us restless and almost panicky. But when Monday morning rolls around, we once again feel pacified.

Do some of these behaviors seem to describe you? If so, the following quiz may indicate whether your difficulty in managing your free time means you that you have "leisure phobia."

TEST ·

1 It bothers me to waste time.
True False

2 I get more fun out of my job than I do from my free-time activities.
True False

③ I am an impatient person.
True False

④ I really don't need as much playtime as the average person seems to need.
True False

⑤ I enjoy working and playing rapidly.
True False

⑥ I usually get bored sooner than most others on a long train or plane trip.
True False

⑦ When I play, I try harder to win than the average person.
True False

⑧ I usually thrive on activities that keep me on the go and require my full attention.
True False

⑨ I consider myself an assertive person.
True False

⑩ I usually have difficulty finding satisfying things to do in my spare time.
True False

SCORING

Give yourself 1 point for each "True" response.

A score of 7 points or less: You are free enough of anxiety to enjoy your leisure time.

A score of 8 points or more: You have a tendency toward the common malady of our time, "hurry sickness." You probably struggle to enjoy your free time.

EXPLANATION ·

This quiz is based on the clinical analysis of people who become frustrated with unstructured time on their hands. Researchers have determined that there are some helpful tools we can employ to overcome this fear of freedom.

First, be sure your leisure time is not too crowded with things to do. Leave plenty of time between activities and try to keep pressure off. If you have something planned for the afternoon, relax and enjoy a late breakfast or brunch. Try to see this not as wasting time but as giving yourself a chance to let go and unwind. Try to engage in an activity that you don't normally have time for, like going on a long bike ride, or making a big dinner that requires lots of preparation. You'll feel good about your accomplishments, and you'll also satisfy your internal requirements for being productive.

And bear in mind some ancient wisdom. An old Chinese proverb says: "To be for one day entirely at leisure is to be for one day an immortal." Will you have your day of immortality?

Are You Burned Out?

Burnout is a modern affliction. It affects all types of people, especially those who work under pressure, deal frequently with others, and expect a lot from themselves. It is particularly prevalent among those who tend to set unrealistic goals for themselves, a by-product of having an unflappable drive to succeed and an excess of external pressure. Often such people grow bored with and unresponsive to their work, taking too long to make even the simplest decisions, and completing the most basic tasks in twice the usual time. For burnout victims, life is not as fulfilling as it might be.

Some critics say that the burnout syndrome is nothing new, that it is simply depression with a new label. But there is evidence that burnout differentiates itself from depression, and that both its cause and remedy are distinctive.

Psychologist Herbert Freudenberger discusses the unique qualities of this modern-day malady in his book *Burn-Out: The High Cost of High Achievement*. In it, he describes how burnout occurs in students, workers, and family members, and offers sound solutions to combat it.

T E S T ·

To find out if you are fighting with the frazzles, take the following quiz, which is adapted from Freudenberger's book. Rate yourself in terms of the five-point scale that follows each question, where 1 equals "a little bit" and 5 equals "very much so."

1 Do you seem to be working harder and accomplishing less?
A little bit   1   2   3   4   5   **Very much so**

2 Do you tire more easily?
A little bit   1   2   3   4   5   **Very much so**

3 Do you often get the blues for no apparent reason?
A little bit   1   2   3   4   5   **Very much so**

4 Do you forget appointments, deadlines, and/or personal possessions?
A little bit   1   2   3   4   5   **Very much so**

5 Have you become increasingly irritable?
A little bit   1   2   3   4   5   **Very much so**

6 Have you grown more disappointed in those around you?
A little bit   1   2   3   4   5   **Very much so**

7 Do you see close friends and family members less frequently than you used to?
A little bit   1   2   3   4   5   **Very much so**

8 Do you suffer physical symptoms like pains and headaches?
A little bit   1   2   3   4   5   **Very much so**

9 Do you find it hard to laugh when the joke is on you?
A little bit   1   2   3   4   5   **Very much so**

10 Does sex seem more trouble than it's worth?
A little bit   1   2   3   4   5   **Very much so**

SCORING

Where do you stand on the Burnout Scale? To tally your score, add the total number of points from each response.

A score of 0–15 points: You may be stressed out on occasion, but generally you're doing fine.

A score of 16–24 points: You're a candidate for burnout. You may want to take a step back and assess how to relax a bit.

A score of 25–29 points: You're beginning to burn out and should think about changing your work environment or lifestyle to give yourself more breathing room.

A score of 30 points or more: Cool it! You're suffering from burnout. Take whatever steps are necessary to alleviate some stress—you're in a dangerous situation that may pose a threat to your physical and mental well-being.

EXPLANATION

It has been said that next to the job of air-traffic controller, the occupation of police officer is the most stressful. Dr. William Kroes, former head of stress research at the National Institute of Occupational Safety (NIOS), concluded that there is more burnout among police officers than any other profession or occupation.

But burnout isn't only connected to a job. It can occur in anyone in a state of fatigue or frustration brought about by a devotion to a cause, a way of life, or a relationship that has failed to produce expected rewards. There are times when we all experience some minor burnout, when we are less than enthusiastic about shouldering our continual job responsibilities, but in time we usually snap out of it and once again take on our tasks.

If your score is high or if you have frequent periods of minor burnout, don't ignore the warning signs. This stressful state is reversible no matter how severe it is. Sometimes all that is needed to re-motivate you is a breather from the constant pressure or monotony of your life patterns. This can mean taking a vacation, getting a new job assignment, meeting new people, or getting a new perspective on your goals. Try to learn exactly what it is you have done in the past that seemed to revitalize you, then concentrate on doing it more often.

CHAPTER 6

THE SMELL OF SUCCESS

✏️ Are You Too Rigid?

If you ever watched the TV series *The Odd Couple*, you surely noticed a sharp contrast between the two lead characters. Oscar is the laid-back, flexible type, while Felix is just the opposite—proper, exacting, and highly organized. For entertainment purposes, they were cast as extremes. If you watched several episodes, you'd have noticed that the rigid one always seemed to suffer the most when things went wrong.

In real life, rigidity poses the same problems. People who tend to be overly conscientious perfectionists can be hard on those who can't keep up with their demands, and as a result, tough on themselves, too. Most of us are neither extremely exacting nor extremely easygoing. Instead, we are usually a mix of both. Still, just as people are classified as introverts or extraverts, submissive or dominant, people can also be categorized as rigid or flexible. When people are uptight, however, stress is often a factor. Fortunately, we can learn to spot this tendency and modify it.

TEST

Where do you stand on the rigidity scale? The following quiz is based on various personality tests used to measure authoritarianism, dominance, and other traits that define the "uptight" personality.

1. It's hard for me to quickly adapt to change, such as a new job, friend, or neighborhood.
   A. *Rarely*
   B. *Sometimes*
   C. *Often*

2. It bugs me when my surroundings are not neat and orderly.
   A. *Rarely*
   B. *Sometimes*
   C. *Often*

3. I like to make lists of things to do.
   A. *Rarely*
   B. *Sometimes*
   C. *Often*

4. I tend to feel dissatisfied or upset when I don't finish a task.
   A. *Rarely*
   B. *Sometimes*
   C. *Often*

5. When on vacation, I get upset if things don't go as planned.
   A. *Rarely*
   B. *Sometimes*
   C. *Often*

6. When someone takes advantage of me, it bothers me for a long time.
   A. *Rarely*
   B. *Sometimes*
   C. *Often*

7. I tend to store used or old things since they may be useful someday.
   A. *Rarely*
   B. *Sometimes*
   C. *Often*

8. I become uncomfortable when people don't replace things the way I left them.
   A. *Rarely*
   B. *Sometimes*
   C. *Often*

9 I am strongly conscientious about fulfilling my obligations.
A. *Rarely*
B. *Sometimes*
C. *Often*

10 I am meticulous about caring for my possessions.
A. *Rarely*
B. *Sometimes*
C. *Often*

SCORING

To tally your score, give yourself 1 point for each "a" response, 2 points for each "b" response, and 3 points for each "c" response.

A score of 8–14 points: You are lax, laid-back, and a threat to no one. You may want to consider developing more self-discipline and structure in your daily activities.

A score of 14–19 points: You are generally easygoing, but you have your moments of verve and pluck.

A score of 20–25 points: You stand your ground, but you also give in now and then for the sake of smooth relationships with others.

A score of 26–30 points: You suffer from "hardening of the categories"—once you've made up your mind, nothing can change it. Try to learn to relax, develop more empathy for others, and be more open to new ideas.

EXPLANATION

Rigidity is influenced by one's biological makeup. Look at two babies. One may be tense, abrupt in its movements, and fussing for more comfort. The other is placid, adaptable to changes in light and noise levels, and generally content. The babies have different inherited temperaments that affect their personalities. The fussy baby will probably be more rigid in adulthood.

Aside from biology, most obstinance is a learned response to frustration. Much of it is based on fear. A rigid person's behavior is saying, in effect, "If things don't go as planned, I'm afraid it will be bad for me." They fear they will be unable to cope with the change. Flexible people, on the other hand, are less riled by change and adapt more readily.

Rigidity, which is more common in men than in women, is essentially a reluctance to trust others and to understand their points of view. Rigid types tend to enjoy highly structured work that calls for strict standards—they often work in science, accounting, the military, and research. At the other extreme are the more yielding types who shun protocol and organized ways of doing things. While the problems of being too uptight are evident, being too docile also has its disadvantages. People who are too flexible can be disorganized and lacking in self-discipline. Too much of either extreme, of course, is not desirable, and most of us can be found somewhere in the middle.

The best course of action would be to find that happy middle ground between a disciplined, organized standard of living and a freewheeling spontaneity. If you can figure out how to combine both, you will be able to reap the rewards that both personalities have to offer.

✏️ How High Is Your Power Motive?

The next time you watch a baseball game, take note of the manager. He is the power center from whom all crucial commands flow, and all eyes are on him. His use of power is constructive and authorized. But can you imagine if someone tried to give orders to a group that disputed his authority? Such a person would probably be labeled a compulsive tyrant.

Interpersonal power is the capacity to influence others while resisting their influence on you. Dozens of books are written each year on how to gain control and mastery over others. As a personality trait, power is neither positive nor negative—like fire, it can be used for well-being or destruction. When a mother stands firms with an unruly six-year-old who won't bathe, when a policeman directs traffic around an accident, when a teacher demands silence, that's power used constructively. The lust for power, on the other hand, becomes psychoneurotic or even illegal when one seeks to gain an advantage at the expense of others.

In his work at Harvard University, Professor David McClelland studied the power motive in thousands of subjects. He concluded that the will to power is a human necessity much like the need for recognition, achievement, or love. Over the course of his extensive studies, he identified three characteristics of people with a high power drive: they act in vigorous and determined ways to exert their power, they spend a lot of time thinking about ways to alter the behavior and thinking of others, and they care very much about their personal standing with others.

If any of the above descriptions sound like you, it might well mean that you are compulsive about having power over others. This quiz may provide some insight.

TEST ·

1 I strive to show competence in any group I join.
   A. *False*
   B. *Somewhat true*
   C. *Very true*

2 I enjoy a job in which I can do things my way.
   A. *False*
   B. *Somewhat true*
   C. *Very true*

3 I like to be the center of attention when with others.
A. *False*
B. *Somewhat true*
C. *Very true*

4 It irritates me when people try to dominate me.
A. *False*
B. *Somewhat true*
C. *Very true*

5 I don't take embarrassments easily.
A. *False*
B. *Somewhat true*
C. *Very true*

6 I dislike taking advice from others.
A. *False*
B. *Somewhat true*
C. *Very true*

7 It's important for me to do things better than others.
A. *False*
B. *Somewhat true*
C. *Very true*

8 I've always been good at selling others on ideas or a point of view.
A. *False*
B. *Somewhat true*
C. *Very true*

9 I like to ask tough questions that are hard to answer.
A. *False*
B. *Somewhat true*
C. *Very true*

10 At work, it would be hard for me to do a task that was meant for a subordinate.
A. *False*
B. *Somewhat true*
C. *Very true*

SCORING ·

Give yourself 1 point for each "a" response, 2 points for each "b" response, and 3 points for each "c" response.

A score of 10–14 points: You have a low power drive and are generally content with allowing others to control situations that involve you.

A score of 15–22 points: You have a more moderate power need and show flexibility in expressing it, and, at times, yielding to it.

A score of 23–30 points: You're motivated by a compulsive drive for power. Do you spend a lot of time wondering if others will "one-up" you? Do you find that people turn away from you? Try to get used to giving in to others once in a while. You may be surprised to find that an occasional nod to submission won't devastate your self-image, and it might gain you a few more friends to boot.

EXPLANATION

Since competition and the struggle to move ahead play such a significant part in our lives, many philosophers and behavioral experts see power as the most fundamental of all human motives. Dr. Alfred Adler, a colleague of Sigmund Freud, believed this. He discarded Freud's notion that sex was the primary drive in man and maintained that mastery over others was the main force in human affairs. As helpless infants, he argued, we develop an inferiority complex, then struggle all our lives to gain power in order to compensate for it.

According to Dr. Adler, becoming powerful is like reaching for an ideal. Some might argue that Adler was the first therapist to advocate the power of positive thinking. You might be tempted to debunk the idea that each of us strives for power when you think of a gracious, soft-spoken homebody, or an unassuming co-worker who simply minds his own business. But all people exert power in their own ways, whether it be through the determination to avoid contests with combative types, or in turning the other cheek in order to keep oneself out of a fray. Power can present itself in numerous guises, but the desire for it is indeed a universal trait that exists in degrees in all of us.

✏️ How People-Sensitive Are You?

Everyone knows someone with extremely thin skin—a fretful type who gets nervous about how people will react to his or her actions. Super-sensitive people are acutely attuned to what others say and think. As a result, other people are quite guarded in their presence, fearful of unwittingly touching a nerve.

Supremely sensitive people are an extreme, of course, but we all share varying degrees of social sensitivity. This trait is called "interpersonal orientation." It describes one's awareness of others in a social setting.

Research done at Tufts University, in Medford, Massachusetts, by Walter Swap and Jeffrey Rubin, discloses some interesting facts on the subject. Over a period of two years they tested some nine hundred students and developed an interpersonal orientation scale. Some of the items on the scale are adapted for use in our quiz.

TEST ·

If you wonder how your social sensitivity compares with that of other people, take the following assessment.

1. I would rather discuss my personal problems with others than ponder them by myself.
   True False

2. I wouldn't ever buy something I suspected was stolen.
   True False

3. It is important for me to work with people I like, even if it means taking on a job that requires less responsibility.
   True False

4. When someone does me a favor I usually feel a duty to return it.
   True False

5 My friends and I seem to share the same musical interests.
True False

6 I consider myself to be more forgiving than the average person.
True False

7 I often wonder what a person sitting next to me on a bus or train might do for a living.
True False

8 When I am spending time with someone, I am usually the first to reveal something personal about myself.
True False

9 It seems that the more time I spend with someone the more I grow to like him or her.
True False

10 If a panhandler asks me for money or food, it bothers me to say no.
True False

SCORING

To tally your score, give yourself 1 point for each "True" response. Keep in mind that neither of the extreme scores is desirable.

A score of 8–10 points: You are high in interpersonal orientation. The comments and actions of others affect your morale to a large degree.

A score of 5–7 points: You are average and in the desirable range with respect to social sensitivity.

A score of 0–4 points: You are low on interpersonal orientation and tend not to focus on the innuendoes of human interaction. You are relatively unaffected by others in the quest to achieve your own ends. You're probably a competitive, assertive person who has limited social needs.

EXPLANATION ·

The quiz is a social sensitivity scale. Each "True" answer indicates the presence of interpersonal orientation. Although some items appear unrelated at face value, the findings show that people with high interpersonal orientation levels feel the items on the quiz accurately describe them.

A person with a high score on this quiz is very aware of others. He is interested in and reactive to their behavior and tends to take their judgments personally. He is responsive to slights as well as compliments and, when rebuffed, gets moody and may sulk. He has more social anxiety than the average individual.

Sometimes, highly interpersonal-oriented people are not easy to deal with. They can be so reactive to others that they become very choosy in forming friendships. People with lower levels of this trait, on the other hand, are less attuned to those around them. They are more concerned with relationships that will promote their personal goals. They are not strongly influenced by the actions of others. They are usually drawn to "thing-oriented" jobs in such fields as engineering, accounting, and science.

Do You Quit or Keep Chugging: How Persevering Are You?

Perseverance is the energy that drives the human spirit. It keeps the soldier tracking his target, the lover pursing his beloved, and the athlete moving toward the goal line.

Perseverance, like all traits, exists in degrees. Would you perform an action repeatedly until you finally achieved success? Would you spend half a lifetime pondering the solution to a problem? Such persistence has played a large part in the success of noted men and women in various fields. Take Thomas Edison, for example. In 1879, after several thousand trials in his search for the right filament, he succeeded in inventing the light bulb. Persistence was present to a large degree in the accomplishments of others as well, such as Madame Marie Curie, who discovered radium, Dr. Jonas Salk, who gave us the vaccine for polio, and Alexander Graham Bell, inventor of the telephone.

Illustrious scientists are not the only ones who have proved that tenacity is necessary to achieve our goals. All of us struggle with problems in which persistence may mean the difference between happiness and gloom, life and death.

Tenacity has been widely studied in college settings, where students must continually muster the will to meet the challenges of ever-mounting schoolwork. A number of Persistence Disposition Questionnaires (PDQs) have been devised to measure the tendency to keep trying. One such study was conducted by B. N. Mukherjee when he was a professor of psychology at York University in Toronto. The items in the following quiz are adapted from his research, which was written up in the *Indian Journal of Psychology*.

Do you rise to a challenge or call it quits? To learn what your persistence index is, take the following assessment.

T E S T ·

1. Little can be gained by people who attempt to do things that are too difficult for them.
True False

2. Compared with others, I hate to lose at anything.
True False

3. The stronger the chance of failing at something, the less determined I am to keep at it.
True False

4. I am known to be a stickler for fighting for my rights.
True False

5 It's better to accomplish many easy jobs than to attempt a few that are very difficult.
True False

6 Luck is an important factor in determining whether one succeeds.
True False

7 Compared with others, I set high goals for myself.
True False

8 People who get ahead work only with their heads rather than with their hands.
True False

9 Regardless of whether I work for myself or someone else, there's no change in my level of ambition.
True False

10 I procrastinate more than my friends when faced with an unpleasant job.
True False

SCORING ·

To tally your score, give yourself 1 point for each response that matches yours.

① *False* ② *True* ③ *False* ④ *True* ⑤ *False* ⑥ *False* ⑦ *True* ⑧ *True* ⑨ *False* ⑩ *False*

A score of 8–10 points: You are very tenacious and work hard to achieve your goals.

A score of 4–7 points: You have an average degree of persistence.

A score of 0–3 points: You give up too easily! When things become difficult, try to stick it out.

You may be surprised to discover that a little effort can yield results that are more positive than you'd imagined.

EXPLANATION ·

Persistence was found to be a bona fide personality trait by Dr. J. P. Guilford, formerly of the University of Southern California. In his book *Personality*, he calls it the "desire to succeed." It's connected to ambition and a compulsion to achieve. Persistent people usually have strong needs for recognition and prestige. They like to make things happen quickly, and they believe that making money is an important goal in life. They rarely bypass a chance to excel at something, even if it is difficult. Generally, they don't believe that attempting many easy goals is the same thing as striving to reach a few difficult ones. They also don't take failures well—when failure occurs, they often double their efforts to succeed the next time.

Luck or miracles rarely factor into the persistent person's idea of how success will occur—rather, they set high aspirations for themselves and then become dedicated to achieving them. Persevering types also tend to procrastinate far less than the average person, and exhibit entrepreneurial tendencies, working harder on their own than under someone else's command. The perseverance trait is commonly found in artists, who practice diligently to perfect their art, students who study hard (and tend to become over-learners, studying more than necessary to pass exams), and salespeople, who sell far beyond their quotas. Tenacious people are more likely to use their head than their hands whenever possible in tackling a tough job. Keep in mind that although highly persistent people aren't necessarily successful, most successful people are highly persistent.

✏ Are You Too Pushy?

When emotions run high, even the most democratic and well-meaning among us may, occasionally, insist that others see things our way. But if you know someone who acts like this consistently, you may be dealing with an authoritarian personality—one who likes to be the boss and take charge. Psychologists have labeled such people "F" types, because the original tests of authoritarianism were based on traits of fascist personalities.

Could you be an "F" type and not realize it? Take the following quiz to find out.

TEST ······························

1 I like people to be definitive when they say things.
   A. *Disagree*
   B. *Disagree somewhat*
   C. *Agree somewhat*
   D. *Agree*

2 Incompetence at home or on the job irritates me.
   A. *Disagree*
   B. *Disagree somewhat*
   C. *Agree somewhat*
   D. *Agree*

3 I like to drive quickly.
   A. *Disagree*
   B. *Disagree somewhat*
   C. *Agree somewhat*
   D. *Agree*

4 I don't mind standing out in a group.
   A. *Disagree*
   B. *Disagree somewhat*
   C. *Agree somewhat*
   D. *Agree*

5 I am argumentative compared with most of my friends or co-workers.
   A. *Disagree*
   B. *Disagree somewhat*
   C. *Agree somewhat*
   D. *Agree*

6 I make up my mind quickly and easily when faced with difficult work decisions.
A. *Disagree*
B. *Disagree somewhat*
C. *Agree somewhat*
D. *Agree*

7 I am intolerant when someone at work does something I think is foolish.
A. *Disagree*
B. *Disagree somewhat*
C. *Agree somewhat*
D. *Agree*

8 I don't like to accept advice from others.
A. *Disagree*
B. *Disagree somewhat*
C. *Agree somewhat*
D. *Agree*

9 Compared with my co-workers, I am more critical of the way people do things.
A. *Disagree*
B. *Disagree somewhat*
C. *Agree somewhat*
D. *Agree*

10 If it were possible, I'd rather give a lecture than hear one.
A. *Disagree*
B. *Disagree somewhat*
C. *Agree somewhat*
D. *Agree*

SCORING ·

To tally your score, give yourself 1 point for each "a" response, 2 points for each "b" response, 3 points for each "c" response, and 4 points for each "d" response.

A score of 10–20 points: You possess few authoritarian traits, and probably get along well with others. Some people may perceive you as passive, however.

A score of 21–30 points: You possess an average degree of bossiness. You are neither a pushover nor a tyrant.

A score of 31–40 points: You are highly domineering and may want to ask yourself whether this is the type of person you wish to be. You may be gradually turning off others by being too pushy. You'll spot the adverse effects of your behavior if you notice greater friction between yourself and others, fewer invitations to meetings and other gatherings, and a rash of fading friendships. These are all early warning signs that you are coming across as too heavy-handed. It may be time to lighten up and graciously accept it when someone else has his way.

EXPLANATION

The preceding quiz was adapted from a study conducted by sociologist J. J. Ray at New South Wales University in Australia. He found that authoritarian people tend to feel that most of the quiz items accurately describe them. Such types have a cluster of traits in common: They are highly conventional and tend to be intolerant and even somewhat prejudiced. They also tend to desire power in order to secure a sense of elevated social status.

Psychologists R. W. Adorno and E. Frenkel-Brunswik coined the term "F-type" to denote an authoritarian personality. Oddly enough, highly domineering people are usually conformists who have limited imaginations. Being more "herd-minded" than the average person, they are submissive to authority and suspicious of groups other than their own. Overall, "F" types are not very trusting—because they see the world as menacing and unfriendly.

Autocratic personalities dislike ambiguity and indecisiveness and prefer situations and conclusions that are clear-cut, with no shades of gray. They are critical, impatient with perceived incompetence in others, and vigorously argumentative about their point of view. They seek to be served rather than to serve and dislike sharing responsibility in team projects—they would rather assume the full burden of a course of action.

"F" types usually come from rigid parents who make strong demands on their children to do things "just so." As leaders, they like to come to quick conclusions. They feel uneasy with uncertainty and tend to encourage dependence from their subordinates. Thus, those who struggle beneath authoritative types rarely develop individuality or initiative, but instead, learn to be passive and submissive.

CHAPTER 7

THOUGHT IN ACTION

✏ Could You Be Hypnotized?

A number of years ago, the actor Zero Mostel needed surgery for a leg injury that he'd sustained in a car accident. For medical reasons, he couldn't receive the usual anesthetic before the operation and hypnosis was tried instead. The comic was kept comfortable in a trance, and the procedure was over within a few hours.

Stories like this one garner national attention and raise the hope of many who suffer from one ailment or another that perhaps hypnosis might work for them. But surveys show that only a small percentage of sufferers actually seek out hypnosis, because it still carries the reputation of being eccentric and somewhat occult.

But hypnosis is not as mysterious as many believe. The fact is, hypnosis occurs often in everyday living and only seems outlandish because we have labeled it as such. Each one of us passes through a momentary hypnotic state each night, as we go from wakefulness to sleep. You may recognize this "twilight zone" if you've ever heard a sound, like a phone ringing, and couldn't distinguish whether you were dreaming it or actually hearing it. Drivers often lapse into a dreamy mood on long stretches of highway, babies are lulled to sleep by rocking and humming, students daydream at lectures, and music lovers doze off at mellow concerts.

We are all amenable to hypnotic states. Yet skepticism about hypnosis still prevails. Perhaps this is because most of us first witnessed hypnosis as entertainment. We saw it as a sort of sideshow practiced by charlatans. But in the domain of dedicated professionals, it is a respected cure for such chronic problems as nail biting, smoking, obesity, and insomnia. It has proved to be an invaluable asset when life-threatening symptoms do not react well to anesthesia, and has improved such conditions as malnutrition, vomiting, uncontrollable hiccuping, and hypertension. What's more, it places no undue strain on the heart, liver, kidney, or lungs.

TEST ·

If what you've heard about hypnosis has piqued your interest, you may be wondering if you'd be a good subject. The following quiz should help provide the answer. It identifies traits of good hypnosis candidates and is based on research conducted at Stanford University.

1 I am female.
   True False

2 I am over fifty years of age.
   True False

3 I am above average
   in intelligence.
   True False

4 I am an original thinker.
   True False

5 I am emotionally stable.
   True False

6 I tend to be more of an
   optimist than a pessimist.
   True False

7 I am somewhat suspicious
   of the motives of other
   people.
   True False

8 I am relatively free of depression.
True False

9 I have a good imagination.
True False

10 I am a fairly independent person.
True False

SCORING ·······························

To tally your score, give yourself 1 point for each response that matches yours.

① *True* ② *False* ③ *True* ④ *False* ⑤ *True* ⑥ *True* ⑦ *False* ⑧ *True* ⑨ *True* ⑩ *False*

A score of 3 points or less: You may be hard to hypnotize.

A score of 4 points or more: You will likely enter a trance without much resistance. The closer your score is to 10, the more likely you are to be a good hypnotherapy subject. If you would like to find a qualified hypnotist in your area, call your local psychiatric association.

EXPLANATION ····························

Even if you received a low score on this quiz, it doesn't mean that you can't be hypnotized. Many people who are low on the hypnotizability scale can be so deeply motivated to use hypnosis that they become excellent subjects for it. Read on to find out who has the easiest time falling under the hypnotist's spell. Each statement refers back to the questions on the quiz.

① *True.* Females are somewhat more suggestible, and hence, more hypnotizable than males.

② *False*. If you are over fifty years old, you are less likely to be hypnotized, since susceptibility to hypnosis diminishes as you age.

③ *True*. Intelligence is correlated with hypnotizability.

④ *False*. Conventional thinkers—rather than "break away" original thinkers—make the best hypnosis clients.

⑤ *True*. People who are unstable are usually harder to hypnotize.

⑥ *True*. Those with a cheerful, uplifting attitude about life usually respond best to hypnosis.

⑦ *False*. A trance-like state is difficult to achieve with persons who are overly cautious about the world and those around them.

⑧ *True*. People who struggle with depression usually need more pre-hypnotic conditioning than those who are happy.

⑨ *True*. If you have an active imagination, you're more likely to do well in hypnosis.

⑩ *False*. Independent-minded individuals often do not make good hypnosis subjects. One must be somewhat willing to depend on others in order to be a good candidate.

How Far Does Your Imagination Stretch?

Ralph Waldo Emerson once said: "The quality of the imagination is to flow, and not to freeze." Imagination, the ability to visualize things in our mind's eye, is a fundamental part of mental life. It is crucial not just in creating works of art, but in anticipating situations and in problem-solving. It's a fanciful way of going beyond the here and now.

Christopher Columbus had to imagine the world as round before he set out on his epic voyage of discovery. And Albert Einstein, who once remarked, "I rarely think in words at all," had to imagine a universe where everything is relative before he theorized about the relativity of space and time.

But imagination varies from person to person. Like Einstein, some of us think almost exclusively in mental images while others think in words. In fact, about three out of every ten people would probably have trouble forming a mental image in any situation.

TEST ·

If you've never had your imagination tested, or would like to test it again, take the following quiz. It is based on several imagination tests, including one developed at Yale University.

1 I can tell a white lie without becoming flustered.
   A. *Rarely*
   B. *Sometimes*
   C. *Often*

2 I cry at the movies.
   A. *Rarely*
   B. *Sometimes*
   C. *Often*

3 I can visualize patterns and images in clouds, mountains, wallpaper patterns, etc.
   A. *Rarely*
   B. *Sometimes*
   C. *Often*

4 I get ideas that I think would make a good movie or book.
   A. *Rarely*
   B. *Sometimes*
   C. *Often*

5 When I retell a story, I tend to embellish it somewhat in order to make it more interesting.
   A. *Rarely*
   B. *Sometimes*
   C. *Often*

6 I vividly imagine extreme life situations, such as being stranded on a deserted island, or winning the lottery.
A. *Rarely*
B. *Sometimes*
C. *Often*

7 I worry about a possible accident when someone who is usually punctual is very late.
A. *Rarely*
B. *Sometimes*
C. *Often*

8 I enjoy abstract art.
A. *Rarely*
B. *Sometimes*
C. *Often*

9 I like to read fiction or stories about the supernatural.
A. *Rarely*
B. *Sometimes*
C. *Often*

10 When I awaken from a vivid dream it takes me a few seconds to return to reality.
A. *Rarely*
B. *Sometimes*
C. *Often*

SCORING

To tally your score, give yourself 1 point for each "a" response, 2 points for each "b" response, and 3 points for each "c." People with active imaginations tend to respond to many of the items with an answer of "Often."

A score of 10–15 points: You're a concrete thinker based in reality. While it is not impossible for you to imagine situations, you prefer a practical, realistic approach to life. You would benefit from stretching your imagination. Perhaps taking a course in creative writing or art will expand your way of thinking and boost your imaginative skills.

A score of 16–23 points: You have an average level of imagination. A balance between practicality and creativity allows you to actualize your ideas and see your fantasies take flight.

A score of 24–30 points: You have a very active imagination. It is a powerful force within you, but be careful to keep it somewhat in check to avoid becoming impractical. If your creative mind already runs wild, try to control it somewhat by being more practical and conservative in your daily decision-making.

EXPLANATION

Human imagination has excited the interest of psychologists since the early 1950s. Experts are now confident that it plays a key role in mental health. There is evidence that those who have difficulty visualizing scenarios or who are discouraged from using their imagination productively tend to become rigid or insecure, and often display various symptoms of neurosis.

Still, an overactive imagination can also be problematic—it can put you out of touch with reality and create difficulties in dealing with responsibility. Researchers believe that a distinct advantage exists for behavior-therapy patients who can form mental images. Imagination is often at the core of treatments for phobia, obsessions, and bad habits. In these situations, patients are asked to imagine those things that cause them anxiety or create other problems for them. They are then taught to relax while still imagining the distressing situation or object.

Do imaginative people have more fun? Probably. They tend to enrich their experiences through creative thinking. Witness the child who receives a new toy and gets almost as much joy out of playing with the box as with the toy itself. The child imagines the box as any number of things and incorporates it into play fantasies.

If your imagination index is fairly low, take heart. Studies show that imagination can be improved. The imaginative powers of children can be strengthened and expanded through a series of games and play exercises. Surely, adults can broaden their minds in a similar fashion—by engaging in activities that require them to think about and perceive the world in new and unusual ways. California psychologist Dr. Richard DeMille's work has verified this. DeMille's interest in imagination may well have been stimulated by his father, Cecil B. DeMille, the famous movie director.

✐ Do You Live in the Perfect Tense?

Any reasonable soul knows that no one is perfect, right? Wrong! There are die-hards among us who strive for perfection with the belief that such a happy state is entirely attainable. But, to quote poet Alexander Pope, "Whoever thinks a faultless piece to see, thinks what ne'er was, nor is, nor e'er shall be." Perfectionists are playing a game that cannot be won. Of course, striving for the best isn't a negative activity. It only becomes a problem when it strains our relationships with others and when it runs us, exhausted, into the ground.

Studies show that "unsatisfy-ables" are compulsive people who become entangled in details. They suffer from what psychoanalyst Karen Horney has called the "tyranny of the should," an attitude that they should have done better at anything they attempted to do.

TEST ·

Do you have perfectionist tendencies? The following quiz might tell.

1. After I finish a challenging job I feel a letdown.
   A. *Disagree*
   B. *Agree somewhat*
   C. *Strongly agree*

2. If I can't do a thing well, I usually won't do it at all.
   A. *Disagree*
   B. *Agree somewhat*
   C. *Strongly agree*

3. Even if I could get away with it, I still couldn't knowingly allow errors to remain in my work.
   A. *Disagree*
   B. *Agree somewhat*
   C. *Strongly agree*

4. On the bus, at parties, in stores, and in other public places, I catch myself critically sizing up strangers' looks, dress, or grooming.
   A. *Disagree*
   B. *Agree somewhat*
   C. *Strongly agree*

5. I feel ashamed when I appear weak or foolish to others.
   A. *Disagree*
   B. *Agree somewhat*
   C. *Strongly agree*

6. My parents were hard to please and generally critical of me.
   A. *Disagree*
   B. *Agree somewhat*
   C. *Strongly agree*

7. I am unsatisfied if I only do an average job.
   A. *Disagree*
   B. *Agree somewhat*
   C. *Strongly agree*

8. As a student, I was never really content with my grades.
   A. *Disagree*
   B. *Agree somewhat*
   C. *Strongly agree*

9. I'm a compulsive type of person—I like to be neat, exact, and organized.
   A. *Disagree*
   B. *Agree somewhat*
   C. *Strongly agree*

10. I usually feel uncomfortable revealing my shortcomings, even to close friends and relatives.
    A. *Disagree*
    B. *Agree somewhat*
    C. *Strongly agree*

⑪ I would feel a strong urge
to level a slightly tilted
hanging picture.
A. *Disagree*
B. *Agree somewhat*
C. *Strongly agree*

⑫ It would bother me if I
had to postpone a job that
I had already started.
A. *Disagree*
B. *Agree somewhat*
C. *Strongly agree*

SCORING

To tally your score, give yourself 1 point for each "a" response, 2 points for each "b" response, and 3 points for each "c" response.

A score of 12–19: You are laid-back and do not generally feel pulled by perfectionist tendencies.

A score of 20–28: Your drive for perfection is average—you're not totally laid-back, but neither are you always a fuss-budget about details.

A score of 29–36: Watch out, mellow types! You strive constantly for perfection and are often uncomfortable when things are not "just so." Your perfectionist tendencies may make more laid-back types a little uneasy.

EXPLANATION

Dr. David D. Burns is a leading authority on this subject. In his work, at the University of Pennsylvania School of Medicine, Burns found that perfectionists use "all or nothing" thinking: They can't readjust their performance standards even when there's plenty of leeway to do so. They have difficulty relishing the fruits of their (or anyone else's) labor—only flawless results will fly. Perfectionists often live by the credo, "No pain, no gain." This unrelenting attitude makes them the fastidious, nitpicking picture straighteners among us.

The truth is that perfectionism is a projection of how such types feel about themselves—incomplete, imperfect, and inviting of criticism unless they hit the bull's-eye every time. An interesting finding shows that all this striving may not get perfectionists any farther than the average person—often people who stop at nothing to be flawless end up paying the price mentally and emotionally. Read on for more detailed explanations about perfectionist tendencies as they relate to each quiz item.

① Perfectionists often feel a kind of anti-climactic, downcast feeling after they have expended much energy and drive on a job.

② People who strive for perfection do not take failures well. Often they will not attempt to do something if there is a possibility of doing it poorly.

③ Perfectionists are deeply concerned about flaws in their work. They often spend inordinate amounts of time checking for errors before handing in an assignment.

④ People who have extremely high standards for themselves often rate others on a similar scale and see them from a critical point of view.

⑤ As hard as perfectionists are on themselves, they are very sensitive to evaluation by others.

⑥ Parents who are overly demanding and can't tolerate even slight deviations from their high standards often raise over-strivers.

⑦ Perfectionists have trouble accepting anything they do as "just average."

⑧ As adults, perfectionists often report that they could have done better in their school years.

⑨ An obsessive-compulsive personality is one component of perfectionism.

⑩ Those who aim to be perfect often have "disclosure anxiety"— they find it painful to reveal their weaknesses to anyone.

⑪ People with perfectionist tendencies are uncomfortable when things are askance or askew.

⑫ Perfectionists do not feel satisfied with loose ends or half-finished tasks. They have all-or-nothing attitudes, and strive for closure in whatever they do.

✏ What Are Your Dreams Telling You?

Sigmund Freud called dreams the "royal road" to the unconscious. As the foremost interpreter of dreams, he saw them as mirrors that reflect the reality within us even though, at times, they may be heavily disguised by symbolism and abstraction. For those who have tried psychoanalysis, the realization is clear enough: Dreams can suggest the absurdities in our lives, reveal the true motives behind our actions, and confront us with the paradoxes of our beliefs.

These nocturnal adventures are a barometer of our emotional lives. More often than not, people who have continuously disturbed dream patterns are afflicted with more than their share of adjustment difficulties. If you haven't paid much attention to your dreams lately, perhaps this is a good time to find out what they're saying about you.

TEST

To learn what your dream patterns reveal about your personality, take the following quiz, adapted from the work of R. Corriere and J. Hart.

1 I sometimes gain a better understanding of myself through a dream.
True False

2 My dreams are generally pleasant.
True False

3 I sometimes solve a problem through a dream.
True False

4 I can recall my dreams at least twice a week.
True False

5 I have the same dream about eight or nine times per year.
True False

6 I have disturbing dreams or nightmares about eight or nine times per year.
True False

7 A bad mood from a dream sometimes lingers into the next day for several hours.
True False

8 I dream in color.
True False

9 I cry, scream, or shout in my dreams about two or three times per year.
True False

10 I abruptly awaken from a dream about once a month.
True False

SCORING

To tally your score, give yourself 1 point for each response that matches yours.

① *True* ② *True* ③ *True* ④ *True* ⑤ *False* ⑥ *False* ⑦ *False* ⑧ *True* ⑨ *False* ⑩ *False*

A score of 8–10 points: Your dreams indicate that you are healthy and well-adjusted.

A score of 5–7 points: Your dreams are sometimes disturbing, but that need not indicate a grave problem. Perhaps you are trying to solve a dilemma while you are asleep, or you are preoccupied with some task that must be done the next day. For example, a nightmare about numbers may merely be your brain's way of reminding you that you need to pay a bill.

A score of 0–4 points: You may be grappling with a problem during the waking state, and because you are unable to find an evident solution, you try to resolve the issue during sleep. If your dreams are particularly upsetting, try to clear your mind before going to bed.

EXPLANATION

Scientists first began to study dreams in the mid-1800s. In 1900, Freud introduced his theory that dreams are the key to the unconscious. The theory revolutionized the world of psychology. Freud attempted to unravel the roots of his patients' neuroses by analyzing their dreams. Until 1953, little was done to study dreams scientifically. It was then that Professor Nathaniel Kleitman and his student Eugene Aserinsky of the University of Chicago discovered that a sleeping person's rapid eye movements (REMs) indicate that he is dreaming. Since then, numerous sleep clinics have sprung up around the world.

It is difficult to determine what our dreams mean because they are symbolic, and often we remember only a portion of them. But there are certain markers that tend to have general significance, and if you know how to spot them, they can help you interpret what your dreams mean. An item-by-item explanation of the quiz follows—its helps outline what you should look for in your dreams.

① *True.* Dreams often present a chance to understand our true feelings about something which, in our waking state, may remain hidden from us.

② *True.* A good feeling during a dream usually indicates that you are content.

③ *True.* Problem-solving in dreams is often reported by productive thinkers who continue to ponder a problem even in their sleep.

④ *True.* Generally speaking, those who can recall at least a portion of their dreams tend to have healthier personalities than those who can't.

⑤ *False.* A repetitive dream is a sign that the dreamer is struggling with a vexing problem or conflict and has not yet resolved it.

⑥ *False.* Dreams that produce strong affects often reflect the dreamer's insecurities and fears (although some bad dreams do result from viewing something disturbing on television before going to bed).

⑦ *False.* Dream moods that last into the daytime indicate that the dreamer has sentiments that have not been adequately harmonized with the rest of his or her personality.

⑧ *True.* The tendency to dream in color suggests that the dreamer has rich creative and imaginative skills.

⑨ *False.* Calm dreams and sound sleep have always been associated with good mental health.

⑩ *False.* Freud taught that when we awaken abruptly from a dream it is because our internal "dream censor" has been unable to disguise its true meaning, namely, an antisocial wish.

✏️ How Do We React When Disaster Strikes?

It seems that the human race has inherited adversity as a condition for its survival. At 8:45 a.m. on September 11, 2001, a massive terrorist attack on the World Trade Center in New York plunged the nation into sudden anguish. Some 3,000 lives were lost and hundreds of people were injured. The world faced the ravages of the terrorists' fury. How did we cope?

Studies of behavior in crisis are not rare, but a survey conducted several years ago revealed some unusual findings. Nearly 3,500 victims of more than twenty-five catastrophic events—including the atomic bombings at Hiroshima and Nagasaki during World War II—were interviewed by the Federal Civil Defense Administration (FCDA) and the Disaster Research Group of the National Academy of Science. The survivors were queried extensively about their behavior during the crises and their responses were, at times, quite surprising.

TEST ·

The following quiz is based on the aforementioned study. Can you predict how people would behave when disaster strikes?

1 An overall reaction of mass panic is likely.
True False

2 Disputes will arise about who shall assume a leadership role.
True False

3 A rash of crime, particularly looting, assaults, and petty theft, will occur.
True False

4 A significant number of people will break down mentally and/or emotionally and be unable to function.
True False

5 The psychological after-effects last for years, even a lifetime.
True False

6 People usually react with incapacitating depression and despair.
True False

7 Problems with crowd control will arise when people flee the scene.
True False

8 Victims commonly react by becoming more concerned with themselves than with others.
True False

9 People tend to respond promptly to a warning that a threat to their life is imminent.
True False

10 There is much disorientation, chaos, and physical affliction, all of which persists throughout the period of stress.
True False

SCORING

To tally your score, give yourself 1 point for each "False" response.

Most people answer 3 or 4 questions correctly. If you answered 6 or more accurately, you have an above-average awareness of how people would behave in a crisis.

EXPLANATION

It is difficult for most people to predict how they or others would react should they be faced with catastrophe. Here is an item-by-item explanation of the quiz, which should help shed some light. All items are false.

① The FCDA found that mass panic is not a typical response to disaster. If emotional upset occurs, it usually centers on concern for missing loved ones, not the disaster itself. Children taken from their mothers during the World War II air raids in England were more damaged psychologically by the separation than by the experience of the bombing itself.

② Groups do not remain leaderless for long. Our first tendency is to look for established authorities. If these people are not available, individuals will inevitably assume or be given leadership status.

③ Although catastrophe will incite isolated instances of anti-social or criminal behavior, it is much rarer or shorter in duration than is generally supposed.

④ Maladaptive behavior is a much less frequent response to disaster than is believed. When it occurs, it usually fades in a relatively short time and for the most part, survivors are docile and sensitive to the needs of others.

⑤ It is common to underestimate the resiliency of people who have experienced a great and sudden tragedy. Although some will develop "survivor syndrome" (guilt about having escaped while others died), most people will return to a normal lifestyle within a reasonable period of time.

⑥ The FCDA study showed that depression and despair, although present among survivors of a catastrophe, do not prevent sufferers from performing their duties.

⑦ Contrary to popular notions, movement away from a disaster area is usually significantly less pronounced than movement toward it. The National Academy of Science found that within minutes of a disaster, scores of people tend to converge on a devastated area. Participants in this "conversion action" are typically those seeking loved ones, those who want to assist, and curiosity seekers.

⑧ The net result of a natural disaster is often social solidarity. Sharing a common threat to survival produces a breakdown of social barriers and prompts spontaneous displays of generosity and caring.

⑨ Unfortunately, people are usually reluctant to heed warnings. They tend to disbelieve the gravity of a situation unless they have already been through well-rehearsed warning drills. It's estimated that no more than 25 percent of the population would take shelter within fifteen to thirty minutes of being warned about impending danger.

⑩ Although most people who endure a catastrophe suffer some transient emotional upsets such as nausea, diarrhea, or the "shakes," such reactions do not incapacitate them from responding realistically to the event. In fact, many rescues in disaster situations are made by the survivors themselves.

✐ Are You an Unbiased Voter?

You probably have a pretty good sense of your political views, but are you sure you are set for the next round of presidential or local elections? The true motivations behind voters' choices are worth their weight in gold. Studies show that people have many offbeat reasons for selecting the candidates they do. A politician is evaluated less often for his or her professional qualifications than you might think. And often people are elected by default—because they are deemed the least incompetent of the lot.

T E S T ·

To see if you are truly plugged in to your political persuasions, take the following quiz.

1. A businessperson would probably do a good job running the country.
True False

2. It's best to vote for someone who is already financially well off, because he or she will be less tempted to make money on the sly.
True False

3. If a less-privileged person were elected to Congress, it would take him or her a long time to get accustomed to moving in such "high" circles.
True False

4. The child of a banker or doctor would probably be a better president than the child of a laborer.
True False

5. Only the well-educated are fit for the monumental task of running a nation.
True False

6. The government would probably be a more honest institution if more working-class people were elected to office.
True False

7. The country is best run by people raised in a political family.
True False

8. It is not necessary for a president to be knowledgeable in all areas because he or she is likely to be surrounded by experts.
True False

9. Our better universities probably attract the best applicants, and graduates of these institutions would therefore be the best politicians.
True False

10. We need more ordinary people in Congress— people who've led the sort of lives that most of us are familiar with.
True False

SCORING ·

To tally your score, give yourself 1 point for each response that matches yours.

① *True* ② *True* ③ *True* ④ *True* ⑤ *True* ⑥ *False* ⑦ *True* ⑧ *True* ⑨ *True* ⑩ *False*

This quiz assesses our political attitudes by testing our levels of "social deference." Oftentimes voters opt for those candidates who seem to be more knowledgeable or financially secure than the voter deems himself to be. This impression that the candidate is somehow "better" than the voter leads the voter to put faith in, and ultimately defer to, the people he supports.

A score of 8–10 points: You have a high level of social deference.

A score of 5–7 points: You have a moderate level of social deference.

A score of 0–4 points: You have a low level of social deference.

EXPLANATION ·

Your vote in upcoming elections will reflect how you feel deep down about who should be in government. A candidate's social class is a surprisingly powerful influence. Some political analysts have speculated that presidents such as Franklin D. Roosevelt and John F. Kennedy were elected because voters were favorably impressed by the wealthy upper class these men represented. This social deference was a more important factor earlier in political history than it is today, but it still prevails in the United States and, to a larger extent, in other parts of the world.

In Europe, for example, surveys show that voters are greatly swayed by office seekers' social class, which is probably due to the enduring tradition of aristocracy that's bound up with the European ruling class. One study, conducted by Australian sociologist John Ray, showed that European candidates from the upper classes were positively affected by their social standing.

Of course, one's social background does not determine his or her ability to govern. Class position is not the same thing as competence, and it's a risk to assume that they go hand in hand. Still, consciously or not, voters are all too often impressed by a candidate's social, rather than political, position.

How a citizen casts his vote strongly reflects his life circumstances. A person who is unhappy, financially strapped, or at a lower economic level is more likely to be socially deferent. According to the late Murray Edelman, former Professor Emeritus of political science at the University of Wisconsin, people who lack stable and gratifying roles in life—such as satisfying professional or family situations—are especially vulnerable to persuasion. They are more likely to seek a candidate, usually an incumbent, to fulfill their needs. When considering potential leaders they look to someone who has established roots such as elevated social standing, strong finances, and a solid family background.

CHAPTER 8

YOUR EMOTIONAL WELLNESS

✏️ Are You Plugged-in to Life?

Sue had a bad day at work. It was one of those, "Stop the world, I want to get off" days. They happen now and again for most of us, but unfortunately some people feel this way all the time.

Sociologists call this condition "alienation," the opposite of feeling one with the world. A strong cynicism makes one feel gloomily pessimistic and distrustful of others' sincerity. People who feel alienated don't see themselves as part of society. Like Ebenezer Scrooge, they pull away and become embittered social isolates. Often they "tune out" through alcohol, drugs, and fantasy; for them, these outlets are the anesthetics for life's rigors.

A Gallup Organization youth survey found that one of the six major reasons teens resort to drinking is because it provides a feeling of escape from their problems. Such alienated youth often come from homes with firm disciplinarian techniques but weak displays of affection. Often the teens' parents themselves feel alienated from others because of a lack of social or business success.

People who move frequently may also develop feelings of estrangement. A recent study of eighth-grade children of United States Air Force personnel found that these less-rooted children projected a sense of isolation and felt different from other children who were more geographically stable. The mobile child has lower self-esteem and tends to identify more with adults than with peers.

If you have never really felt a complete sense of oneness with all of mankind, you're not alone. Few of us do. But the following quiz may shed some light on the degree of alienation you feel.

TEST

The quiz items are adapted from the work of Dr. John Ray at New South Wales University in Australia, who has studied alienation in all kinds of people from various backgrounds.

1. These days a person doesn't really know who he can count on.
True False

2. Human nature is fundamentally cooperative.
True False

3. In spite of what some people say, on average, the lot of humanity is getting worse.
True False

4. Most public officials are not really interested in the problems of ordinary people.
True False

5. It is difficult for people like myself to have much influence on public affairs.
True False

6. Life is difficult and risky; the odds of finding success and fulfillment are largely a matter of chance.
True False

7 When you get right down to it, no one cares much what happens to you.
True False

8 In this society, most people can find contentment.
True False

9 There are more rational than irrational people in the world.
True False

10 Considering everything that is going on these days, things still look bright for the younger generation.
True False

SCORING ·

To tally your score, give yourself 1 point for each response that matches yours.

① *True* ② *False* ③ *True* ④ *True* ⑤ *True* ⑥ *True* ⑦ *True* ⑧ *False* ⑨ *False* ⑩ *False*

A score of 8 points or more: You are more cynical and alienated than most people. You view others with suspicion, and generally like to set your course by relying on your own standards rather than those of others. You might consider reexamining your attitudes about life, either on your own or with the help of a counselor.

A score of 4–7 points: You show an average degree of identification with others. You feel enough of a connection with those around you to make you a happy, contributing member of society.

A score of 3 points or less: You are very traditional in your values and attitudes and not likely to be adventurous in plotting your life patterns. You are highly optimistic about life and feel secure in conforming to norms laid down by your social group.

EXPLANATION ·

Why do people become alienated? Famed Harvard psychologist B. F. Skinner, founder of modern behaviorism, called alienation a loss of faith, or "nerve." He saw the resulting despair as a sense of doubt or powerlessness in which people feel they can't change or influence their destiny. "They lack something to believe in or to be devoted to ... these reactions immobilize men of good will," he said.

No one really knows how an attitude of alienation or cynicism begins. Some say it is socially derived, and that we absorb misanthropic attitudes from others. Freudians tell us that cynicism starts early in life, probably before age three, as a result of frustrated oral needs. Regardless of its cause, if one has a strong motivation to change, cynicism can often be reversed.

Young people who join cults are often thought to typify alienated youth. These individuals strongly believe that society cannot fulfill their need for security. They see themselves as different from those who lead conventional lives. But such people usually expect too much from the cults they join, and often find their way back into mainstream society.

✐ Would You Resist Psychotherapy?

In the United States alone, an estimated 30 million people a year suffer some form of mental illness—and many of these people do not seek help. The millions who don't receive attention are often plagued by indecisiveness and hesitation about psychotherapy. Some reasons for this hesitation include a faulty understanding of just what the process entails. But most of the resistance comes from deeper attitudes associated with shame, fear, and the tarnished social image they feel will result from being a patient. These notions block many needy people from getting the care that can help them.

TEST ·

Would you enter therapy if you were told you needed it? More importantly, would you possess the attitudes necessary to benefit from it? To find out, take the following quiz, which is based on the work of psychologists E. Fischer and J. Le B. Turner.

1 I probably wouldn't vote for anyone who had struggled with an emotional problem in the past.
True False

2 Building a strong character is the best way to overcome mental illness.
True False

3 Like many other things, emotional difficulties tend to work themselves out.
True False

4 When getting help, the main caution is to avoid getting the wrong advice.
True False

5 Keeping my mind on a job is a good remedy for avoiding worries.
True False

6 Having been a psychiatric patient is a serious blot on a person's life.
True False

7 I would see a psychotherapist only after I'd tried for a long while to solve my own problems.
True False

8 It's probably best not to know everything about myself.
True False

9 Compared with my friends, I am a very closed person.
True False

10 People who go to a psychotherapist could have helped themselves if they had tried harder.
True False

SCORING

To tally your score, give yourself 1 point for each "True" response.

A score of 6 points of more: You're likely to be resistant to therapy. The closer your score is to 10, the more resistant you will be.

A score of 5 points or less: You would be open to receiving psychotherapy if necessary.

Research shows that women tend to be more accepting of psychotherapy than men. This probably has a lot to do with social conditioning—men usually try hard to live up to an image of independence, and tend not to ask someone else for help.

EXPLANATION

Read on for more detailed explanations of the items on the quiz.

① *False.* Those who believe that an emotional crisis has lasting effects on one's judgment have difficulty believing that one can regain stability after an emotional upset. These people tend to make poor prospects for psychotherapy.

② *False.* Character has little to do with mental health. Regrettably, those who think otherwise may someday suffer needlessly because of this attitude.

③ *False.* More often than not, a serious mental disturbance tends to worsen with time.

④ *False.* Poor advice can be detrimental, but a competent therapist will minimize the danger of this happening.

⑤ *False.* It is wishful thinking to believe that distractions, like a job or love affair, will lead to resolution of a personal crisis.

⑥ *False.* People with poor attitudes toward psychotherapy often use social stigma about mental illness as an excuse to avoid treatment.

⑦ *False.* Procrastinators often reflect fear or resistance about changing themselves. They usually break with therapy too soon to be helped.

⑧ *False.* People who aren't receptive to new insights into themselves don't benefit from treatment.

⑨ *False.* Studies confirm that those who feel comfortable in revealing themselves stand the best chance of benefiting from psychotherapy.

⑩ *False.* Trying harder to "cure" yourself isn't enough to solve fairly serious emotional problems. This notion merely provides the resistant person with yet another reason for staying away from therapy.

No matter how you scored on this quiz, keep in mind that if your motivation to be helped is high enough, your chances of solving your problems are greatly increased.

✏️ Can You Spot the Signs of Creeping Alcoholism?

The American Council on Alcoholism in Alexandria, Virginia, reports that 10 percent of the United States' population (some 20 million people) has a serious problem with alcohol. In addition to being a mental health problem, excessive drinking can also lead to or exacerbate physical ailments like diabetes, hypertension, and liver disease. If you've noticed changes in your drinking patterns lately, observe them carefully—you may be a candidate for addiction.

TEST ··

To find out if your drinking habits have the potential to turn into a problem, take the following quiz.

1. I'll have a drink before going to a gathering where I know liquor will be served.
   True False

2. I drink when I'm feeling blue.
   True False

3. I'll have a drink before and/or after a stressful event.
   True False

4. I tend to drink more than my friends do.
   True False

5. I'll have more than three drinks per day, even when alone.
   True False

6. I occasionally tipple in the morning before going to work or school.
   True False

7. I imbibe to steady my nerves.
   True False

8. I gulp my alcoholic beverages.
   True False

9. I feel it is necessary to have two or more drinks at certain times, like before lunch, at dinner, or after work.
   True False

10. I have boozed to the point of feeling ill.
    True False

SCORING ··

To tally your score, give yourself 1 point for each "True" response.

A score of 5 or more points: You may be developing a drinking problem. Take steps immediately to intervene before your drinking turns into an addiction. You might consider talking to a trusted friend or therapist.

A score of 4 points or less: Your drinking habits seem to be under control. If you think a friend or loved one would score high on this quiz, you might want to consider having a conversation with that person about his or her drinking.

EXPLANATION ····································

Authorities at the Menninger Foundation for Psychiatry in Topeka, Kansas, believe that most alcoholics have undiagnosed mental disturbances and drink to quell or cover up these problems. In addition, alcoholics bear the distinction of profoundly affecting others in their family circle. Each alcoholic adversely affects about six people he knows, bringing the total number of people who can use alcohol-related support resources to 120 million.

Alcoholism costs the American economy some $50 billion annually, to say nothing of its toll in human suffering. Over-indulging is not restricted to the United States, either. The addiction can be found worldwide. Both France and Russia, for example, have declared that alcoholism is their number one public health concern.

The American grassroots organization MADD (Mothers Against Drunk Driving) has probably done more to publicize the abuse of alcohol within the past twenty-five years than any other civic group. Its campaigns are aimed primarily at teenagers who drink and drive. In this age group, liquor is far and away the main substance addiction, exceeding that of tobacco and drugs. The age group from seventeen to twenty-five consumes proportionately far more cigarettes, liquor, and drugs than that of any other age bracket. As a result, this group is the prime target for peddlers of such products.

✏️ How Self-Conscious Are You?

Of all living creatures, man is the only one who is self-conscious. This ability to reflect upon ourselves as an object can be used constructively to correct our faulty behavior. But, if carried to extremes, self-consciousness can be a hindrance.

Research done by Dr. P. A. Pilkonis while at Stanford University revealed two types of self-consciousness: private and public. Being privately self-conscious involves a feeling about yourself that is usually unfavorable, such as "I'm fat," "I'm lazy," or "I'm shallow." Public self-consciousness, on the other hand, reflects your sensitivity about how others will judge or think about you. In this age of style and image, where there is more emphasis on form than on substance, a common type of public self-consciousness is concern about one's appearance. Judging from the billions of dollars spent yearly on clothes and cosmetics, this is uppermost in the minds of many people.

T E S T ·

To gauge your own level of public self-consciousness, take the following quiz.

1 I probably wouldn't sing solo at a party.
   A. *Disagree*
   B. *Somewhat agree*
   C. *Strongly agree*

2 I would feel uneasy if someone watched me work.
   A. *Disagree*
   B. *Somewhat agree*
   C. *Strongly agree*

3 It makes me feel "nervous" if a stranger nearby makes a fool of himself.
   A. *Disagree*
   B. *Somewhat agree*
   C. *Strongly agree*

4 One of the last things I do before I go out is look in the mirror.
   A. *Disagree*
   B. *Somewhat agree*
   C. *Strongly agree*

5 I would probably refuse to go up onto a stage if I were picked from an audience.
A. *Disagree*
B. *Somewhat agree*
C. *Strongly agree*

6 I would feel conspicuous if I were first to arrive or first to leave a small party of friends.
A. *Disagree*
B. *Somewhat agree*
C. *Strongly agree*

7 In public, I would feel conspicuous if I spent more than a few seconds in front of a mirror.
A. *Disagree*
B. *Somewhat agree*
C. *Strongly agree*

8 On a crowded bus, I would feel embarrassed if I offered my seat to someone who loudly declined it.
A. *Disagree*
B. *Somewhat agree*
C. *Strongly agree*

SCORING ·

To tally your score, give yourself 1 point for each "a" response, 2 points for each "b" response, and 3 points for each "c" response.

A score of 19–24 points: You possess a great deal of public self-consciousness. It's possible that you are too sensitive to what others think of you. You are also likely to be susceptible to feelings of rejection.

A score of 12–18 points: You have an average degree of public self-consciousness. You're aware of others' perceptions of you, but not to the point that it stifles your self-expression or shakes your self-confidence.

A score of 8–11 points: Your level of public self-consciousness is very low. People in this category may lack awareness of how they appear to others and/or may show too little concern for what people think of them.

EXPLANATION ·

Public or social self-consciousness starts in infancy. When a child faces a situation that challenges his self-image, like being criticized or scolded for being rude to others, it tends to heighten his concern about being judged negatively. Being raised by overly critical adults usually results in excessive public as well as private self-consciousness. This trait often leads to introversion.

But public self-consciousness isn't always as bad as it may seem. Some publicly self-conscious people have a good image of themselves and are not privately self-conscious at all. They can be loners who nevertheless engage in constructive pursuits. Well-known people who have been publicly self-conscious include Abraham Lincoln, Thomas Edison, and Ludwig van Beethoven.

However, extreme public self-consciousness can be practically immobilizing. Those who are constantly having self-reflective thoughts are often shy, socially insecure, and sensitive to criticism. They avoid competition. Often, they are charitable to almost everyone except themselves. Charlie Chaplin's vivid portrayal of the forlorn tramp exemplifies such a person. He tries hard to please everyone he meets. Like many who are painfully self-conscious, Chaplin's character is a lovable person with many fine qualities. The trouble is that he and others like him rarely believe in their own positive qualities.

Those who are very self-aware are often silent around others. But they can learn to become more assertive and outgoing. One study conducted at Stanford University showed that quiet people who are encouraged to speak while in a group can change the way the group perceives them. When the subjects were silent, group members tended to ignore or minimize their position in the group. But when they began to express ideas and opinions, others' attitudes changed. Many subjects went from exhibiting a strong degree of public self-consciousness and shyness to assuming a leadership position within the group.

✏️ Are You Bound for a Coronary?

One day an upholsterer who was repairing chairs in a doctors' reception room commented that the seats were worn out only on the front edges. This chance remark caused cardiologists Meyer Friedman and Ray Rosenman, at Mt. Zion Medical Center in San Francisco, to wonder about the traits of their cardiac patients—were they overly anxious and therefore leaning forward in their chairs, rubbing away the fabric? After several studies they found evidence that peoples' personalities did indeed affect their behavior, and as a natural result, their health. For the first time they isolated, defined, and named the specific behavior pattern closely associated with coronary heart disease, which they labeled "A-Type." Their subsequent book, *A-Type Behavior and Your Heart*, came to significantly influence the way we think about how our actions affect our heart.

TEST ·

The A-Type personality has a compulsive sense of urgency combined with an intensely competitive drive. B-Types, who are at the other end of the spectrum, tend to be calmer, more patient, and more adaptable (and consequently gentler on their hearts). To find out if your personality type might lead to some troubles with your ticker, take the following quiz.

1 I tend to do things rapidly, such as walking, eating, and getting dressed.
True False

2 I find it satisfying to do many things at the spur of the moment and without much reflection.
True False

3 I often have little time to have my hair cut or styled.
True False

4 I frequently face interruptions and unexpected or last-minute changes.
True False

5 I am impatient and sometimes even angry when someone ahead of me drives slowly.
True False

6 I often do two or more things at once, such as reading while eating, typing while talking on the phone, or scanning a magazine while watching TV.
True False

7 I hate to waste time.
True False

8 I usually arrive just a few minutes before my train or plane is due to depart.
True False

9 Compared to most of my friends, I lose my temper easily.
True False

10 I am a competitive person.
True False

SCORING ·

To tally your score, give yourself 1 point for each "True" response.

A score of 8-10: Watch out heart—you tend towards being an A-Type.

A score of 4–7: You are about average, though you may exhibit A-Type behavior on occasion.

A score of 0-3: You are a B-Type personality, and relatively easygoing.

EXPLANATION ·

The A-Type is a stressed, often angry or frustrated individual. His compulsive sense of urgency, more graphically called "hurry sickness," compels him to achieve more in less time.

People who have A-Type personalities evaluate their merit by numeration. For example, if an A-Type were a lawyer, he or she might mention how many cases were handled in the past year; if he or she were a real-estate broker, how many houses were sold; if a gardener, how many lawns were mowed.

It must be said that most of the world's achievers are A-Types. According to Dr. Friedman's findings, they succeed despite their self-created stress. Still, there are some quietly achievement-minded individuals who exhibit B-Type behavior and get ahead. Some notable B-Types include Abraham Lincoln, Ronald Reagan, and Jimmy Carter.

On the physical level, A's have a tougher time with their coronary health. They tend to metabolize cholesterol more slowly than do B's, which gives them a greater propensity for clogged arteries. This seems to be a genetic factor, though B-Types have been known to adapt A-Type behavior (and symptoms) when under increased amounts of stress.

Although being an A-Type is a considerably riskier existence than being a B, there are ways that A's can train themselves to adopt B-Type characteristics. By learning to relax, eat healthfully, and set realistic life goals, many A-Types have successfully overcome their natural tendencies and protected themselves against further heart disease and damage.

TEST YOUR EMOTIONAL INTELLIGENCE

INTRODUCTION

What is emotional intelligence, also known as EQ? It is a bit like common sense—it is a skill, an innate, very perceptive way of looking at yourself and at other people. It doesn't matter how much education you have, or how varied and rich your life and work experiences may have been, or how high your IQ score is—none of these things will predict if you have been blessed with emotional intelligence.

You can see living, breathing examples of this every day. Brilliant, successful individuals have no people skills, while an individual with fewer advantages seems to get along well with everyone. And the thing the Ivy League university president lacks but the neighborhood handyman possesses is more than charm or charisma.

According to psychologists Dr. Travis Bradberry and Dr. Jean Greaves, authors of The Emotional Intelligence Quick Book, emotional intelligence is a combination of skills. Self-awareness and self-management are characteristic traits of the person who possesses EQ. Then there are social awareness and relationship management, which relate to how the person with EQ interacts with other people. Of course, some people by nature are more emotionally intelligent than others. Nonetheless, you can become more emotionally intelligent by paying attention to your emotions and behavior and managing them, while also understanding what motivates other people and working at improving your relationships with others.

Each EQ test comes with a scoring system that will help you to gauge your emotional intelligence. Based on the scores in the individual tests, you will be able to judge if your EQ needs some work.

As you work to boost your emotional intelligence, some discomfort will probably be involved. You will have to take a long, candid look at yourself and assess your own positive and negative qualities, then set out to improve yourself. Along the way there are all the other people you will encounter. Not all of them will be pleasant. A nineteenth-century Italian saint, John Bosco, once said that the most difficult penance is putting up with tiresome people. Yet the only way to become more emotionally intelligent is to make that open and honest assessment of yourself, while practicing how to get along with just about everyone else.

The fifty quizzes included in this small book are designed to make you more aware of yourself and your relationships with others—in the family, in the workplace, in friendships, and in romantic relationships. Answer the questions honestly and you will be surprised by what you can learn about your own level of emotional intelligence. And if your score in some of the tests isn't as high as you'd like, then you will know what facets of your EQ need work.

Have fun getting emotionally smarter!

CHAPTER 1

ON THE JOB

Every morning, when you walk into your workplace, you are walking into an emotional mine field. And it's not just your boss and co-workers you have to keep an eye on, it's also clients, vendors, service staff, even the cashier in the cafeteria. All of them come to work every day with their issues, worries, ambitions, aggravations, and resentments. And so do you. We are still a long way from replacing the human work force with robots, so as long as you work with people, you also have to deal with their emotions, and, for that matter, you have to deal with your emotions, too.

You've probably encountered the co-worker who keeps his or her emotions bottled up. In moments of success, he or she is cool and aloof. In moments of crisis, he or she is detached. Such people can be very rigid about process and procedures, which makes them difficult to work with. Furthermore, workers of this type tend to give off an unfriendly vibe: you probably won't see them playing softball at the company summer picnic or singing carols at the holiday party.

At the other end of the spectrum is the co-worker who never has an unexpressed emotion. Joy, frustration, success, or despair—he or she lets it all out. It can be exhausting for such a person's co-workers (not to mention noisy).

In 2002, Wendy Alfus Rothman, a member of The Employment Roundtable, wrote a short piece entitled "Developing Emotional Intelligence in the Workplace." In her essay, Rothman said, "Developing emotional intelligence in the workplace means acknowledging that emotions are always present, and doing something intelligent with them."

In the quizzes that follow, you'll be presented with questions and scenarios intended to help you handle your own emotions on the job, while staying attuned to the emotions of the people around you.

An emotionally intelligent employee or manager does a good job even in a stressful situation; works well as part of a team; motivates, perhaps even inspires others; and maintains cordial, productive relationships with co-workers and superiors. That sounds like a tall order, but the cornerstone of emotional intelligence is keeping the most violent emotions in check, learning to be empathetic, and responding appropriately to a variety of unexpected situations in the workplace.

The "On the Job" quizzes are designed to help you understand and work with even difficult people, while also helping you become a better employee or manager.

✎ How Well Do You Cooperate with Others?

1 I like things done in a certain way, so it is difficult for me to work with others.

Completely true   *Somewhat true/false*   *Completely false*

     Mostly true   *Mostly false*

2 I become angry if someone else is the center of attention.

Completely true   *Somewhat true/false*   *Completely false*

     Mostly true   *Mostly false*

3 I must follow the same routine every day.

Completely true   *Somewhat true/false*   *Completely false*

     Mostly true   *Mostly false*

4 If people offend me, I snub them.

Completely true   *Somewhat true/false*   *Completely false*

     Mostly true   *Mostly false*

5 Lack of structure upsets me.

Completely true   *Somewhat true/false*   *Completely false*

     Mostly true   *Mostly false*

6 I am most comfortable when I am in charge.

Completely true   *Somewhat true/false*   *Completely false*

     Mostly true   *Mostly false*

7 I often worry that I am being taken advantage of.

Completely true   *Somewhat true/false*   *Completely false*

     Mostly true   *Mostly false*

8 I do my best work when I work on my own.

Completely true   *Somewhat true/false*   *Completely false*

     Mostly true   *Mostly false*

9 I can be intimidating.

Completely true   *Somewhat true/false*   *Completely false*

     Mostly true   *Mostly false*

10 Most people do not meet my standards.

Completely true   *Somewhat true/false*   *Completely false*

     Mostly true   *Mostly false*

SCORING

Each answer is awarded a specific number of points.

Completely true: *1 point*
Mostly true: *2 points*
Somewhat true/false: *3 points*
Mostly false: *4 points*
Completely false: *5 points*

50–40: You work well with others.
39–30: You're basically a team player.
Below 30: You'll never be first pick at the office softball game.

How Responsible Are You?

1 I am rarely late for an appointment.

Completely true   *Somewhat true/false*   *Completely false*

Mostly true   *Mostly false*

2 I am not afraid of responsibility.

Completely true   *Somewhat true/false*   *Completely false*

Mostly true   *Mostly false*

3 I prefer a busy, fast-paced job.

Completely true   *Somewhat true/false*   *Completely false*

Mostly true   *Mostly false*

4 I like to be productive all day.

Completely true   *Somewhat true/false*   *Completely false*

Mostly true   *Mostly false*

5 At work, I follow up on all my assignments to monitor how they are progressing.

Completely true   *Somewhat true/false*   *Completely false*

Mostly true   *Mostly false*

6 I enjoy working with my hands.

Completely true   *Somewhat true/false*   *Completely false*

Mostly true   *Mostly false*

7 I do my best to meet deadlines.

Completely true   *Somewhat true/false*   *Completely false*

Mostly true   *Mostly false*

8 I have good control over my impulses.

Completely true   *Somewhat true/false*   *Completely false*

Mostly true   *Mostly false*

9 My work habits are fairly consistent.

Completely true   *Somewhat true/false*   *Completely false*

Mostly true   *Mostly false*

10 I enjoy problem-solving.

Completely true   *Somewhat true/false*   *Completely false*

Mostly true   *Mostly false*

SCORING ·

Each answer is awarded a specific number of points.

Completely true: *5 points*
Mostly true: *4 points*
Somewhat true/false: *3 points*
Mostly false: *2 points*
Completely false: *1 point*

50–40: You're a responsible, trustworthy individual.
39–30: You're a fairly responsible person.
Below 30: You're not the best choice for an important assignment or a tight deadline.

✏️ How Do You Function at Work?

1 Even in a crisis, I stay composed and clearheaded.

Completely true   *Somewhat true/false*   *Completely false*

Mostly true   *Mostly false*

2 Deadlines do not freak me out.

Completely true   *Somewhat true/false*   *Completely false*

Mostly true   *Mostly false*

3 If I make a mistake, I admit it.

Completely true   *Somewhat true/false*   *Completely false*

Mostly true   *Mostly false*

4 I make a sincere effort to meet my commitments.

Completely true   *Somewhat true/false*   *Completely false*

Mostly true   *Mostly false*

5 I believe that staying organized is the key to good job performance.

Completely true   *Somewhat true/false*   *Completely false*

Mostly true   *Mostly false*

6 I welcome new ideas and new ways of doing things.

Completely true   *Somewhat true/false*   *Completely false*

Mostly true   *Mostly false*

7 I can juggle more than one assignment at a time.

Completely true   *Somewhat true/false*   *Completely false*

Mostly true   *Mostly false*

8 If the requirements of a project change, I can adapt.

Completely true   *Somewhat true/false*   *Completely false*

Mostly true   *Mostly false*

9 To achieve my goals, I'm not afraid to take calculated risks.

Completely true   *Somewhat true/false*   *Completely false*

Mostly true   *Mostly false*

10 I am interested in new methods and new technologies that will improve my job performance.

Completely true   *Somewhat true/false*   *Completely false*

Mostly true   *Mostly false*

SCORING ·

Each answer is awarded a specific number of points.

Completely true: *5 points*
Mostly true: *4 points*
Somewhat true/false: *3 points*
Mostly false: *2 points*
Completely false: *1 point*

50–40: You're a valuable, reliable employee.
39–30: You have something to contribute in the workplace.
Below 30: You're not functioning at an especially high level on the job.

✏️ How Confident Are You?

1 I would never sing a solo at a party.

Completely true *Somewhat true/false* *Completely false*

Mostly true *Mostly false*

2 Before I leave the house, I check myself in the mirror.

Completely true *Somewhat true/false* *Completely false*

Mostly true *Mostly false*

3 I would never be part of the studio audience on a game show—I'm afraid I'd get called up onstage.

Completely true *Somewhat true/false* *Completely false*

Mostly true *Mostly false*

4 If someone does or says something foolish, I feel very uncomfortable.

Completely true *Somewhat true/false* *Completely false*

Mostly true *Mostly false*

5 I make mistakes if someone watches me work.

Completely true *Somewhat true/false* *Completely false*

Mostly true *Mostly false*

6 I don't feel comfortable wearing bright colors or stylish clothes.

Completely true *Somewhat true/false* *Completely false*

Mostly true *Mostly false*

7 I am never at ease undressing in a locker room or walking around in my bathing suit at the beach.

Completely true   *Somewhat true/false*   *Completely false*

Mostly true   *Mostly false*

8 At office meetings, I rarely offer a suggestion.

Completely true   *Somewhat true/false*   *Completely false*

Mostly true   *Mostly false*

9 When dealing with rude people, it is easier for me to walk away silently than to confront them.

Completely true   *Somewhat true/false*   *Completely false*

Mostly true   *Mostly false*

10 I have trouble standing up for myself.

Completely true   *Somewhat true/false*   *Completely false*

Mostly true   *Mostly false*

SCORING ·

Each answer is awarded a specific number of points.

Completely true: *1 point*
Mostly true: *2 points*
Somewhat true/false: *3 points*
Mostly false: *4 points*
Completely false: *5 points*

50–40: You're a self-assured person.
39–30: You're more or less confident.
Below 30: A little assertiveness training wouldn't hurt.

✏️ What Type of Employee Are You?

1 I think of myself as a team player.

Completely true   *Somewhat true/false*   *Completely false*

Mostly true   *Mostly false*

2 I like having clearly defined goals.

Completely true   *Somewhat true/false*   *Completely false*

Mostly true   *Mostly false*

3 I feel a sense of accomplishment when my peers praise my problem-solving skills.

Completely true   *Somewhat true/false*   *Completely false*

Mostly true   *Mostly false*

4 The thing I dislike most in the workplace is incompetence.

Completely true   *Somewhat true/false*   *Completely false*

Mostly true   *Mostly false*

5 In my ideal career, I'd keep learning new skills.

Completely true   *Somewhat true/false*   *Completely false*

Mostly true   *Mostly false*

6 When I'm interacting with coworkers, the best approach for me is to be impartial and professional.

Completely true   *Somewhat true/false*   *Completely false*

Mostly true   *Mostly false*

7 When I'm doing problem-solving, what I value most is finding new ways to prevent the problem from recurring.

Completely true   *Somewhat true/false*   *Completely false*

Mostly true   *Mostly false*

8 When I'm making a decision, I make a logical assessment of all the facts.

Completely true   *Somewhat true/false*   *Completely false*

Mostly true   *Mostly false*

9 The best reward my employer could give me would be more managerial authority.

Completely true   *Somewhat true/false*   *Completely false*

Mostly true   *Mostly false*

10 Talking with new employees or clients often generates new ideas.

Completely true   *Somewhat true/false*   *Completely false*

Mostly true   *Mostly false*

SCORING ·

Each answer is awarded a specific number of points.

Completely true: *1 point*
Mostly true: *2 points*
Somewhat true/false: *3 points*
Mostly false: *4 points*
Completely false: *5 points*

50–40: Call the next job candidate, please.
39–30: You're not ideal on the job, but you're a smart bet.
Below 30: You're the perfect employee.

✐ What Is Your Personality in the Workplace?

Mark the circle that corresponds to where on the continuum between each of the word/phrase pairs you fall. If you mark 1 or 5, then you identify most strongly with one of the words or phrases in the pair; 2 or 4 less so; 3 you are neutral.

1 methodical ① • ② • ③ • ④ • ⑤ confused

2 communicative ① • ② • ③ • ④ • ⑤ reserved

3 volunteer for assignments ① • ② • ③ • ④ • ⑤ never volunteer for assignments

4 eager for change ① • ② • ③ • ④ • ⑤ like a routine

5 takes direction ① • ② • ③ • ④ • ⑤ hates criticism

6 self-assured ① • ② • ③ • ④ • ⑤ nervous

7 cooperative ① • ② • ③ • ④ • ⑤ resentful

8 prompt ① • ② • ③ • ④ • ⑤ late

9 office door open ① • ② • ③ • ④ • ⑤ office door closed

10 ambitious ① • ② • ③ • ④ • ⑤ apathetic

SCORING ·

50–40: You're the worst job candidate ever.
39–30: You're not even a runner-up.
Below 30: You're a five-star applicant.

✏ How Do You Handle Stress?

1 I have a strong personality.

Completely true   *Somewhat true/false*   *Completely false*

Mostly true   *Mostly false*

2 I suffer from mood swings, more so than most people.

Completely true   *Somewhat true/false*   *Completely false*

Mostly true   *Mostly false*

3 I lash out in stressful situations.

Completely true   *Somewhat true/false*   *Completely false*

Mostly true   *Mostly false*

4 When I feel stressed, I refuse to take on more assignments and responsibilities.

Completely true   *Somewhat true/false*   *Completely false*

Mostly true   *Mostly false*

5 In my circle of friends, I'm known as the perfectionist.

Completely true   *Somewhat true/false*   *Completely false*

Mostly true   *Mostly false*

6 I worry about my health.

Completely true   *Somewhat true/false*   *Completely false*

Mostly true   *Mostly false*

7 I use food or alcohol to help me get through stressful times.

Completely true   *Somewhat true/false*   *Completely false*

Mostly true   *Mostly false*

8 When I'm anxious, I get nauseous.

Completely true   *Somewhat true/false*   *Completely false*

Mostly true   *Mostly false*

9 Stress makes me physically and emotionally exhausted.

Completely true   *Somewhat true/false*   *Completely false*

Mostly true   *Mostly false*

10 When I'm under stress, I find it hard to sit still and relax.

Completely true   *Somewhat true/false*   *Completely false*

Mostly true   *Mostly false*

SCORING ·

Each answer is awarded a specific number of points.

Completely true: *1 point*
Mostly true: *2 points*
Somewhat true/false: *3 points*
Mostly false: *4 points*
Completely false: *5 points*

50–40: You're composed even in stressful situations.
39–30: You handle stress reasonably well.
Below 30: At the first sign of stress, you're ready to crawl under the bed and assume the fetal position.

✏️ Do You Have a Persuasive Personality?

1 I try to be courteous to everyone I meet.

Completely true   *Somewhat true/false*   *Completely false*

     Mostly true   *Mostly false*

2 Usually, I find it easy to bring people around to my point of view.

Completely true   *Somewhat true/false*   *Completely false*

     Mostly true   *Mostly false*

3 Usually, I can talk people into doing what I want them to do.

Completely true   *Somewhat true/false*   *Completely false*

     Mostly true   *Mostly false*

4 When making a point, I try to be as clear as possible so everyone will understand what I am trying to explain.

Completely true   *Somewhat true/false*   *Completely false*

     Mostly true   *Mostly false*

5 I am rarely nervous when talking to a stranger.

Completely true   *Somewhat true/false*   *Completely false*

     Mostly true   *Mostly false*

6 I believe most people think I am friendly.

Completely true   *Somewhat true/false*   *Completely false*

     Mostly true   *Mostly false*

7 I think most people enjoy my company.

Completely true   *Somewhat true/false*   *Completely false*

   Mostly true   *Mostly false*

8 I enjoy attending parties and other social functions.

Completely true   *Somewhat true/false*   *Completely false*

   Mostly true   *Mostly false*

9 I have a lot of influence over my family and friends.

Completely true   *Somewhat true/false*   *Completely false*

   Mostly true   *Mostly false*

10 I have always been a good salesperson.

Completely true   *Somewhat true/false*   *Completely false*

   Mostly true   *Mostly false*

SCORING ·

Each answer is awarded a specific number of points.

Completely true: *5 points*
Mostly true: *4 points*
Somewhat true/false: *3 points*
Mostly false: *2 points*
Completely false: *1 point*

50–40: You have an outgoing, charismatic personality
39–30: You have some persuasive skills.
Below 30: There's no future for you in sales or politics.

CHAPTER 2

YOUR
SOCIAL LIFE

"**N**o man is an island," wrote the 17th-century English poet, John Donne. In other words, we are all part of a community, and the community functions best when its members possess self-awareness.

People who are self-aware have a clear, just understanding of their strengths and weaknesses, their potential, their desires, and how these aspects of their personality can affect other people. We have all had encounters with people who hold long, loud conversations on their cellphone on a train or plane or bus—places where the rest of the passengers can't escape the big-mouthed bore. Anyone with the slightest sense of self-awareness would know to lower his or her voice, or find a more private setting for the phone conversation—the rest room, or perhaps the rear of the vehicle, someplace where he or she will not be disruptive.

Then there are individuals who are slaves to their emotions. Whatever they feel, they express; whether it is the most appropriate time or place to vent their emotions doesn't phase such people. For generations, parents have instructed their children not to discuss religion or politics in public, but the socially clueless go beyond these taboos, droning on and on about their salary, their jobs, their current and past relationships, even the most intimate details of their family life. Nor do such people notice that their insensitive monologue has made just about everyone within earshot feel uncomfortable, even mortified.

Finally, there are the people so caught up in themselves that they cannot empathize with others. Imagine being confined to a hospital bed, and receiving a string of visitors who aren't interested in your condition but only want to talk about their own aches and pains, or their last visit to their doctor, or their most current ailment. Such people are so self-absorbed that even when confronted with a seriously ill friend or relative, they can only think of themselves.

The three types of people we've described are the socially clueless. They have no sense of how they are perceived, or how they have embarrassed or offended the people around them.

The "Your Social Life" quizzes that follow are intended to help you be more aware of what you are doing and saying, control your emotions, and become more empathetic.

✏️ How Social Are You?

1 I have many friends and acquaintances.

Completely true   *Somewhat true/false*   *Completely false*

Mostly true   *Mostly false*

2 In my spare time, I enjoy socializing with family and friends, attending dinner parties, and going to movies.

Completely true   *Somewhat true/false*   *Completely false*

Mostly true   *Mostly false*

3 I am happy to help someone, and I don't expect anything in return.

Completely true   *Somewhat true/false*   *Completely false*

Mostly true   *Mostly false*

4 I am a sympathetic person.

Completely true   *Somewhat true/false*   *Completely false*

Mostly true   *Mostly false*

5 I find it easy to make new friends at a new workplace.

Completely true   *Somewhat true/false*   *Completely false*

Mostly true   *Mostly false*

6 I enjoy interacting with people.

Completely true   *Somewhat true/false*   *Completely false*

Mostly true   *Mostly false*

7 I am moved by stories of people who are sick, suffering, or needy.

Completely true   *Somewhat true/false*   *Completely false*

          Mostly true   *Mostly false*

8 I feel at ease in a crowd.

Completely true   *Somewhat true/false*   *Completely false*

          Mostly true   *Mostly false*

9 There are times when I am emotional.

Completely true   *Somewhat true/false*   *Completely false*

          Mostly true   *Mostly false*

10 I enjoy doing volunteer work.

Completely true   *Somewhat true/false*   *Completely false*

          Mostly true   *Mostly false*

SCORING

Each answer is awarded a specific number of points.

Completely true: *5 points*
Mostly true: *4 points*
Somewhat true/false: *3 points*
Mostly false: *2 points*
Completely false: *1 point*

50–40: You're a charismatic people person.
39–30: You have average people skills.
Below 30: You don't appear on any party planner's A list.

✏ What Kind of Friend Are You?

1 If I knew for a fact that a friend's spouse was having an affair, I would say nothing.

Completely true   *Somewhat true/false*   *Completely false*

Mostly true   *Mostly false*

2 If I found that a friend and I no longer enjoyed each other's company, I'd ignore his/her phone calls, e-mails, or invitations.

Completely true   *Somewhat true/false*   *Completely false*

Mostly true   *Mostly false*

3 If my spouse or partner developed an annoying habit, I would threaten to leave unless he/she changed.

Completely true   *Somewhat true/false*   *Completely false*

Mostly true   *Mostly false*

4 If friends at work took credit for my work, I would get back at them by taking credit for something they did.

Completely true   *Somewhat true/false*   *Completely false*

Mostly true   *Mostly false*

5 If a friend borrowed something that has great sentimental value to me and failed to return it, I would cut off him/her without a word of explanation.

Completely true   *Somewhat true/false*   *Completely false*

Mostly true   *Mostly false*

6 If my date seemed ill at ease, I would decide there is no chemistry between the two of us and never call him/her again.

Completely true   *Somewhat true/false*   *Completely false*

Mostly true   *Mostly false*

7 If a friend at work was given the promotion I was angling for, I would tell myself I really didn't want that stupid promotion anyway.

Completely true   *Somewhat true/false*   *Completely false*

Mostly true   *Mostly false*

8 When a friend talks about another one of my friends behind his/her back, I join in.

Completely true   *Somewhat true/false*   *Completely false*

Mostly true   *Mostly false*

9 If my best friend says he/she has no time to socialize because of obligations at work, I would assume my friend doesn't like me anymore.

Completely true   *Somewhat true/false*   *Completely false*

Mostly true   *Mostly false*

10 If my best friend's lover has dumped him/her, I would worry that I might get dumped, too.

Completely true   *Somewhat true/false*   *Completely false*

Mostly true   *Mostly false*

SCORING ·

Each answer is awarded a specific number of points.

Completely true: *5 points*
Mostly true: *4 points*
Somewhat true/false: *3 points*
Mostly false: *2 points*
Completely false: *1 point*

50–40: You're the worst friend in history.
39–30: You're still not great friend material.
Below 30: You're the one to hang out with.

✏ Are You a People Person?

1 I try to comfort people who are upset or going through a difficult time.

Completely true   *Somewhat true/false*   *Completely false*

       Mostly true   *Mostly false*

2 If asked, I am happy to help a friend get organized.

Completely true   *Somewhat true/false*   *Completely false*

       Mostly true   *Mostly false*

3 I am happiest among people I know very well.

Completely true   *Somewhat true/false*   *Completely false*

       Mostly true   *Mostly false*

4 One of my favorite things is helping two people become friends.

Completely true   *Somewhat true/false*   *Completely false*

Mostly true   *Mostly false*

5 If I help someone, I don't expect any kind of payment in return.

Completely true   *Somewhat true/false*   *Completely false*

Mostly true   *Mostly false*

6 If someone helps me, I express my appreciation immediately.

Completely true   *Somewhat true/false*   *Completely false*

Mostly true   *Mostly false*

7 I socialize with my friends as often as possible.

Completely true   *Somewhat true/false*   *Completely false*

Mostly true   *Mostly false*

8 I enjoy volunteering in my community.

Completely true   *Somewhat true/false*   *Completely false*

Mostly true   *Mostly false*

9 Conflict between people makes me uncomfortable.

Completely true   *Somewhat true/false*   *Completely false*

Mostly true   *Mostly false*

10 I am always happy to help one of my neighbors.

Completely true   *Somewhat true/false*   *Completely false*

Mostly true   *Mostly false*

SCORING ·

Each answer is awarded a specific number of points.

Completely true: *5 points*
Mostly true: *4 points*
Somewhat true/false: *3 points*
Mostly false: *2 points*
Completely false: *1 point*

50–40: You're well-adjusted and sympathetic.
39–30: More often than not, you're helpful and friendly.
Below 30: You're a borderline recluse.

✏ Are You
a Party Animal?

Mark the circle that corresponds to where on the continuum between each of the word/phrase pairs you fall. If you mark 1 or 5,
then you identify most strongly with one of the words or phrases
in the pair; 2 or 4 less so; 3 you are neutral.

❶ boisterous ① • ② • ③ • ④ • ⑤ shy

❷ chatty ① • ② • ③ • ④ • ⑤ quiet

❸ outgoing ① • ② • ③ • ④ • ⑤ reserved

❹ hands-on ① • ② • ③ • ④ • ⑤ hands off

❺ center of attention ① • ② • ③ • ④ • ⑤ wallflower

❻ dance ① • ② • ③ • ④ • ⑤ sit down

❼ great wine ① • ② • ③ • ④ • ⑤ bottled water

❽ tells jokes ① • ② • ③ • ④ • ⑤ doesn't get jokes

⑨ warm ① • ② • ③ • ④ • ⑤ remote

⑩ having fun ① • ② • ③ • ④ • ⑤ killing time

S C O R I N G ·

50–40: Why were you even invited?
39–30: You're a borderline party pooper.
Below 30: People always invite you to the party, but they should probably take your car keys.

✏ How Good Are Your Manners?

① In conversation, I rarely speak loudly.

Completely true   *Somewhat true/false*   *Completely false*

Mostly true   *Mostly false*

② I rarely use foul language.

Completely true   *Somewhat true/false*   *Completely false*

Mostly true   *Mostly false*

③ I try to be respectful of elderly people.

Completely true   *Somewhat true/false*   *Completely false*

Mostly true   *Mostly false*

④ Even if I believe my opinion is important, I rarely interrupt a discussion.

Completely true   *Somewhat true/false*   *Completely false*

Mostly true   *Mostly false*

5 I never smack my lips or chew with my mouth open when eating.

Completely true   *Somewhat true/false*   *Completely false*

Mostly true   *Mostly false*

6 Usually I knock on the door before entering a room.

Completely true   *Somewhat true/false*   *Completely false*

Mostly true   *Mostly false*

7 Even if I can't find a trash barrel, I will not drop a candy wrapper or used tissue on the street.

Completely true   *Somewhat true/false*   *Completely false*

Mostly true   *Mostly false*

8 The words "please," "thank you," and "excuse me" are a basic part of my vocabulary.

Completely true   *Somewhat true/false*   *Completely false*

Mostly true   *Mostly false*

9 I try not to make noise in a church or a library.

Completely true   *Somewhat true/false*   *Completely false*

Mostly true   *Mostly false*

10 If something I've said or done offends someone else, then I apologize.

Completely true   *Somewhat true/false*   *Completely false*

Mostly true   *Mostly false*

SCORING ·

Each answer is awarded a specific number of points.

Completely true: *5 points*
Mostly true: *4 points*
Somewhat true/false: *3 points*
Mostly false: *2 points*
Completely false: *1 point*

50–40: You're courteous and considerate.
39–30: More often than not, you're thoughtful.
Below 30: You're crass and insensitive.

✏ Are You Neighborly?

① I socialize with my neighbors.

    Completely true   *Somewhat true/false*   *Completely false*

          Mostly true   *Mostly false*

② If my neighbor's dog got out, I'd try to bring him home.

    Completely true   *Somewhat true/false*   *Completely false*

          Mostly true   *Mostly false*

③ If I have a problem with one of my neighbors, I'd speak to him or about it politely.

    Completely true   *Somewhat true/false*   *Completely false*

          Mostly true   *Mostly false*

④ If I saw someone suspicious casing my neighbor's house, I'd call the police.

    Completely true   *Somewhat true/false*   *Completely false*

          Mostly true   *Mostly false*

5 I don't mind collecting my neighbors' mail while they are out of town.

Completely true   *Somewhat true/false*   *Completely false*

Mostly true   *Mostly false*

6 If the noise level of a neighbor's party got out of hand, I would walk over and ask them to keep it down.

Completely true   *Somewhat true/false*   *Completely false*

Mostly true   *Mostly false*

7 I'm cordial, even to neighbors I do not like.

Completely true   *Somewhat true/false*   *Completely false*

Mostly true   *Mostly false*

8 When a new family moves onto the block, I go over and introduce myself.

Completely true   *Somewhat true/false*   *Completely false*

Mostly true   *Mostly false*

9 If a neighbor is working outdoors and needs help, I offer my assistance.

Completely true   *Somewhat true/false*   *Completely false*

Mostly true   *Mostly false*

10 If I saw smoke coming from a neighbor's house, I would call 911, then run over to see if they were safe.

Completely true   *Somewhat true/false*   *Completely false*

Mostly true   *Mostly false*

SCORING ·

Each answer is awarded a specific number of points.

Completely true: *5 points*
Mostly true: *4 points*
Somewhat true/false: *3 points*
Mostly false: *2 points*
Completely false: *1 point*

50–40: You're a beloved and valued member of the community.
39–30: You show signs of a neighborly spirit.
Below 30: You'll never win the neighborhood's Good Samaritan Award.

CHAPTER 3

MIND VERSUS EMOTIONS

Your emotions are important. They are a vital source of communication with others. A small child's laugh tells us that he or she feels happy and safe with us. A friend's look of anxiety is a call for help. And the confused expression on the face of stranger in the middle of a bustling city street is your opportunity to be a good Samaritan.

Just as important is the human mind, our capability to use our reason to think through problems. Our mind, our reason, our intelligence enable us to learn from past experiences and use what we have learned to respond successfully when we encounter new experiences.

Most of us go through life with a fairly well-balanced sense of when to respond to a situation emotionally and when to respond rationally. But there are individuals who tend to be ruled by their emotions or by their intellect. For example, let's say that your family gives you a new car for your birthday. You are filled with happiness, excitement, gratitude—all positive emotions, and this is the moment to let them out. An overly emotional person, however, might surrender to his or her impulses, jump into the car, and head off immediately on a cross-country road trip. An overly rational person might start quizzing his or her family about the details of the warranty.

Emotions and reason co-exist in every person. Some people may have a tendency to be overly emotional or overly analytical. There are even individuals who make a conscious choice to give free reign to their emotions—they believe it makes their responses to people and situations more authentic, while others all but suppress their emotions in favor of cool, detached, rational approach to life's experiences. Both extremes have a common problem— egotism. The extreme emotionalist and the extreme rationalist are so convinced that their way is the right way, that they have lost all sense of consideration for other people, who will probably be uncomfortable with the over-the-top emotions of the one and the cold analysis of the other.

Emotional Intelligence rejects extremes. The "Mind vs. Emotions" quizzes that follow are designed to help you identify how you respond to people and situations. If you find that you tend to be too emotional or too rational, you might want to consider ways that you can bring such tendencies into balance.

✏️ How Tough Are You Emotionally?

1 If someone else cries, I get teary.

Completely true   *Somewhat true/false*   *Completely false*

    Mostly true   *Mostly false*

2 It's not unusual for me to share details of my personal life with strangers.

Completely true   *Somewhat true/false*   *Completely false*

    Mostly true   *Mostly false*

3 An emotional movie can make me cry.

Completely true   *Somewhat true/false*   *Completely false*

    Mostly true   *Mostly false*

4 Even after I've made a decision, my family and friends can persuade me to change my mind.

Completely true   *Somewhat true/false*   *Completely false*

    Mostly true   *Mostly false*

5 If someone is rude to me, I feel bad for days afterward.

Completely true   *Somewhat true/false*   *Completely false*

    Mostly true   *Mostly false*

6 My heart rules my head.

Completely true   *Somewhat true/false*   *Completely false*

    Mostly true   *Mostly false*

7 I take offense easily.

Completely true   *Somewhat true/false*   *Completely false*

Mostly true   *Mostly false*

8 I tend to dwell on bad news.

Completely true   *Somewhat true/false*   *Completely false*

Mostly true   *Mostly false*

9 I often feel insecure.

Completely true   *Somewhat true/false*   *Completely false*

Mostly true   *Mostly false*

10 What my family, friends, and coworkers think of me is very important.

Completely true   *Somewhat true/false*   *Completely false*

Mostly true   *Mostly false*

SCORING ·

Each answer is awarded a specific number of points.

Completely true: *1 point*
Mostly true: *2 points*
Somewhat true/false: *3 points*
Mostly false: *4 points*
Completely false: *5 points*

50–40: You don't let emotions get the better of you.
39–30: You're somewhat in control of your emotions.
Below 30: You're an insecure, emotional wreck.

✏️ How Impulsive Are You?

1 I'm usually the first person to answer the phone or the door.

Completely true   *Somewhat true/false*   *Completely false*

Mostly true   *Mostly false*

2 It is better to act on impulse than to analyze a situation thoroughly.

Completely true   *Somewhat true/false*   *Completely false*

Mostly true   *Mostly false*

3 My emotions guide my actions.

Completely true   *Somewhat true/false*   *Completely false*

Mostly true   *Mostly false*

4 Usually I rush through my work.

Completely true   *Somewhat true/false*   *Completely false*

Mostly true   *Mostly false*

5 I am not afraid to express my emotions or to say what's on my mind.

Completely true   *Somewhat true/false*   *Completely false*

Mostly true   *Mostly false*

6 Books of philosophy, economics, or other theoretical fields bore me.

Completely true   *Somewhat true/false*   *Completely false*

Mostly true   *Mostly false*

7 I like being the center of attention.

Completely true   *Somewhat true/false*   *Completely false*

  Mostly true   *Mostly false*

8 I am willing to experiment and take risks.

Completely true   *Somewhat true/false*   *Completely false*

  Mostly true   *Mostly false*

9 There are more important things in life than deadlines.

Completely true   *Somewhat true/false*   *Completely false*

  Mostly true   *Mostly false*

10 I am adventurous.

Completely true   *Somewhat true/false*   *Completely false*

  Mostly true   *Mostly false*

SCORING ·

Each answer is awarded a specific number of points.

Completely true: *5 points*
Mostly true: *4 points*
Somewhat true/false: *3 points*
Mostly false: *2 points*
Completely false: *1 point*

50–40: On a dare, you would bungee-jump off the Golden Gate Bridge.
39–30: Your impulses are somewhat under control.
Below 30: You're thoughtful—you look before you leap.

✏️ How Intellectual Are You?

1 Ideas interest me more than putting them to practical use.

Completely true *Somewhat true/false* *Completely false*

Mostly true *Mostly false*

2 I often contemplate the future of humankind.

Completely true *Somewhat true/false* *Completely false*

Mostly true *Mostly false*

3 I try to understand the mystery and complexity of life.

Completely true *Somewhat true/false* *Completely false*

Mostly true *Mostly false*

4 I need time to myself, especially after socializing.

Completely true *Somewhat true/false* *Completely false*

Mostly true *Mostly false*

5 Justice is more important than mercy.

Completely true *Somewhat true/false* *Completely false*

Mostly true *Mostly false*

6 Given a choice, I prefer to stay home and read a book than go to a party.

Completely true *Somewhat true/false* *Completely false*

Mostly true *Mostly false*

7 I avoid social obligations.

Completely true *Somewhat true/false* *Completely false*

Mostly true *Mostly false*

8 I cannot live or work in a noisy environment.

Completely true   *Somewhat true/false*   *Completely false*

Mostly true   *Mostly false*

9 Every situation in life can be improved if it is thoroughly analyzed.

Completely true   *Somewhat true/false*   *Completely false*

Mostly true   *Mostly false*

10 I have no trouble grasping new philosophical or scientific theories.

Completely true   *Somewhat true/false*   *Completely false*

Mostly true   *Mostly false*

SCORING ·

Each answer is awarded a specific number of points.

Completely true: *5 points*
Mostly true: *4 points*
Somewhat true/false: *3 points*
Mostly false: *2 points*
Completely false: *1 point*

50–40: You're cerebral and standoffish.
39–30: Your head and your heart seem to be working in balance.
Below 30: You're an emotional and thoughtless mess.

✎ What Type of Person Do You Admire?

Mark the circle that corresponds to where on the continuum between each of the word/phrase pairs you fall. If you mark 1 or 5, then you identify most strongly with one of the words or phrases in the pair; 2 or 4 less so; 3 you are neutral.

1. technician ① • ② • ③ • ④ • ⑤ artist

2. college professor ① • ② • ③ • ④ • ⑤ kindergarten teacher

3. researcher ① • ② • ③ • ④ • ⑤ handyperson

4. physicist ① • ② • ③ • ④ • ⑤ rancher

5. mathematician ① • ② • ③ • ④ • ⑤ musician

6. economist ① • ② • ③ • ④ • ⑤ dancer

7. investor ① • ② • ③ • ④ • ⑤ consumer

8. independently wealthy ① • ② • ③ • ④ • ⑤ entrepreneur

9. dog breeder ① • ② • ③ • ④ • ⑤ dog owner

10. theater critic ① • ② • ③ • ④ • ⑤ actor

SCORING ·

50–40: You're a hands-on, independent, artsy type.
39–30: You're artsy with a touch of brainiac go-getter.
Below 30: You're ambitious and cerebral.

✏️ Are You Cool and Detached?

1 I try to be impartial and fair-minded in my decisions.

Completely true   *Somewhat true/false*   *Completely false*

Mostly true   *Mostly false*

2 Objective criticism of people and ideas is always a good thing.

Completely true   *Somewhat true/false*   *Completely false*

Mostly true   *Mostly false*

3 Decisions should not be made on the basis of feelings.

Completely true   *Somewhat true/false*   *Completely false*

Mostly true   *Mostly false*

4 I plan how I will spend each day.

Completely true   *Somewhat true/false*   *Completely false*

Mostly true   *Mostly false*

5 In making a decision, I rely more on my own experiences that some abstract standard.

Completely true   *Somewhat true/false*   *Completely false*

Mostly true   *Mostly false*

6 I like to put things in order.

Completely true   *Somewhat true/false*   *Completely false*

Mostly true   *Mostly false*

7 I stick to my principles.

Completely true   *Somewhat true/false*   *Completely false*

Mostly true   *Mostly false*

8 My workplace is usually neat and clean.

Completely true   *Somewhat true/false*   *Completely false*

Mostly true   *Mostly false*

9 At work, I can see ways productivity could be improved.

Completely true   *Somewhat true/false*   *Completely false*

Mostly true   *Mostly false*

10 Generally speaking, I can see how a particular event will play out.

Completely true   *Somewhat true/false*   *Completely false*

Mostly true   *Mostly false*

SCORING ·

Each answer is awarded a specific number of points.

Completely true: *5 points*
Mostly true: *4 points*
Somewhat true/false: *3 points*
Mostly false: *2 points*
Completely false: *1 point*

50–40: You're completely dependable.
39–30: You're reliable in most situations.
Below 30: You're probably not at your best in an orderly work environment.

✎ Are You an Extrovert?

1 I do not get excited easily.

Completely true   *Somewhat true/false*   *Completely false*

Mostly true   *Mostly false*

2 I do not reveal much about myself to other people.

Completely true   *Somewhat true/false*   *Completely false*

Mostly true   *Mostly false*

3 At a party, I prefer to be at the periphery of the crowd, rather than in the center.

Completely true   *Somewhat true/false*   *Completely false*

Mostly true   *Mostly false*

4 I enjoy taking long walks alone.

Completely true   *Somewhat true/false*   *Completely false*

Mostly true   *Mostly false*

5 I am not comfortable talking about my feelings.

Completely true   *Somewhat true/false*   *Completely false*

Mostly true   *Mostly false*

6 I prefer being with a small group of close friends rather than at a large party full of strangers.

Completely true   *Somewhat true/false*   *Completely false*

Mostly true   *Mostly false*

7 I am most at ease with my family.

Completely true   *Somewhat true/false*   *Completely false*

Mostly true   *Mostly false*

8 I prefer following convention.

Completely true   *Somewhat true/false*   *Completely false*

Mostly true   *Mostly false*

9 My habits are fairly consistent.

Completely true   *Somewhat true/false*   *Completely false*

Mostly true   *Mostly false*

10 There are things about me that even my family does not know.

Completely true   *Somewhat true/false*   *Completely false*

Mostly true   *Mostly false*

SCORING ·

Each answer is awarded a specific number of points.

Completely true: *5 points*
Mostly true: *4 points*
Somewhat true/false: *3 points*
Mostly false: *2 points*
Completely false: *1 point*

50–40: You keep most people at arm's length.
39–30: You're friendly, but you're never the life of the party.
Below 30: You're outgoing, and have genuine people skills.

✏️ How Independent-Minded Are You?

1 Human existence may be meaningless.

Completely true   *Somewhat true/false*   *Completely false*

Mostly true   *Mostly false*

2 I consider myself to be unconventional.

Completely true   *Somewhat true/false*   *Completely false*

Mostly true   *Mostly false*

3 It is foolish for each generation to carry on their family, ethnic, and religious traditions.

Completely true   *Somewhat true/false*   *Completely false*

Mostly true   *Mostly false*

4 I don't care what others think of me.

Completely true   *Somewhat true/false*   *Completely false*

Mostly true   *Mostly false*

5 Intellectual curiosity is a prime motivating force in my life.

Completely true   *Somewhat true/false*   *Completely false*

Mostly true   *Mostly false*

6 I enjoy avant-garde music.

Completely true   *Somewhat true/false*   *Completely false*

Mostly true   *Mostly false*

7 Most of my opinions are not popular.

Completely true   *Somewhat true/false*   *Completely false*

Mostly true   *Mostly false*

8 Living in a wealthy neighborhood would make me uncomfortable.

Completely true   *Somewhat true/false*   *Completely false*

       Mostly true   *Mostly false*

9 There is nothing wrong with being outspoken.

Completely true   *Somewhat true/false*   *Completely false*

       Mostly true   *Mostly false*

10 I consider myself to be an idealist.

Completely true   *Somewhat true/false*   *Completely false*

       Mostly true   *Mostly false*

SCORING ·

Each answer is awarded a specific number of points.

Completely true: *5 points*
Mostly true: *4 points*
Somewhat true/false: *3 points*
Mostly false: *2 points*
Completely false: *1 point*

50–40: You're a borderline misanthrope.
39–30: You're independent-minded, but not obnoxiously so.
Below 30: You're conventional, but personable.

✏️ Are You a Brainiac?

1 Doing theoretical research all day would be my dream job.

Completely true   *Somewhat true/false*   *Completely false*

Mostly true   *Mostly false*

2 When others panic, I stay calm.

Completely true   *Somewhat true/false*   *Completely false*

Mostly true   *Mostly false*

3 Strong displays of emotion make me uncomfortable.

Completely true   *Somewhat true/false*   *Completely false*

Mostly true   *Mostly false*

4 Intellectual pursuits are my primary pastime.

Completely true   *Somewhat true/false*   *Completely false*

Mostly true   *Mostly false*

5 I often think about the purpose of my life.

Completely true   *Somewhat true/false*   *Completely false*

Mostly true   *Mostly false*

6 I want people to think of me as competent.

Completely true   *Somewhat true/false*   *Completely false*

Mostly true   *Mostly false*

7 I often use words and phrases most people do not understand.

Completely true   *Somewhat true/false*   *Completely false*

Mostly true   *Mostly false*

8 I have always been good at the sciences.

Completely true   *Somewhat true/false*   *Completely false*

Mostly true   *Mostly false*

9 Detachment is an important character trait.

Completely true   *Somewhat true/false*   *Completely false*

Mostly true   *Mostly false*

10 As a child, I was more comfortable with adults than with children my own age.

Completely true   *Somewhat true/false*   *Completely false*

Mostly true   *Mostly false*

SCORING ·

Each answer is awarded a specific number of points.

Completely true: *5 points*
Mostly true: *4 points*
Somewhat true/false: *3 points*
Mostly false: *2 points*
Completely false: *1 point*

50–40: You will probably win a Nobel Prize.
39–30: You're smarter than average.
Below 30: You may have other positive qualities.

✏️ Do You Live in a Fantasy World?

1 People find me impressive.

Completely true   *Somewhat true/false*   *Completely false*

Mostly true   *Mostly false*

2 I spend most of my time pursuing one or two highly specialized interests.

Completely true   *Somewhat true/false*   *Completely false*

Mostly true   *Mostly false*

3 Someday I will be famous.

Completely true   *Somewhat true/false*   *Completely false*

Mostly true   *Mostly false*

4 I am an influential person.

Completely true   *Somewhat true/false*   *Completely false*

Mostly true   *Mostly false*

5 My family and friends don't do anything without seeking my advice.

Completely true   *Somewhat true/false*   *Completely false*

Mostly true   *Mostly false*

6 The jealousy of others has kept me from being more successful.

Completely true   *Somewhat true/false*   *Completely false*

Mostly true   *Mostly false*

7 I am interested in the paranormal.

Completely true   *Somewhat true/false*   *Completely false*

          Mostly true   *Mostly false*

8 I am psychic.

Completely true   *Somewhat true/false*   *Completely false*

          Mostly true   *Mostly false*

9 I am prophetic.

Completely true   *Somewhat true/false*   *Completely false*

          Mostly true   *Mostly false*

10 I can relate to wizards.

Completely true   *Somewhat true/false*   *Completely false*

          Mostly true   *Mostly false*

SCORING ·

Each answer is awarded a specific number of points.

Completely true: *5 points*
Mostly true: *4 points*
Somewhat true/false: *3 points*
Mostly false: *2 points*
Completely false: *1 point*

50–40: You're seriously self-deluded.
39–30: You're quirky.
Below 30: You have remained in touch with reality.

✎ Are You a Cynic or an Optimist?

1 I don't know who I can trust.

Completely true   *Somewhat true/false*   *Completely false*

Mostly true   *Mostly false*

2 I believe that, at heart, human beings only look out for Number One.

Completely true   *Somewhat true/false*   *Completely false*

Mostly true   *Mostly false*

3 I believe people are getting nastier and more selfish.

Completely true   *Somewhat true/false*   *Completely false*

Mostly true   *Mostly false*

4 Our elected officials only care about their jobs and their perks —they don't care about the ordinary citizens of this country.

Completely true   *Somewhat true/false*   *Completely false*

Mostly true   *Mostly false*

5 Voting in local, state, and national elections is pointless.

Completely true   *Somewhat true/false*   *Completely false*

Mostly true   *Mostly false*

6 Being happy and successful in life is a matter of luck. Nothing I do will change that.

Completely true   *Somewhat true/false*   *Completely false*

Mostly true   *Mostly false*

7 No one cares what happens to me.

Completely true   *Somewhat true/false*   *Completely false*

Mostly true   *Mostly false*

8 In our society, there are few opportunities for people to build happy, meaningful lives for themselves.

Completely true   *Somewhat true/false*   *Completely false*

Mostly true   *Mostly false*

9 Most people are irrational.

Completely true   *Somewhat true/false*   *Completely false*

Mostly true   *Mostly false*

10 Things will only get worse for the next generation.

Completely true   *Somewhat true/false*   *Completely false*

Mostly true   *Mostly false*

SCORING ·

Each answer is awarded a specific number of points.

Completely true: *5 points*
Mostly true: *4 points*
Somewhat true/false: *3 points*
Mostly false: *2 points*
Completely false: *1 point*

50–40: You're cranky, irritable, and bad-tempered.
39–30: You have bouts of cynicism and optimism.
Below 30: You always looks on the bright side of life.

LOVE AND RELATIONSHIPS

Romance is complicated. It is fraught with so many emotions—love and desire, of course, but also uncertainty about commitment, fear of rejection, and disappointment if the relationship is not developing in the way you or your partner would like. Taking the cold analytical approach doesn't work—you can't dissect love like a laboratory frog. And surrendering entirely to emotions doesn't work either—at some point the people involved have to assess their chances of being a happy, successful couple. For these reasons, many experts in Emotional Intelligence consider romance the acid test of a person's EQ.

The key to having a loving relationship is coming from a loving home. If you grew up in a family that loved and supported and nurtured you, then the odds are excellent that you have the skills (for lack of a better word) to be a good romantic partner and eventually a good spouse.

Pity people who grew up in a dysfunctional family, where anger, violence, neglect, and abuse were routine. Thanks to the twisted lessons they learned about relationships, they have little chance of finding true love. But it is not hopeless: if they are willing to abandon those destructive ideas and habits, break the chain of dysfunctional relationships they witnessed as children and teenagers, and learn to be gentle and caring, then their chance of finding a loving partner increases substantially.

At the core of a healthy relationship is caring about the partner's happiness. In the most successful relationships, each partner wants the other to feel safe, content, appreciated, loved. If you are in such a relationship, you have been blessed. If you would like to find such a relationship, the "Love and Relationship" section may help. The quizzes encourage the qualities already present in your personality that demonstrate that you are good candidate for a serious relationship, or throw the spotlight on facets of your personality that may need some work.

✏️ Are You Ready for Love?

1 I often become infatuated with someone.

Completely true　　*Somewhat true/false*　　*Completely false*

Mostly true　　　　　*Mostly false*

2 I find it easy to say "I love you."

Completely true　　*Somewhat true/false*　　*Completely false*

Mostly true　　　　　*Mostly false*

3 I am at ease hugging men, women, and children.

Completely true　　*Somewhat true/false*　　*Completely false*

Mostly true　　　　　*Mostly false*

4 It has never been difficult for me to establish a long-term, loving relationship.

Completely true　　*Somewhat true/false*　　*Completely false*

Mostly true　　　　　*Mostly false*

5 I would require certain conditions in a relationship.

Completely true　　*Somewhat true/false*　　*Completely false*

Mostly true　　　　　*Mostly false*

6 A couple does not have to do everything together, or share the same opinions on every subject.

Completely true　　*Somewhat true/false*　　*Completely false*

Mostly true　　　　　*Mostly false*

7 I know I am worthy of love.

Completely true　　*Somewhat true/false*　　*Completely false*

Mostly true　　　　　*Mostly false*

8 When I'm alone with my romantic partner, I often experience intense feelings of sexual desire.

Completely true   *Somewhat true/false*   *Completely false*

       Mostly true   *Mostly false*

9 When I give a gift to my partner, I do not expect to receive one in return.

Completely true   *Somewhat true/false*   *Completely false*

       Mostly true   *Mostly false*

10 If my partner asked about my past relationships, I would be honest.

Completely true   *Somewhat true/false*   *Completely false*

       Mostly true   *Mostly false*

SCORING ·

Each answer is awarded a specific number of points.

Completely true: *5 points*
Mostly true: *4 points*
Somewhat true/false: *3 points*
Mostly false: *2 points*
Completely false: *1 point*

50–40: You're a keeper; anyone would be proud to take you home to meet the folks.

39–30: You're a pretty good bet.

Below 30: There are lots of good fish in the sea, so a prospective love interest might be seriously tempted to throw you back.

✎ How Important Is Love in Your Life?

1 My main goal in life is to find my true love.

Completely true   *Somewhat true/false*   *Completely false*

Mostly true   *Mostly false*

2 I do not like living alone.

Completely true   *Somewhat true/false*   *Completely false*

Mostly true   *Mostly false*

3 I have been happiest when I have been in a relationship.

Completely true   *Somewhat true/false*   *Completely false*

Mostly true   *Mostly false*

4 I am not afraid to let someone get close to me.

Completely true   *Somewhat true/false*   *Completely false*

Mostly true   *Mostly false*

5 I want to raise a family.

Completely true   *Somewhat true/false*   *Completely false*

Mostly true   *Mostly false*

6 I enjoy socializing.

Completely true   *Somewhat true/false*   *Completely false*

Mostly true   *Mostly false*

7 I enjoy spending private time with the person I love.

Completely true   *Somewhat true/false*   *Completely false*

Mostly true   *Mostly false*

8 It is important to me to be considerate of other people.

Completely true   *Somewhat true/false*   *Completely false*

Mostly true   *Mostly false*

9 I believe I am a loving person.

Completely true   *Somewhat true/false*   *Completely false*

Mostly true   *Mostly false*

10 I get somewhat depressed when I am not in a romantic relationship.

Completely true   *Somewhat true/false*   *Completely false*

Mostly true   *Mostly false*

SCORING ·

Each answer is awarded a specific number of points.

Completely true: *5 points*
Mostly true: *4 points*
Somewhat true/false: *3 points*
Mostly false: *2 points*
Completely false: *1 point*

50–40: For you, love cannot come along soon enough.
39–30: You're ready for love, but it's not critical.
Below 30: You probably won't have a date on New Year's Eve.

✏️ Are You in the Mood for Love?

Mark the circle that corresponds to where on the continuum between each of the word/phrase pairs you fall. If you mark 1 or 5, then you identify most strongly with one of the words or phrases in the pair; 2 or 4 less so; 3 you are neutral.

1. go dancing ① • ② • ③ • ④ • ⑤ go to a hockey game

2. bouquet of flowers ① • ② • ③ • ④ • ⑤ fifth of vodka

3. romantic ① • ② • ③ • ④ • ⑤ formal

4. spontaneous ① • ② • ③ • ④ • ⑤ controlling

5. dinner for two ① • ② • ③ • ④ • ⑤ a night out with friends

6. ready to commit ① • ② • ③ • ④ • ⑤ reviewing options

7. affectionate ① • ② • ③ • ④ • ⑤ undemonstrative

8. courtship ① • ② • ③ • ④ • ⑤ friendship

9. bistro ① • ② • ③ • ④ • ⑤ food cart

10. St. Valentine's Day ① • ② • ③ • ④ • ⑤ St. Patrick's Day

SCORING

50–40: You are not in the mood.
39–30: If you found love now, you could take it or leave it.
Below 30: Oh yeah, you are so in the mood.

✏ Are You Over Your Ex?

1 Many times during the day I feel the urge to call my ex.

Completely true   *Somewhat true/false*   *Completely false*

Mostly true   *Mostly false*

2 The cards and gifts my ex gave me are special to me.

Completely true   *Somewhat true/false*   *Completely false*

Mostly true   *Mostly false*

3 I think of my ex often, especially when I am alone.

Completely true   *Somewhat true/false*   *Completely false*

Mostly true   *Mostly false*

4 Since the breakup, I have avoided my friends.

Completely true   *Somewhat true/false*   *Completely false*

Mostly true   *Mostly false*

5 I can't go to restaurants or theaters or parks I visited with my ex.

Completely true   *Somewhat true/false*   *Completely false*

Mostly true   *Mostly false*

6 It bothers me if my family or friends mention my ex in conversation.

Completely true   *Somewhat true/false*   *Completely false*

Mostly true   *Mostly false*

7 I often think of the good times I had with my ex.

Completely true   *Somewhat true/false*   *Completely false*

Mostly true   *Mostly false*

8 I am not ready for a new relationship.

Completely true   *Somewhat true/false*   *Completely false*

        Mostly true   *Mostly false*

9 Sometimes I think the breakup was my fault.

Completely true   *Somewhat true/false*   *Completely false*

        Mostly true   *Mostly false*

10 If my ex called, I would try to make up with him/her.

Completely true   *Somewhat true/false*   *Completely false*

        Mostly true   *Mostly false*

SCORING ·

Each answer is awarded a specific number of points.

Completely true: *5 points*
Mostly true: *4 points*
Somewhat true/false: *3 points*
Mostly false: *2 points*
Completely false: *1 point*

50–40: You're so not over your ex.
39–30: You're getting there, but you're not over your ex yet.
Below 30: You're ready for the next, hopefully happier, relationship.

CHAPTER 5

THE HAPPINESS FACTOR

Emotionally intelligent people are happy people. Happy people have a loving family, a wide circle of friends and acquaintances. They work well with others, which makes them more productive at work and often leads them to do volunteer work in their communities. Happy people attract other people, they tend to be given more responsibility, and they are generally regarded as an asset in any organization to which they belong.

It's interesting to note that happy people are not all wealthy, nor are they all especially good looking, nor do they belong to the high-level professions. Wealth can vanish overnight; good looks fade over time; and holding on to a high-powered job can be a precarious business. Happy people know that these things are superficial and fleeting, so they ground their happiness in the things that last: family, friends, personal ethics, a generous spirit.

Why are happy people happy? Because they possess Emotional Intelligence. They are in control of their emotions, and they can assess and respond appropriately to the emotions of others. In other words, they have people skills.

Furthermore, happy people are not only productive, they are satisfied with their lives. This is not to say that every day is a day of fairy tale perfection for happy people—they have problems, challenges, sorrows, just like everyone else. But they love the people around them, and they are grateful for the blessings they already possess.

Unhappy people, on the other hand, tend to be aggressive, resentful, brimming over with negative emotions—particularly the feeling that they are unappreciated, not respected, and not being rewarded as they deserve. Not surprisingly, co-workers, neighbors, even family members find the chronically unhappy person unpleasant to be around.

The "Happiness Factor" quizzes that follow have been designed to measure your level of happiness with your life. A few of you will find that you are genuinely happy. And a few will confirm what you already knew—that you are just seething with dissatisfaction. But most who take these quizzes will fall in the middle, which gives you an opportunity to assess what you can do to become a happier, more contented person.

✏️ Are You Happy?

1 I have a positive self-image.

Completely true　　*Somewhat true/false*　　*Completely false*

Mostly true　　*Mostly false*

2 I make enough money to pay my bills and splurge on special things from time to time.

Completely true　　*Somewhat true/false*　　*Completely false*

Mostly true　　*Mostly false*

3 My work is fulfilling.

Completely true　　*Somewhat true/false*　　*Completely false*

Mostly true　　*Mostly false*

4 I enjoy one or two hobbies.

Completely true　　*Somewhat true/false*　　*Completely false*

Mostly true　　*Mostly false*

5 I love my family.

Completely true　　*Somewhat true/false*　　*Completely false*

Mostly true　　*Mostly false*

6 My life is satisfying.

Completely true　　*Somewhat true/false*　　*Completely false*

Mostly true　　*Mostly false*

7 I make time to visit with my family and friends.

Completely true　　*Somewhat true/false*　　*Completely false*

Mostly true　　*Mostly false*

8 I usually sleep well at night.

Completely true   *Somewhat true/false*   *Completely false*

          Mostly true   *Mostly false*

9 I smile much more often than I frown.

Completely true   *Somewhat true/false*   *Completely false*

          Mostly true   *Mostly false*

10 I have complaints from time to time, but I'm not a whiner.

Completely true   *Somewhat true/false*   *Completely false*

          Mostly true   *Mostly false*

SCORING ·

Each answer is awarded a specific number of points.

Completely true: *5 points*
Mostly true: *4 points*
Somewhat true/false: *3 points*
Mostly false: *2 points*
Completely false: *1 point*

50–40: You're a very happy person.
39–30: You're happy most of the time.
Below 30: You're the neighborhood grouch.

✏️ How Do You See Yourself?

Mark the circle that corresponds to where on the continuum between each of the word/phrase pairs you fall. If you mark 1 or 5, then you identify most strongly with one of the words or phrases in the pair; 2 or 4 less so; 3 you are neutral.

1. loser ① • ② • ③ • ④ • ⑤ winner

2. prestige does not bring happiness ① • ② • ③ • ④ • ⑤ prestige brings happiness

3. emotional ① • ② • ③ • ④ • ⑤ logical

4. instinct ① • ② • ③ • ④ • ⑤ facts

5. impulsive ① • ② • ③ • ④ • ⑤ analytical

6. outgoing ① • ② • ③ • ④ • ⑤ aloof

7. extravagant ① • ② • ③ • ④ • ⑤ cautious

8. conventional ① • ② • ③ • ④ • ⑤ unconventional

9. respect tradition ① • ② • ③ • ④ • ⑤ reject tradition

10. socially awkward ① • ② • ③ • ④ • ⑤ socially at ease

SCORING ·

50–40: You have a solid sense of self-esteem, plus you're thoughtful, sociable, and a bit of a free spirit.
39–30: You're balanced, with no extremes of behavior.
Below 30: You're nervous and ill at ease in almost all social situations.

✏ How Low Is Your Self-Esteem?

1 All it takes is one mistake and I berate myself as a stupid loser.

Completely true   *Somewhat true/false*   *Completely false*

Mostly true   *Mostly false*

2 Every time I strive for something, challenges and obstacles get in my way.

Completely true   *Somewhat true/false*   *Completely false*

Mostly true   *Mostly false*

3 I feel that doing my best is not good enough.

Completely true   *Somewhat true/false*   *Completely false*

Mostly true   *Mostly false*

4 I am fixated on my problems.

Completely true   *Somewhat true/false*   *Completely false*

Mostly true   *Mostly false*

5 Family, friends, work, and day-to-day life all bore me.

Completely true   *Somewhat true/false*   *Completely false*

Mostly true   *Mostly false*

6 I worry about things no one else worries about.

Completely true   *Somewhat true/false*   *Completely false*

Mostly true   *Mostly false*

7 The unhappiness of someone I love makes me unhappy, too.

Completely true   *Somewhat true/false*   *Completely false*

Mostly true   *Mostly false*

8 The opinions of other people can make me feel bad about myself.

Completely true   *Somewhat true/false*   *Completely false*

Mostly true   *Mostly false*

9 Nothing I've ever attempted has been a success.

Completely true   *Somewhat true/false*   *Completely false*

Mostly true   *Mostly false*

10 If someone does not praise my work, then I know it is no good.

Completely true   *Somewhat true/false*   *Completely false*

Mostly true   *Mostly false*

SCORING

Each answer is awarded a specific number of points.

Completely true: *5 points*
Mostly true: *4 points*
Somewhat true/false: *3 points*
Mostly false: *2 points*
Completely false: *1 point*

50–40: Your self-esteem is nonexistent.
39–30: Your self-esteem needs some work.
Below 30: You're capable and self-confident.

✏️ How Big of a Slacker Are You?

1 It's not unusual for me to put off work, chores, or errands.

Completely true   *Somewhat true/false*   *Completely false*

Mostly true   *Mostly false*

2 In school, if I didn't get around to studying, I cheated on my exams.

Completely true   *Somewhat true/false*   *Completely false*

Mostly true   *Mostly false*

3 I can lie around doing nothing for hours.

Completely true   *Somewhat true/false*   *Completely false*

Mostly true   *Mostly false*

4 Typically, I begin a task, like washing the dishes, then walk away before the job is done.

Completely true   *Somewhat true/false*   *Completely false*

Mostly true   *Mostly false*

5 Watching TV is my favorite activity.

Completely true   *Somewhat true/false*   *Completely false*

Mostly true   *Mostly false*

6 I rarely meet a deadline.

Completely true   *Somewhat true/false*   *Completely false*

Mostly true   *Mostly false*

7 If a task can be postponed, I will postpone it.

Completely true   *Somewhat true/false*   *Completely false*

Mostly true   *Mostly false*

8 Usually I am late for work.

Completely true   *Somewhat true/false*   *Completely false*

Mostly true   *Mostly false*

9 I would rather eat out than cook a meal.

Completely true   *Somewhat true/false*   *Completely false*

Mostly true   *Mostly false*

10 I like to sleep late in the morning.

Completely true   *Somewhat true/false*   *Completely false*

Mostly true   *Mostly false*

SCORING ·

Each answer is awarded a specific number of points.

Completely true: *5 points*
Mostly true: *4 points*
Somewhat true/false: *3 points*
Mostly false: *2 points*
Completely false: *1 point*

50–40: You're the king of the slackers.
39–30: You have lots of slacker potential.
Below 30: There's no time for you to be a slacker—you're too busy being productive.

✏ What Makes You Happy?

Mark the circle that corresponds to where on the continuum between each of the word/phrase pairs you fall. If you mark 1 or 5, then you identify most strongly with one of the words or phrases in the pair; 2 or 4 less so; 3 you are neutral.

1 sociable ① • ② • ③ • ④ • ⑤ solitary

2 family ① • ② • ③ • ④ • ⑤ coworkers

3 friends ① • ② • ③ • ④ • ⑤ acquaintances

4 home cooking ① • ② • ③ • ④ • ⑤ takeout

5 read a book ① • ② • ③ • ④ • ⑤ nap on the couch

6 volunteer ① • ② • ③ • ④ • ⑤ watch a movie

7 play with the kids ① • ② • ③ • ④ • ⑤ watch the game

8 help a neighbor ① • ② • ③ • ④ • ⑤ do it yourself

9 date night ① • ② • ③ • ④ • ⑤ channel surfing

10 bottle of wine ① • ② • ③ • ④ • ⑤ bag of chips

SCORING ·

50–40: You're a couch potato.
39–30: You appreciate at least some of the good things in life.
Below 30: You appreciate the good things in life.

✏ Are Your Emotions in Charge of You?

❶ Confronting someone who is angry terrifies me.

Completely true   *Somewhat true/false*   *Completely false*

Mostly true   *Mostly false*

❷ Hugging or kissing people makes me uncomfortable.

Completely true   *Somewhat true/false*   *Completely false*

Mostly true   *Mostly false*

❸ I am self-conscious about my personal appearance or the way I behave around other people.

Completely true   *Somewhat true/false*   *Completely false*

Mostly true   *Mostly false*

❹ I am afraid to let myself cry.

Completely true   *Somewhat true/false*   *Completely false*

Mostly true   *Mostly false*

❺ If someone insults me, I dwell on the slight for days.

Completely true   *Somewhat true/false*   *Completely false*

Mostly true   *Mostly false*

❻ A loss or a disappointment, even one that occurred many years ago, can make me profoundly sad.

Completely true   *Somewhat true/false*   *Completely false*

Mostly true   *Mostly false*

7 I get depressed easily.

Completely true   *Somewhat true/false*   *Completely false*

        Mostly true   *Mostly false*

8 I often experience feelings of jealousy.

Completely true   *Somewhat true/false*   *Completely false*

        Mostly true   *Mostly false*

9 A minor difficulty often makes me overreact.

Completely true   *Somewhat true/false*   *Completely false*

        Mostly true   *Mostly false*

10 When I'm under pressure, I freak out.

Completely true   *Somewhat true/false*   *Completely false*

        Mostly true   *Mostly false*

SCORING ·

Each answer is awarded a specific number of points.

Completely true: *5 points*
Mostly true: *4 points*
Somewhat true/false: *3 points*
Mostly false: *2 points*
Completely false: *1 point*

50–40: Your emotions are in charge.
39–30: Your emotions still have too much influence.
Below 30: Your emotions have learned there's a new sheriff in town.

✏️ How Impulsive Are You?

1 If I were unhappy at work, I would quit my job, even if I did not have another one lined up.

Completely true   *Somewhat true/false*   *Completely false*

Mostly true   *Mostly false*

2 On Friday afternoon, if a friend invited me to an all-expenses-paid weekend vacation, I would go.

Completely true   *Somewhat true/false*   *Completely false*

Mostly true   *Mostly false*

3 When I shop, it is not unusual for me to buy things I want but don't need.

Completely true   *Somewhat true/false*   *Completely false*

Mostly true   *Mostly false*

4 I would go skydiving if someone dared me.

Completely true   *Somewhat true/false*   *Completely false*

Mostly true   *Mostly false*

5 Sometimes, when I see an attractive stranger, I ask him/her out on a date.

Completely true   *Somewhat true/false*   *Completely false*

Mostly true   *Mostly false*

6 I have been known to go away for a weekend without telling my family what I'm doing.

Completely true   *Somewhat true/false*   *Completely false*

Mostly true   *Mostly false*

7 I would probably have a romantic fling if I knew my spouse wouldn't find out about it.

Completely true　　*Somewhat true/false*　　*Completely false*

Mostly true　　　*Mostly false*

8 In high school, I played hooky about once a month.

Completely true　　*Somewhat true/false*　　*Completely false*

Mostly true　　　*Mostly false*

9 I took my bonus and blew it all at the racetrack.

Completely true　　*Somewhat true/false*　　*Completely false*

Mostly true　　　*Mostly false*

10 I hate a routine.

Completely true　　*Somewhat true/false*　　*Completely false*

Mostly true　　　*Mostly false*

SCORING ·

Each answer is awarded a specific number of points.

Completely true: *5 points*
Mostly true: *4 points*
Somewhat true/false: *3 points*
Mostly false: *2 points*
Completely false: *1 point*

50–40: Impulsiveness guides your life.
39–30: You often surrender to impulse.
Below 30: You know the difference between spontaneity and impulsiveness.

CHAPTER 6

THE REAL YOU

If you were asked to describe your main quality, what would it be? Genuine? Impulsive? Reserved? Open? Do you worry too much? Are you a thrill seeker? Do you think of yourself as a confidant person? Do you find yourself all too often giving in to feelings of anger? How independent or unconventional are you?

Think of what gets you excited, what motivates you, what brings out your passion. Now try to understand why these things are so important to you. What do you get out of them? How do they make you feel? What is it about that feeling that you long to experience it again and again? This is an especially important exercise if you are indulging in negative experiences.

An essential step in increasing your emotional intelligence is to have a firm idea of the type of person you are. Of course, self-assessment can be tough—it is not much fun to confront your personal demons, to admit your shortcomings, but it is the only way to improve and to boost your EQ.

Daniel Goleman, the author of Emotional Intelligence, wrote, "Emotional Intelligence is the capacity for recognizing our own feelings." It is those feelings that compel us to bottle-up our emotions (perhaps out of fear of rejection?), to go sky-diving (because our day-to-day life is so unfulfilling?), or to enjoy the company of other people (which is a sign of sound Emotional Intelligence).

The following quizzes are intended to help you uncover the real you. If you have a tendency toward unhealthy emotions or unhelpful emotional responses, these quizzes may be useful in spotlighting them. And once you are aware of any emotional difficulties, you can take steps to correct them. Emotional Intelligence is most often defined as being sensitive to the emotional needs of others, but Emotional Intelligence is also about self-awareness, of being sensitive to your own emotional needs.

✏️ How Would You Describe Your Behavior?

Mark the circle that corresponds to where on the continuum between each of the word/phrase pairs you fall. If you mark 1 or 5, then you identify most strongly with one of the words or phrases in the pair; 2 or 4 less so; 3 you are neutral.

1 genuine ① • ② • ③ • ④ • ⑤ false

2 rational ① • ② • ③ • ④ • ⑤ impulsive

3 spontaneous ① • ② • ③ • ④ • ⑤ structured

4 prompt ① • ② • ③ • ④ • ⑤ tardy

5 outgoing ① • ② • ③ • ④ • ⑤ standoffish

6 caring ① • ② • ③ • ④ • ⑤ distant

7 tidy ① • ② • ③ • ④ • ⑤ disorganized

8 chatty ① • ② • ③ • ④ • ⑤ reserved

9 prepare ① • ② • ③ • ④ • ⑤ improvise

10 open ① • ② • ③ • ④ • ⑤ closed off

SCORING ·

50–40: You have impetuous tendencies, and no clue as to how to act around other people.

39–30: You have a few quirks, but you're still a good choice as a friend.

Below 30: You're balanced, grounded, probably fun to be around.

✏️ Are You Plagued by Anxiety?

1 People who know me consider me a very serious person.

Completely true   *Somewhat true/false*   *Completely false*

Mostly true   *Mostly false*

2 When I'm away on vacation or a business trip, I think about my home often.

Completely true   *Somewhat true/false*   *Completely false*

Mostly true   *Mostly false*

3 At night, it is often difficult for me to fall asleep.

Completely true   *Somewhat true/false*   *Completely false*

Mostly true   *Mostly false*

4 Disappointing or making someone angry will bother for days or even weeks afterward.

Completely true   *Somewhat true/false*   *Completely false*

Mostly true   *Mostly false*

5 I am extremely conscientious about all my responsibilities.

Completely true   *Somewhat true/false*   *Completely false*

Mostly true   *Mostly false*

6 I hate it when I make a mistake.

Completely true   *Somewhat true/false*   *Completely false*

Mostly true   *Mostly false*

7 When I leave the house, I often return to double-check that I have turned off the stove and securely locked the door.

Completely true   *Somewhat true/false*   *Completely false*

Mostly true   *Mostly false*

8 I avoid getting a physical because I worry that my doctor will find that I have a serious illness or condition.

Completely true   *Somewhat true/false*   *Completely false*

Mostly true   *Mostly false*

9 Among strangers, I feel self-conscious and uninteresting.

Completely true   *Somewhat true/false*   *Completely false*

Mostly true   *Mostly false*

10 If someone is not friendly to me, I worry that I offended him/her in some way.

Completely true   *Somewhat true/false*   *Completely false*

Mostly true   *Mostly false*

SCORING ·

Each answer is awarded a specific number of points.

Completely true: *5 points*
Mostly true: *4 points*
Somewhat true/false: *3 points*
Mostly false: *2 points*
Completely false: *1 point*

50–40: You're a nervous wreck.
39–30: You suffer from a bit too much anxiety.
Below 30: You're as cool and calm as a glass of water.

✏️ Are You a Compulsive Thrill Seeker?

1 When I was a child, I liked to steal things.

Completely true   *Somewhat true/false*   *Completely false*

Mostly true   *Mostly false*

2 I get bored easily.

Completely true   *Somewhat true/false*   *Completely false*

Mostly true   *Mostly false*

3 I'm at my best in a big, noisy party.

Completely true   *Somewhat true/false*   *Completely false*

Mostly true   *Mostly false*

4 In school, I often defied my teachers.

Completely true   *Somewhat true/false*   *Completely false*

Mostly true   *Mostly false*

5 In stressful situations, I get headaches and become nauseous.

Completely true   *Somewhat true/false*   *Completely false*

Mostly true   *Mostly false*

6 I'll often go away on vacation without telling my family and friends where I'm going.

Completely true   *Somewhat true/false*   *Completely false*

Mostly true   *Mostly false*

7 The need for excitement has led me to do some crazy things.

Completely true   *Somewhat true/false*   *Completely false*

Mostly true   *Mostly false*

8 I enjoy taking risks.

Completely true   *Somewhat true/false*   *Completely false*

Mostly true   *Mostly false*

9 I enjoy reading thrillers.

Completely true   *Somewhat true/false*   *Completely false*

Mostly true   *Mostly false*

10 If I haven't done something exciting or risky in a while, I become depressed.

Completely true   *Somewhat true/false*   *Completely false*

Mostly true   *Mostly false*

SCORING ·

Each answer is awarded a specific number of points.

Completely true: *5 points*
Mostly true: *4 points*
Somewhat true/false: *3 points*
Mostly false: *2 points*
Completely false: *1 point*

50–40: You're a compulsive thrill seeker.
39–30: You're adventurous, but not insanely so.
Below 30: You know how to have a good time without risking a trip to the hospital, or jail.

✏ How Self-Confident Are You?

1. At a restaurant, I add up the check and count my change.

   Completely true   *Somewhat true/false*   *Completely false*

   Mostly true   *Mostly false*

2. It is impossible for me to start a conversation with a stranger.

   Completely true   *Somewhat true/false*   *Completely false*

   Mostly true   *Mostly false*

3. My boss intimidates me.

   Completely true   *Somewhat true/false*   *Completely false*

   Mostly true   *Mostly false*

4. I've had a hard life, but that has made me a stronger person.

   Completely true   *Somewhat true/false*   *Completely false*

   Mostly true   *Mostly false*

5. No one thinks of me as assertive.

   Completely true   *Somewhat true/false*   *Completely false*

   Mostly true   *Mostly false*

6. I never gamble.

   Completely true   *Somewhat true/false*   *Completely false*

   Mostly true   *Mostly false*

7. It is difficult for me to get over times when I've screwed up.

   Completely true   *Somewhat true/false*   *Completely false*

   Mostly true   *Mostly false*

8. I don't like my job, but I'm afraid a new job might turn out to be even worse.

Completely true   *Somewhat true/false*   *Completely false*

        Mostly true   *Mostly false*

9. Even among my friends, I rarely contribute much to a conversation.

Completely true   *Somewhat true/false*   *Completely false*

        Mostly true   *Mostly false*

10. I worry more than most people I know.

Completely true   *Somewhat true/false*   *Completely false*

        Mostly true   *Mostly false*

SCORING ·

Each answer is awarded a specific number of points.

Completely true: *5 points*
Mostly true: *4 points*
Somewhat true/false: *3 points*
Mostly false: *2 points*
Completely false: *1 point*

50–40: Your self-confidence is almost nil.
39–30: You have some self-confidence, but not very much.
Below 30: You're the mayor of Self-Confidence Town.

✏️ Are You an Angry Person?

1 I don't like it when people tell me what to do.

Completely true   *Somewhat true/false*   *Completely false*

    Mostly true   *Mostly false*

2 There is nothing wrong with standing up to authority figures, such as a police officer.

Completely true   *Somewhat true/false*   *Completely false*

    Mostly true   *Mostly false*

3 I like to be in charge.

Completely true   *Somewhat true/false*   *Completely false*

    Mostly true   *Mostly false*

4 If someone has hurt or offended me, I plot how to get even.

Completely true   *Somewhat true/false*   *Completely false*

    Mostly true   *Mostly false*

5 If someone is bothering me, I let him/her know about it.

Completely true   *Somewhat true/false*   *Completely false*

    Mostly true   *Mostly false*

6 Modest people get walked on.

Completely true   *Somewhat true/false*   *Completely false*

    Mostly true   *Mostly false*

7 It's healthy to release your anger.

Completely true   *Somewhat true/false*   *Completely false*

    Mostly true   *Mostly false*

8 I find it very satisfying to tell off an obnoxious person.

Completely true   *Somewhat true/false*   *Completely false*

      Mostly true   *Mostly false*

9 If people don't like it when I express my anger, that's their problem.

Completely true   *Somewhat true/false*   *Completely false*

      Mostly true   *Mostly false*

10 What other people think of me doesn't concern me at all.

Completely true   *Somewhat true/false*   *Completely false*

      Mostly true   *Mostly false*

SCORING ·

Each answer is awarded a specific number of points.

Completely true: *5 points*
Mostly true: *4 points*
Somewhat true/false: *3 points*
Mostly false: *2 points*
Completely false: *1 point*

50–40: You're a ticking time bomb.
39–30: You're still way too angry.
Below 30: You have your anger under control.

✏️ Are You Lonely?

1 I get lonely if I am not living with a roommate, lover, or spouse.

Completely true   *Somewhat true/false*   *Completely false*

      Mostly true   *Mostly false*

2 I believe that if I were more successful in my career, I would never be lonely.

Completely true   *Somewhat true/false*   *Completely false*

      Mostly true   *Mostly false*

3 When I run into my neighbors, I never know what to say.

Completely true   *Somewhat true/false*   *Completely false*

      Mostly true   *Mostly false*

4 I feel awkward and uncomfortable when I must speak to a stranger, such as a waiter or a sales clerk.

Completely true   *Somewhat true/false*   *Completely false*

      Mostly true   *Mostly false*

5 It seems to me that today most people keep to themselves, so it's harder to make new friends.

Completely true   *Somewhat true/false*   *Completely false*

      Mostly true   *Mostly false*

6 I think of myself as shy.

Completely true   *Somewhat true/false*   *Completely false*

      Mostly true   *Mostly false*

7 Office parties and other large social functions make me ill at ease.

Completely true   *Somewhat true/false*   *Completely false*

        Mostly true   *Mostly false*

8 I have a few close friends, but I'm not sure how to make more.

Completely true   *Somewhat true/false*   *Completely false*

        Mostly true   *Mostly false*

9 I get bored sitting at home evening after evening.

Completely true   *Somewhat true/false*   *Completely false*

        Mostly true   *Mostly false*

10 I would like to have a more active social life.

Completely true   *Somewhat true/false*   *Completely false*

        Mostly true   *Mostly false*

SCORING

Each answer is awarded a specific number of points.

Completely true: *5 points*
Mostly true: *4 points*
Somewhat true/false: *3 points*
Mostly false: *2 points*
Completely false: *1 point*

50–40: You're the living, breathing definition of lonely.
39–30: You need to get out more.
Below 30: You're rarely, if ever, lonely.

✏️ How Conventional Are You?

Mark the circle that corresponds to where on the continuum between each of the word/phrase pairs you fall. If you mark 1 or 5, then you identify most strongly with one of the words or phrases in the pair; 2 or 4 less so; 3 you are neutral.

1. innovate ① • ② • ③ • ④ • ⑤ preserve the status quo

2. atheist ① • ② • ③ • ④ • ⑤ theist

3. individualistic ① • ② • ③ • ④ • ⑤ group-oriented

4. change ① • ② • ③ • ④ • ⑤ tradition

5. militant ① • ② • ③ • ④ • ⑤ authoritarian

6. free-form ① • ② • ③ • ④ • ⑤ structured

7. rebellious ① • ② • ③ • ④ • ⑤ dutiful

8. abstract ① • ② • ③ • ④ • ⑤ concrete

9. defiant ① • ② • ③ • ④ • ⑤ obedient

10. doubt ① • ② • ③ • ④ • ⑤ faith

SCORING ·

50–40: There's no chance of your becoming a rebel.
39–30: You dabble in nonconformity from time to time.
Below 30: You're the classic nonconformist.

✏ How Independent Are You?

1 I like to join organizations.

Completely true   *Somewhat true/false*   *Completely false*

Mostly true   *Mostly false*

2 I prefer to make household and auto repairs myself.

Completely true   *Somewhat true/false*   *Completely false*

Mostly true   *Mostly false*

3 I consider myself to be self-reliant.

Completely true   *Somewhat true/false*   *Completely false*

Mostly true   *Mostly false*

4 When I make a mistake, I admit it; I don't make excuses.

Completely true   *Somewhat true/false*   *Completely false*

Mostly true   *Mostly false*

5 Other people's opinion of me does not matter.

Completely true   *Somewhat true/false*   *Completely false*

Mostly true   *Mostly false*

6 I am not afraid to express an opinion that is contrary to what my family and friends believe.

Completely true   *Somewhat true/false*   *Completely false*

Mostly true   *Mostly false*

7 It is an admirable thing to swim against the current.

Completely true   *Somewhat true/false*   *Completely false*

Mostly true   *Mostly false*

8 I am not self-conscious.

   Completely true   *Somewhat true/false*   *Completely false*

        Mostly true   *Mostly false*

9 Change does not upset me.

   Completely true   *Somewhat true/false*   *Completely false*

        Mostly true   *Mostly false*

10 I love my family and friends, but I am not emotionally needy.

   Completely true   *Somewhat true/false*   *Completely false*

        Mostly true   *Mostly false*

SCORING

Each answer is awarded a specific number of points.

Completely true: *5 points*
Mostly true: *4 points*
Somewhat true/false: *3 points*
Mostly false: *2 points*
Completely false: *1 point*

50–40: You're independent, with lots of self-sufficiency to spare.
39–30: You're a straight shooter.
Below 30: Maybe you're not needy, but you're certainly not independent.

CHAPTER 7

ALL IN THE FAMILY

John Lennon assured us, "All you need is love." Well, in family life love is vital, but it's not all you need. You also need kindness, respect, support, encouragement, patience (lots of patience), and tolerance. And when we say tolerance, we mean it in the old-fashioned sense of "to put up with." The most successful families put up with a lot from each—divergent interests; different tastes in clothing, music, and friends; conflicting opinions on politics, religion, sexuality, and all those other hot-button issues that can set off a ferocious argument around the dinner table. Parents and children, brothers and sisters, have to find some way to put up with one another's irritating habits and annoying opinions by remembering what is essential: they are a family, and they love each other.

Psychologist Maurice Elias suggests that a family take the "neighbor test." Imagine that the entire family is in the middle of a full-blown argument when the door bell rings. A neighbor has come by to visit. What will the family do? In most circumstances, they will be welcoming, friendly, and hospitable to their unexpected guest. Everyone trots out their company manners, and the visit is a lovely time for all. Eventually the neighbor goes home, and Elias asks, "What happens next?" In the worst case, the family picks up the brawl where they left off. But in most cases, the visit has broken the tension and the family returns to its routine and usual civil interaction.

Why did the family end their argument and become pleasant when the neighbor showed up on the doorstep? Because they did not want to expose themselves to neighborhood gossip as "the angry family," or make a friend uncomfortable in their home. They did this by exercising a quality they all possessed—adults, teens, children—and that quality is self-control. Dr. Elias identifies self-control as an important quality for the emotional intelligence of a family, and he urges parents and kids to exercise it at least one day a week by not saying anything to one another that they wouldn't say if a neighbor were in the room.

The "All in the Family" quizzes help you explore your skills as a parent, your preparedness for getting through the kids' teen years, and even the state of your marriage—because family life is much happier if the spark is still there.

✏️ How Are Your Parenting Skills?

1 Just the thought of discussing sex, drugs, and alcohol with my kids makes me uncomfortable.

Completely true   *Somewhat true/false*   *Completely false*

     Mostly true   *Mostly false*

2 My love for my kids changes depending on how they behave.

Completely true   *Somewhat true/false*   *Completely false*

     Mostly true   *Mostly false*

3 Making any demands on young children will make them anxious when they grow older.

Completely true   *Somewhat true/false*   *Completely false*

     Mostly true   *Mostly false*

4 Sometimes a spanking is the only way to control a child.

Completely true   *Somewhat true/false*   *Completely false*

     Mostly true   *Mostly false*

5 If my children misbehave, I correct them at once even if their friends are present.

Completely true   *Somewhat true/false*   *Completely false*

     Mostly true   *Mostly false*

6 I'd rather my kids thought of me as their friend than their parent.

Completely true   *Somewhat true/false*   *Completely false*

     Mostly true   *Mostly false*

7 Being an authority figure is important. Even if I make an obvious mistake, I do not apologize to my kids.

Completely true   *Somewhat true/false*   *Completely false*

Mostly true   *Mostly false*

8 Children must be permitted to make their own mistakes and learn from them.

Completely true   *Somewhat true/false*   *Completely false*

Mostly true   *Mostly false*

9 There are some subjects I will not discuss with my kids.

Completely true   *Somewhat true/false*   *Completely false*

Mostly true   *Mostly false*

10 If my child is having trouble with another child at school, it's the school's responsibility to sort it out.

Completely true   *Somewhat true/false*   *Completely false*

Mostly true   *Mostly false*

SCORING ·

Each answer is awarded a specific number of points.

Completely true: *5 points*
Mostly true: *4 points*
Somewhat true/false: *3 points*
Mostly false: *2 points*
Completely false: *1 point*

50–40: You're completely clueless about raising a child.
39–30: You still need serious guidance about how to be a parent.
Below 30: You're the kind of parent you see in 1960s sitcoms.

Which Word or Phrase Best Describes Your Child?

Mark the circle that corresponds to where on the continuum between each of the word/phrase pairs you fall. If you mark 1 or 5, then you identify most strongly with one of the words or phrases in the pair; 2 or 4 less so; 3 you are neutral.

1. outgoing ① • ② • ③ • ④ • ⑤ unsociable
2. in high spirits ① • ② • ③ • ④ • ⑤ unhappy
3. curious ① • ② • ③ • ④ • ⑤ bored
4. generous ① • ② • ③ • ④ • ⑤ stingy
5. affectionate ① • ② • ③ • ④ • ⑤ standoffish
6. talkative ① • ② • ③ • ④ • ⑤ restrained
7. kind ① • ② • ③ • ④ • ⑤ mean
8. thoughtful ① • ② • ③ • ④ • ⑤ selfish
9. imaginative ① • ② • ③ • ④ • ⑤ irritable
10. loving ① • ② • ③ • ④ • ⑤ withdrawn

SCORING

50–40: Get help now.
39–30: You raised a good kid with lots of potential.
Below 30: You have a happy, well-adjusted kid—keep up the good work.

✏ Who's Responsible for the Kids?

1 Raising the children is primarily the mother's responsibility.

Completely true　　*Somewhat true/false*　　*Completely false*

Mostly true　　*Mostly false*

2 After working all day, the father should not be expected to take care of the kids.

Completely true　　*Somewhat true/false*　　*Completely false*

Mostly true　　*Mostly false*

3 If a woman has a career, her family will suffer.

Completely true　　*Somewhat true/false*　　*Completely false*

Mostly true　　*Mostly false*

4 Women are more nurturing than men.

Completely true　　*Somewhat true/false*　　*Completely false*

Mostly true　　*Mostly false*

5 Most fathers don't know how to care for children.

Completely true　　*Somewhat true/false*　　*Completely false*

Mostly true　　*Mostly false*

6 Parents who send their kids to day care and preschool are letting strangers raise their children.

Completely true　　*Somewhat true/false*　　*Completely false*

Mostly true　　*Mostly false*

7 Children sent to day care develop emotional problems later in life.

Completely true *Somewhat true/false* *Completely false*

Mostly true *Mostly false*

8 If children are sick, their mother should stay home from work to take care of them.

Completely true *Somewhat true/false* *Completely false*

Mostly true *Mostly false*

9 Fathers are clumsy when it comes to changing a diaper or feeding a baby.

Completely true *Somewhat true/false* *Completely false*

Mostly true *Mostly false*

10 Children who come from homes where both parents work are more likely to become delinquents.

Completely true *Somewhat true/false* *Completely false*

Mostly true *Mostly false*

SCORING ·

Each answer is awarded a specific number of points.

Completely true: *5 points*
Mostly true: *4 points*
Somewhat true/false: *3 points*
Mostly false: *2 points*
Completely false: *1 point*

50–40: You exemplify the Stone Age approach to family life and child rearing.

39–30: You're still a little hidebound when it comes to gender roles.
Below 30: You have a flexible, cooperative, shared approach to raising the kids.

✏️ How Well Do You Understand Teenagers?

① Teens have real feelings that should be acknowledged and respected.

Completely true   *Somewhat true/false*   *Completely false*

Mostly true   *Mostly false*

② Even if your teens are moody, they still want to know you love them.

Completely true   *Somewhat true/false*   *Completely false*

Mostly true   *Mostly false*

③ Teens will respect and accept limits on their actions, such as curfews and deadlines, as long as they are reasonable.

Completely true   *Somewhat true/false*   *Completely false*

Mostly true   *Mostly false*

④ Not all teens are rebellious all the time.

Completely true   *Somewhat true/false*   *Completely false*

Mostly true   *Mostly false*

⑤ Parents should make their teen's friends welcome in their home.

Completely true   *Somewhat true/false*   *Completely false*

Mostly true   *Mostly false*

6 In high school, young people need more freedom than they had in grammar school.

Completely true   *Somewhat true/false*   *Completely false*

     Mostly true   *Mostly false*

7 There is nothing wrong with telling teens to get a job so they have their own spending money.

Completely true   *Somewhat true/false*   *Completely false*

     Mostly true   *Mostly false*

8 If you talk honestly about sex and drugs with your teens, they will probably listen.

Completely true   *Somewhat true/false*   *Completely false*

     Mostly true   *Mostly false*

9 Teens do not respect parents who are hypocritical.

Completely true   *Somewhat true/false*   *Completely false*

     Mostly true   *Mostly false*

10 Family dinners are an excellent way to keep up with what your teen is doing.

Completely true   *Somewhat true/false*   *Completely false*

     Mostly true   *Mostly false*

SCORING

Each answer is awarded a specific number of points.

Completely true: *5 points*
Mostly true: *4 points*
Somewhat true/false: *3 points*

Mostly false: *2 points*
Completely false: *1 point*

50–40: You could teach a course on raising teens.
39–30: Overall, you have good teen-raising skills.
Below 30: The teen years are going to be long and ugly in your household.

✏ How Well Do You Know Your Spouse?

1 My spouse's bad moods mystify me—I don't know what sets them off.

Completely true　　*Somewhat true/false*　　*Completely false*

　　　Mostly true　　　　*Mostly false*

2 I never know what type of gift to give my spouse.

Completely true　　*Somewhat true/false*　　*Completely false*

　　　Mostly true　　　　*Mostly false*

3 My spouse wouldn't be interested in a regular date night.

Completely true　　*Somewhat true/false*　　*Completely false*

　　　Mostly true　　　　*Mostly false*

4 My spouse loves taking care of the kids.

Completely true　　*Somewhat true/false*　　*Completely false*

　　　Mostly true　　　　*Mostly false*

5 I know the month of my spouse's birthday, but not the date.

Completely true　　*Somewhat true/false*　　*Completely false*

　　　Mostly true　　　　*Mostly false*

6 Neither my spouse nor I care much about our personal appearance.

Completely true   *Somewhat true/false*   *Completely false*

       Mostly true   *Mostly false*

7 Compliments and spontaneous little gifts are for when you're dating.

Completely true   *Somewhat true/false*   *Completely false*

       Mostly true   *Mostly false*

8 My spouse knows I love him/her. There's no need to say it out loud.

Completely true   *Somewhat true/false*   *Completely false*

       Mostly true   *Mostly false*

9 Making my in-laws feel like they are part of our family doesn't interest me.

Completely true   *Somewhat true/false*   *Completely false*

       Mostly true   *Mostly false*

10 Sometimes I say something critical about my spouse in front of the kids.

Completely true   *Somewhat true/false*   *Completely false*

       Mostly true   *Mostly false*

SCORING ·

Each answer is awarded a specific number of points.

Completely true: *5 points*
Mostly true: *4 points*

Somewhat true/false: *3 points*
Mostly false: *2 points*
Completely false: *1 point*

50–40: You're a troglodyte.
39–30: You need work on your relationship skills.
Below 30: You're a fully evolved human being.

Are You Ready to Introduce Your Kids to the Social Network?

1 When my children express an interest in social networks, I'll introduce them to social networking sites.

Completely true   *Somewhat true/false*   *Completely false*

     Mostly true   *Mostly false*

2 When the kids are young, I'll monitor their social networking activity.

Completely true   *Somewhat true/false*   *Completely false*

     Mostly true   *Mostly false*

3 I've told my kids that what is bad offline is bad online.

Completely true   *Somewhat true/false*   *Completely false*

     Mostly true   *Mostly false*

4 I've set daily limits on how long the kids can be on a social networking site.

Completely true   *Somewhat true/false*   *Completely false*

     Mostly true   *Mostly false*

5 I talk about the sites with my kids to show that I'm interested in their online activities.

Completely true   *Somewhat true/false*   *Completely false*

Mostly true   *Mostly false*

6 My kids cannot join a site that requires their full name, date of birth, or the name of their school.

Completely true   *Somewhat true/false*   *Completely false*

Mostly true   *Mostly false*

7 I have installed safety controls on all our online devices so there are sites the kids are automatically barred from visiting.

Completely true   *Somewhat true/false*   *Completely false*

Mostly true   *Mostly false*

8 I've directed my kids to kid-centric sites.

Completely true   *Somewhat true/false*   *Completely false*

Mostly true   *Mostly false*

9 I spend time online with my kids.

Completely true   *Somewhat true/false*   *Completely false*

Mostly true   *Mostly false*

10 I have the final say on which site(s) my kids can sign onto.

Completely true   *Somewhat true/false*   *Completely false*

Mostly true   *Mostly false*

SCORING

Each answer is awarded a specific number of points.

Completely true: 5 points
Mostly true: 4 points
Somewhat true/false: 3 points
Mostly false: 2 points
Completely false: 1 point

50–40: Yours is a safe, sane approach to introducing kids to social networking.
39–30: You have some good ideas, but should adopt a few more.
Below 30: You're just asking for trouble.

Is There Still a Spark in Your Marriage?

① My spouse and I kiss all the time.

Completely true   Somewhat true/false   Completely false
        Mostly true   Mostly false

② We find ways to spend time alone.

Completely true   Somewhat true/false   Completely false
        Mostly true   Mostly false

③ We have regular date nights.

Completely true   Somewhat true/false   Completely false
        Mostly true   Mostly false

④ Sometimes our parents take the kids for a weekend so we can be alone.

Completely true　　*Somewhat true/false*　　*Completely false*

Mostly true　　*Mostly false*

⑤ We say "I love you" just about every day.

Completely true　　*Somewhat true/false*　　*Completely false*

Mostly true　　*Mostly false*

⑥ My spouse is sexy.

Completely true　　*Somewhat true/false*　　*Completely false*

Mostly true　　*Mostly false*

⑦ I'm not interested in anyone else.

Completely true　　*Somewhat true/false*　　*Completely false*

Mostly true　　*Mostly false*

⑧ We take care of each other.

Completely true　　*Somewhat true/false*　　*Completely false*

Mostly true　　*Mostly false*

⑨ My life would be diminished without my spouse.

Completely true　　*Somewhat true/false*　　*Completely false*

Mostly true　　*Mostly false*

⑩ This is the person I'll spend the rest of my life with.

Completely true　　*Somewhat true/false*　　*Completely false*

Mostly true　　*Mostly false*

SCORING ·

Each answer is awarded a specific number of points.

Completely true: *5 points*
Mostly true: *4 points*
Somewhat true/false: *3 points*
Mostly false: *2 points*
Completely false: *1 point*

50–40: Yours is a grade-A marriage.
39–30: You're still a good match.
Below 30: Make an appointment with a marriage counselor now.

✏️ Is Your Birth Order Having an Impact on Your Life?

➊ Growing up, my brothers and sisters played together all the time. Sometimes we bickered, but for the most part we had fun.

Completely true   *Somewhat true/false*   *Completely false*

Mostly true   *Mostly false*

➋ My parents spoiled my youngest sibling, but they didn't overdo it.

Completely true   *Somewhat true/false*   *Completely false*

Mostly true   *Mostly false*

➌ If my mother had a favorite child, none of us could tell.

Completely true   *Somewhat true/false*   *Completely false*

Mostly true   *Mostly false*

4 I don't believe my parents expected more of their eldest child.

Completely true   *Somewhat true/false*   *Completely false*

Mostly true   *Mostly false*

5 All of my siblings and I excel at different things.

Completely true   *Somewhat true/false*   *Completely false*

Mostly true   *Mostly false*

6 None of my siblings would ever try to steal my boyfriend/girlfriend.

Completely true   *Somewhat true/false*   *Completely false*

Mostly true   *Mostly false*

7 Sometimes we are competitive, but we are never jealous of each other.

Completely true   *Somewhat true/false*   *Completely false*

Mostly true   *Mostly false*

8 The idea that birth order can influence how you develop as a person is a myth.

Completely true   *Somewhat true/false*   *Completely false*

Mostly true   *Mostly false*

9 The most important factor in personal development is coming from a loving, supportive, and understanding family.

Completely true   *Somewhat true/false*   *Completely false*

Mostly true   *Mostly false*

10 A little sibling rivalry is healthy—it convinced us to always try our best.

Completely true   *Somewhat true/false*   *Completely false*

Mostly true   *Mostly false*

S C O R I N G ·

Each answer is awarded a specific number of points.

Completely true: 5 points
Mostly true: 4 points
Somewhat true/false: 3 points
Mostly false: 2 points
Completely false: 1 point

50-40: Birth order is meaningless to you.
39-30: A little tension is detected, but it's not out of control.
Below 30: Isn't it time to give up those resentments from childhood?

✏ How Well Do You Get Along with Your Parents?

1 You live near your parents and visit them almost daily.

Completely true　　*Somewhat true/false*　　*Completely false*

　　　　Mostly true　　　　*Mostly false*

2 You invite your parents to just about every social event you are hosting.

Completely true　　*Somewhat true/false*　　*Completely false*

　　　　Mostly true　　　　*Mostly false*

3 You speak with your parents on the phone every day.

Completely true　　*Somewhat true/false*　　*Completely false*

　　　　Mostly true　　　　*Mostly false*

4 You spend your vacation with your parents and immediate family.

Completely true   *Somewhat true/false*   *Completely false*

Mostly true   *Mostly false*

5 You would give up a boyfriend/girlfriend—even you truly loved him/her—if your parents didn't like him/her.

Completely true   *Somewhat true/false*   *Completely false*

Mostly true   *Mostly false*

6 Your parents know all your friends, all your workplace colleagues, all your neighbors.

Completely true   *Somewhat true/false*   *Completely false*

Mostly true   *Mostly false*

7 Before making even minor decisions, such as purchasing new furniture or a new appliance, you ask your parents for their opinion.

Completely true   *Somewhat true/false*   *Completely false*

Mostly true   *Mostly false*

8 Your parents' approval is very important to you.

Completely true   *Somewhat true/false*   *Completely false*

Mostly true   *Mostly false*

9 If your parents go out of town for any period of time, you miss them terribly.

Completely true   *Somewhat true/false*   *Completely false*

Mostly true   *Mostly false*

10 Your friends have commented on how much time you spend with your parents and have expressed concern that you might be too dependent on them.

Completely true   *Somewhat true/false*   *Completely false*

Mostly true   *Mostly false*

SCORING ·

Each answer is awarded a specific number of points.

Completely true: *5 points*
Mostly true: *4 points*
Somewhat true/false: *3 points*
Mostly false: *2 points*
Completely false: *1 point*

50-40: You and your parents are grown-ups.
39-30: You have a tight bond with your parents, but not in an unhealthy way.
Below 30: Hopelessly clingy.

✏️ How Healthy Is Your Mother-Daughter Relationship?

1 My mother/daughter respects and understands me.

Completely true   *Somewhat true/false*   *Completely false*

Mostly true   *Mostly false*

2 When ever I think of my mother/daughter, I am filled with feelings of love and affection.

Completely true   *Somewhat true/false*   *Completely false*

Mostly true   *Mostly false*

3 My mother/daughter may not always agree with me, but she supports my decisions.

Completely true   *Somewhat true/false*   *Completely false*

Mostly true   *Mostly false*

4 I can have serious, heart-to-heart discussions with my mother/daughter.

Completely true   *Somewhat true/false*   *Completely false*

Mostly true   *Mostly false*

5 I visit with my mother/daughter fairly often, but we respect each other's privacy, too.

Completely true   *Somewhat true/false*   *Completely false*

Mostly true   *Mostly false*

6 My mother/daughter and I often do small favors for one another, or give each other small gifts.

Completely true   *Somewhat true/false*   *Completely false*

Mostly true   *Mostly false*

7 My mother/daughter is honest with me.

Completely true   *Somewhat true/false*   *Completely false*

Mostly true   *Mostly false*

8 My mother/daughter would never purposely hurt my feelings.

Completely true   *Somewhat true/false*   *Completely false*

Mostly true   *Mostly false*

9 If we quarrel, we do not hold a grudge; after our emotions have cooled down, we can talk about the disagreement in a civil, adult manner.

Completely true   *Somewhat true/false*   *Completely false*

Mostly true   *Mostly false*

10 In difficult situations, such as illness or financial trouble, I know I can trust my mother/daughter to help me.

Completely true   *Somewhat true/false*   *Completely false*

Mostly true   *Mostly false*

SCORING ·

Each answer is awarded a specific number of points.

Completely true: *5 points*
Mostly true: *4 points*
Somewhat true/false: *3 points*
Mostly false: *2 points*
Completely false: *1 point*

50-40: Your mother/daughter relationship is loving, trusting and mature. Congratulations!
39-30: Could be better, but not bad at all.
Below 30: Do really plan to rehash these issues for the rest of your life?

✏️ Are You Jealous of Your Siblings?

1 In school, my sibling got the best grades.

Completely true   *Somewhat true/false*   *Completely false*

Mostly true   *Mostly false*

2 I think I am the smartest of my siblings.

Completely true   *Somewhat true/false*   *Completely false*

Mostly true   *Mostly false*

3 My sibling is more athletic than the rest of the family.

Completely true   *Somewhat true/false*   *Completely false*

Mostly true   *Mostly false*

4 My sibling has always had more friends than me.

Completely true   *Somewhat true/false*   *Completely false*

Mostly true   *Mostly false*

5 I think I am more charismatic than my sibling.

Completely true   *Somewhat true/false*   *Completely false*

Mostly true   *Mostly false*

6 My sibling thinks he/she is the best looking person in our family.

Completely true   *Somewhat true/false*   *Completely false*

Mostly true   *Mostly false*

7 My career has been more successful than my siblings'.

Completely true   *Somewhat true/false*   *Completely false*

Mostly true   *Mostly false*

8 At birthdays, my siblings received more gifts than I did on my birthday.

Completely true   *Somewhat true/false*   *Completely false*

          Mostly true   *Mostly false*

9 I was my mother's favorite.

Completely true   *Somewhat true/false*   *Completely false*

          Mostly true   *Mostly false*

10 My sibling received more attention from our parents than I did.

Completely true   *Somewhat true/false*   *Completely false*

          Mostly true   *Mostly false*

SCORING

Each answer is awarded a specific number of points.

Completely true: *5 points*
Mostly true: *4 points*
Somewhat true/false: *3 points*
Mostly false: *2 points*
Completely false: *1 point*

50-40: You are seething with resentment.
39-30: You've got a touch of sibling rivalry, but it's not out of control.
Below 30: You and your siblings are pals.